Proceedings of
the Eighth Annual International
Bilingual Bicultural Education Conference

National Association
for Bilingual Education

NATIONAL CLEARINGHOUSE
FOR BILINGUAL EDUCATION

This document is published by InterAmerica Research Associates, Inc., pursuant to contract NIE 400-80-0040 to operate the National Clearinghouse for Bilingual Education. The National Clearinghouse for Bilingual Education is jointly funded by the National Institute of Education and the Office of Bilingual Education and Minority Languages Affairs, U.S. Department of Education. Contractors undertaking such projects under government sponsorship are encouraged to express their judgment freely in professional and technical matters; the views expressed in this publication do not necessarily reflect the views of the sponsoring agencies.

InterAmerica Research Associates, Inc. d/b/a
National Clearinghouse for Bilingual Education
1300 Wilson Boulevard, Suite B2-11
Rosslyn, Virginia 22209
(703) 522-0710/(800) 336-4560

Cover design by Sans Serif Graphics, Arlington, Virginia
Typesetting by Eagle One Graphics, Inc., Lanham, Maryland

ISBN: 0-89763-054-8
First printing 1981
Printed in USA

10   9   8   7   6   5   4   3   2   1

Contents

Foreword

The proceedings of the first National Conference on Bilingual Education were published in the fall of 1972. The conference, held 14–15 April 1972, in Austin, and cosponsored by the Texas Education Agency, Education Service Center, Region XIII and the United States Office of Education, marked the beginning of an organized, national effort to give bilingual education higher priority.

Dr. Severo Gómez, Associate Commissioner of Education of the Texas Education Agency, made the closing presentation, "Where Do We Go from Here?" Since then, as evinced by the proceedings of the Eighth International Conference on Bilingual Bicultural Education, held in Seattle 4–9 May 1979, bilingual education has grown from revolutionary concept toward established fact.

The journey has not been easy. There have been triumphs and disappointments along the way. But a decade of dedicated efforts to meet the needs of minority language students has resulted in much-needed reform of the traditional monolingual pattern in education.

A new generation of bilingual educators is visibly eager to carry on the work of its precursors. The participation of 3,500 parents, teachers, teacher trainers, and administrators at the NABE conference in Seattle clearly demonstrates that bilingual education programs across the United States remain committed to the educational value of learning in two languages.

The publication of these proceedings reflects the broad issues of concern to us all. The titles of papers presented at the 1979 NABE Conference attest to the current vitality of bilingual education in the United States and elsewhere. In like manner, these proceedings indicate a desire to consolidate the gains of the past while preparing to meet the challenges of the future.

In the section on Foundations, the reader will share the excitement of recognizing the challenges that bilingual educators face today. In the section on Special Populations, the reader will perceive the international scope of bilingual education. Current concerns of bilingual educators in the field are discussed in the last two sections, Curriculum and Pedagogy.

I thank Dr. Juan Juárez, Conference Chairman; Dr. Phillip Gonzales, editor of these proceedings; and Dean Frederick Giles, University of Washington, for their shared leadership in the planning and implementation of a most successful NABE Conference.

Juan D. Solís
NABE President, 1978-79

Introduction

The Eighth Annual International Bilingual Bicultural Education Conference sponsored by the National Association for Bilingual Education provided an opportunity for educators to share ideas about bilingual education, to provide new perspectives on familiar problems, and to draw attention to problems which had not previously been clearly recognized or adequately defined. The 244 concurrent sessions, the forty preconference workshops, the fifteen major session addresses, and the three keynote talks provided a forum for discussion by the more than 3,500 participants of topics relevant to parents, teachers, administrators, and teacher trainers concerned with the bilingual education of children. In addition, these discussions were intended to provide a resource to stimulate further thinking and action long after the participants had dispersed.

This publication of proceedings contains a limited selection of papers presented at the 1979 conference. Naturally, the twenty-one papers could not provide a complete and exhaustive reporting on all topics examined at the conference or of all areas of concern to bilingual educators. Their purpose, rather, is to provide a sampling of papers reflective of the breadth of issues presented and discussed in Seattle during the week of 5-9 May 1979.

The papers in this publication are grouped into four relatively discrete areas: Foundations, Special Populations, Curriculum, and Pedagogy. In part one, Foundations, noted bilingual educators address the issues affecting bilingual schooling. Fillmore discusses classroom use of language and language learning as well as the linguistic proficiency teachers need to make bilingual education "better in the 1980s." Ramírez shares exciting research on bilingual multicultural individuals and suggests that identified characteristics associated with such individuals are needed by future leaders who indeed can "save the world." Arciniega says that while we can be proud of the accomplishments and importance of bilingual education, we need to face the challenge posed by the schools in our society that may be repressing the reform needed to effect better and appropriate schooling for bilingual children. In the final paper in this section, an understanding and appreciation of cultural difference as well as effective participation in divergent cultures are seen by Chávez as important objectives in public education.

In part two, Special Populations, bilingual bicultural education is seen as a worldwide concern which affects the many populations in various and unique ways. In outlining the culturally and linguistically diverse nature of multiethnic Japan, Honna discusses the characteristics and special problems of several groups with language concerns residing in Japan. In the paper by Minaya-Portella and Sanches, the similarities and differences of bilingual education programs in the United States and Peru are contrasted. The concept of bilingual education needs to be expanded to incorporate the language and culture of the Indian peoples who are largely unserved by programs specifically designed to promote language maintenance or language restoration, says Dupris in his paper on the impact of multicultural education. Vásquez suggests that motivation may vary from population to population and that education for the Chicano needs to reflect this population's value system if it is to be effective. St. Clair and Bassett present a sociohistorical overview of the question of language renewal among Native Americans, which introduced a panel discussion conducted as a major session of the 1979 conference.

Part three, Curriculum, includes curricular concerns at the teacher training, vocational, and local educational agency levels. Valencia shares his expertise as a teacher trainer in his paper, which discusses various approaches to bilingual teacher training. Sutman provides comprehensive guidelines for teacher-training curriculum in bilingual education, including discussions of teacher competencies, subject area methodologies and teaching strategies, and ideas regarding classroom management. Gilman, de Frutos; and Christensen explain the reasons for needing a bilingual outreach program in the Reno area and further describe the mechanism for such a homebound tutoring program. A systems approach employed in a community college English as a Second Language/bilingual vocational program is presented as a model for the college-level bilingual curriculum in the paper by Kotesky. Jacobson explains the concurrent approach to bilingual bicultural education and the need for equal importance to be given to both languages in his paper on the "Laredo Experiment." In the final paper in this section, Otheguy, Otto, and Siffeti explore the use of the vernacular language and its possible effects on the learning of English in college-level subject matter courses.

Part four, Pedagogy, includes enlightening information on the current research involving use of tests with bilingual children in Archuleta's and Cervantes' paper on the "misplaced child." Preston discusses semilingualism, its origins, and its educational implications as it relates to the "nonlearner," and offers suggestions regarding instruction that should be provided such children. Met and Thuy provide useful ideas for developing materials designed to meet individual student's needs in a bilingual classroom. In a very practical paper especially meaningful for bilingual teachers, Hansen-Krening suggests language experiences as means of helping promote language development as well as reading skill acquisition. A research study explaining a successful peer-tutoring program in which social factors were found useful in promoting second-language acquisition is explained in the paper by Johnson and August. Finally, interesting research on spelling errors exhibited by bilinguals in two countries is discussed by Staczek.

The editor would like to thank the many individuals who assisted with the publication of the *Proceedings of the Eighth Annual International Bilingual Bicultural Education Conference*. First, the initial reading, screening, and editorial comments of Araceli Furby, José Francisco Villarreal, and Jesús Rodríguez of the University of Washington Bilingual Programs are gratefully acknowledged. Additionally, the many hours of typing, proofreading and correcting done by Diane Collum and the assistance provided by Howard Horstman in the final copy proofreading are certainly appreciated. Finally, a special thanks is extended to the NABE Executive Board for commissioning this publication.

Phillip C. Gonzales

National Association for Bilingual Education
Officers 1978-79

President
Juan D. Solís

President Elect
Carmen Pérez

Vice President
Henry Oyama

Secretary
John Correiro

Treasurer
Ramón Santiago

Past President
María Medina Swanson

Proceedings of the Eighth Annual International Bilingual Bicultural Education Conference

National Association for Bilingual Education

Phillip C. Gonzales
NABE Editor

Foundations

Bilingual Education in the Eighties: Making a Good Thing Better

Lily Wong Fillmore
University of California at Berkeley

This summer marks the end of one decade of involvement in bilingual education in this country. I think those of us in this room who are old enough to have gone through those first ten years will agree with me that it has not been boring. We have experienced the challenge and excitement of turning those vague promises we made in project proposals into working educational programs, and we have experienced the joy of watching the programs we created and the children they served come into their own. We have felt the exhilaration of being in the front ranks of an educational crusade. We have faced and battled a powerful group of critics and detractors who have been trying to convince us that what we are doing is not merely wrong, but downright un-American.

Lately, we have come to the sobering realization that, although we have accomplished a great deal in these first ten years — in figuring out how to establish and conduct bilingual education programs — there is still much that remains to be done. In general, what we have accomplished has been solid and the children we have served have profited from these programs; but we know that we are not doing as good a job as possible. Overall, we have to admit, the results of bilingual education have been mixed.

No doubt each of us has a list of good reasons why this has been the case. We have been operating under incredible handicaps. During these ten years we have had to figure out not only how one ought to conduct bilingual education under ideal conditions, but also how to do it with personnel who, at times, are unsympathetic to what we are trying to do, or who are linguistically and culturally unqualified to serve well in these programs. Not only have we had to design curricula for these programs, we have also had to create from scratch the instructional materials to be used, since nothing appropriate was ready at hand. And we have had to deal with the animosity that these programs engender in people who fear anything they cannot understand.

We know that ten years is a very short time, where educational and social changes are concerned. We have done as much as possible. Looked at in terms of what has been accomplished despite the handicaps under which we have been operating, the achievements are impressive, and we can well be proud of them. Nevertheless, in many places, the fate of bilingual education is uncertain. In California, as in a number of other states where bilingual education has been established by law, each legislative session puts the programs into jeopardy. Each year, a clutch of bills gets thrown into the legislative hopper designed to weaken, diminish, or destroy bilingual education.

Such actions stem basically from fear and a lack of understanding of what bilingual education is all about; they are almost always supported with evidence that bilingual education does not work. It is clear to those of us who believe that bilingual education is the soundest way to educate non-English-speaking children in our society that the only fitting response to such attacks is a strong counterattack. Unfortunately, there has been little agreement among us of late as to what the target of this counterattack ought to be, or what kinds of forces we should pull together. There are those who would go after our opponents by marshalling evidence to prove that they are wrong, i.e., if we come up with the right things to measure, we could prove that indeed bilingual education *has* worked.

But what we are up against is emotional: fear and ignorance are not likely to be dispelled by evidence that calls for any sort of special perceptions, evidence that requires a special effort for it to be recognized. There are others who, while recognizing the emotional tone of the opposition, see the attacks as basically grounded in politics; they have argued that the place to fight back is in the political arena. We should marshal our political forces (and bilingual education has powerful political forces behind it) to secure our ground. We need to demonstrate that the forces which favor bilingual education are mightier than the ones that stand against it. Or so this group would have us feel. But again, we may be underestimating the strength of the opposition. It would be nice to think that right adds to our might, but as the old Chinese saying goes, "Though they may be wrong, they're still mighty powerful strong."

My words have probably sounded pretty pessimistic so far; I don't mean them to, for I am an optimist where bilingual education is concerned. I believe that in the end, faith and common sense will triumph over fear and ignorance. I have faith that bilingual education works, but my common sense tells me that the best plan for dealing with the opposition is to make bilingual education work better.

Along with the rest of you, I have spent these past ten years helping bilingual education works better in the future than it does now. I am going. I have trained teachers, designed material, and done research. At the end of a decade's experience and commitment, I now have a clear idea of what sorts of things I don't yet know that I ought to know; and many of those things, I suspect, are of central importance to our task.

I assume, then, that the best answer to our critics is to make sure that bilingual education works better in the future than it does now. I am convinced that the most direct steps to improvement in bilingual education is through a solid program of hard-nosed research. We need to understand much better than we now do just what processes are involved in teaching students in two languages in the same program, especially when one of the languages is being learned as a second language. Only after achieving such an understanding can we expect to improve the quality of instruction that is offered in the bilingual classroom.

In the rest of this talk, I would like to identify and discuss some questions I believe most urgently need answering in bilingual education. They are not the only ones, of course, but from my perspective as both a linguist and a bilingual educator, they are certainly among the most crucial ones affecting instructional practices in the bilingual classroom.

I will address two issues in the practice of bilingual education that are of particular interest to a linguist. The first I will deal with in some detail: how can the language that is used in the bilingual classroom be chosen and shaped in order to achieve all that it must? The other I will deal with as it relates to the first: what degree of linguistic proficiency is needed to make it possible for a teacher to teach in a bilingual classroom?

Language Usage in the Bilingual Classroom

The question of how language gets used in the bilingual classroom is a key issue in why many programs do not show very good results, either in subject matter instruction or in second-language teaching.

Let us remind ourselves what is involved in language use in any instructional setting. First of all, the language used for instructional purposes must carry informational content. It is the medium by which teachers impart the skills and information that students are expected to acquire, and it is the means by which they determine whether the students have learned what they are supposed to learn. To be successful, such language must follow the principles of conversational cooperation that the philosopher Paul Grice has described: it has to be informative, complete, accurate, relevant, clear, orderly, and direct. In other words, instruction must be presented in language that permits the learner to make sense of the information being presented, and to learn what is being taught. As important as it is for the instructional language to follow the principles of well-formed discourse, it must also be appropriate to the ability level of the learners. That is, its level of difficulty should not exceed the ability of the students to understand, nor should it be too easy.

Most of us would present a lesson in very different language depending on whether we were giving it to high school students or to fourth graders, and we would also be likely to use quite different levels of language depending on whether we were instructing high-achieving or low-achieving students. Speakers take account of the age, ability levels, and experiences of their audience, and they make quite natural adjustments depending on what they believe the listeners' level of understanding to be. Sometimes, of course, the instructional language used in a classroom by the teacher is set at a particular level, based on fixed ideas of what the capability of students at that grade level is. We have all known kindergarten teachers who insist on speaking to their classes as if they were talking to three-year-olds. Also, because the language and general ability levels represented in any classroom tend to vary among students, it is not always easy to take every individual's ability into account in determining at what level instructional language ought to be set.

The ideal instructional situation, then, is one with a homogeneous class of students and a teacher who remains sensitive to their uniformly expanding abilities. But real situations and real teachers usually fall short of that idealization.

Hugh Mehan, in his 1974 study of the language used for instructional purposes in an English monolingual first grade classroom, found that the teacher's instructions used in presenting lessons tended to be vague, ambiguous, and incomplete. Consider, for example, an excerpt from Mehan's transcripts (1974) in which the teacher presented a lesson on spatial relations. She asked the children to draw a line on their papers and then to draw another object in relation to that line.

[Teacher:] Yes. Let's take our green crayon and make a line at the bottom of your paper. Just take your green crayon and make a green line at the bottom.

[Child #1:] Like that?

[Teacher:] Yeah.

[Child #2:] Now what are we going to do?

[Teacher:] Now take your orange crayon and make an orange worm under the green line. Pretend that's grass. Just a little wiggle. Here let me show you on this one. An orange worm.

[Child #2:] Hey, can you make it on yours?

[Child #3:] Under?

[Teacher:] No, I'm watching you make yours.

[Child #3:] Over here?

[Child #1:] Under?

[Teacher:] Listen, I'm going to say it just once. Make an orange worm under the green line.

[Child #2:] Like that?

[Teacher:] Beautiful. Okay. We are going to pretend that green line is the grass, okay? Can you pretend that with me? All right, where is the orange worm?

[Child #4:] Right there.

[Teacher:] Okay, tell me where he is.

[Child #4:] Under the grass.

[Teacher:] Okay, now, would you please make, um, a, a little brown seed under the grass?

[Child #1:] How do you make a little brown seed?

[Child #5:] Easy. You see. You go like this. Simple. A little circle.

[Child #1:] Like that?

[Teacher:] Oh, beautiful.

[Child #3:] Look at mine.

[Child #1:] Under what?

[Teacher:] Under the grass.

She went on in this vein, directing the students to draw other objects—worms, flowers and the sun, below, on, and above the green line they have drawn across the sheet. On numerous occasions the instructions were so imprecise that they were uninterpretable. The children had to ask for clarification and for more information. Between the instructions, the teacher asked the children to describe the location of the objects they had drawn relative to the green line, or the grass. She did this by asking *where* questions, for which she always expected a complete sentence, but she never came right out and asked for it. When the children offered her factually and linguistically correct responses, such as "under the grass," she would let them know that their answers were inadequate. In ordinary circumstances, a speaker hardly ever needs to give complete-sentence responses to questions of the form "Where is the worm?" The full-sentence response, "The worm is under the grass," contains redundant information—information that doesn't need to be mentioned again. A response containing only the information asked for is far more appropriate. In each case in our transcript the teacher tried to get the children to respond with the full form, by asking a question such as "Can you say it in a sentence?" To children at that age and level of understanding, there is a very feeble consciousness of such a metalinguistic notion as the "sentence," certainly nothing strong enough to be teased out with this kind of questioning. What the children understood from this probing no doubt was that the answer they had provided was in some way wrong, either factually or linguistically, but they couldn't understand what it was in their answers that she was rejecting. The transcripts Mehan includes with his report of this research indicate that the children did not generally divine the teacher's objective in this line of prompting. The children in Mehan's classroom episodes had to cooperate and guess to an extraordinary degree to figure out what the teacher was getting at in her presentation of the lesson.

This teacher was by no means doing a bad job. Her students were probably learning from this lesson and profiting from school generally. They had to work hard at times to discover what they were supposed to be learning, but it was well enough within their capability to do so in most cases. They understood the language, they had a general understanding of how people use language in educational settings, and they knew what was expected of them in general in activities of this type.

Imagine now that this was a lesson being given in a bilingual classroom as part of the instruction that is carried out in English each day; and imagine, if you will, that these children were limited English speakers. By being observant they no doubt could figure out what the teacher had in mind when she said, "Let's take out our green crayon and make a line at the bottom of your paper," or "Now take your orange crayon and make an orange worm under the green line." These instructions would be easy enough to interpret since in each case the teacher apparently demonstrated what she wanted the class to do. They wouldn't really need to know what the words "at the bottom of your paper" or "under the green line" meant in order to figure out what behavioral response the teacher was trying to elicit from them: they would only need to watch her or their English-comprehending classmates. But much of this lesson, presented as it was when Mehan observed it, would not have been interpretable. For example: "We are going to pretend that the green line is grass, okay? Can you pretend with me?" That could not have been interpreted by the children in our imaginary bilingual classroom, unless the children knew the meaning of "pretend" and what it meant to give the green line the new name, "grass."

This same lesson, then, which despite its imperfections probably worked well enough in the case of the English-speaking students, would have been quite inadequate in the bilingual classroom where some or all of the students are likely to be unable to comprehend English totally. The question you might be asking at this moment is, "What is our speaker leading up to? Is she going to tell us not to use English in teaching subject matter in the bilingual classroom?" The answer, of course, is "No, not at all." English is obviously a necessary part of bilingual programs in this country. If it were not used for instructional purposes at all, these programs would not be bilingual, and the non-English-speaking students in these programs would have a far more difficult time learning English than they do. In order to learn English efficiently and effectively, learners must hear it used in a variety of settings by a variety of speakers. They need to hear it in the classroom and in the school yard, from teachers and from peers. The English used by teachers in the bilingual classroom for instructional purposes serves a vital function for the students who are in the process of learning that language. It constitutes a part of the essential language input that the learner needs, the linguistic materials on which he is going to be basing his analysis of the structure of this new language.

The process of learning a language requires that one figures out the full set of rules by which it is structured — unconsciously, of course. In order to be able to do that, one must hear the language as it is spoken by its speakers in social situations in which the learner is a participant. English as a second language lessons in which the language itself is the subject matter seldom in themselves provide the right kind of exposure. Students definitely need to experience hearing English in a context in which it is used for presenting other subject matter.

The same goes for the other language that is used in any bilingual classroom. Most, if not all, bilingual programs must include, for integration purposes, some children who are not of the linguistic or ethnic group directly served by the program. These children are frequently recruited for bilingual programs with the promise that the experience will give them a rare and valuable opportunity to pick up a second language. Thus, the lessons they take part in which are carried out in that language are going to have to provide needed input on which to base their learning of it as a second language. In both cases, therefore, the language used for instructional purposes in bilingual classrooms must serve the same dual function: not only must it communicate the information and skills associated with the subject matter being taught, but it must also serve as linguistic input for language learning purposes.

This, then, is what makes bilingual education the complex undertaking that it is; but then nobody ever said it was going to be easy. The kind of talk the teacher engages in, in either language, has to meet the conditions of clarity, precision, orderliness, and the like, that I described for instructional language in general, but it has to meet these conditions at a much higher level than in a monolingual classroom setting. It must be used in such a way that the learners, even though they don't understand at the beginning what is being said, can figure out what the intended message is. Language which serves successfully as input for the process of second language learning is different from ordinary language use in a number of important ways.

First, generally speaking, instructional language is much more richly contextualized than ordinary language. The language that is most useful to language learners, be they first- or second-language learners, must be clearly anchored in the speech situation most of the time. It is talk that pertains to the participants in the speech event, to what they are currently experiencing, to knowledge that they clearly share, and so on. I have found in my own research on second-language learners that speakers talking to such learners tend to limit their topics of conversation to knowledge and experiences that they know are shared between them. There is a noticeable avoidance of topics that do not relate to the immediate situation in which the speech is occurring, perhaps in part because they cannot be certain that other topics are in fact shared, and perhaps in part because they would have difficulty establishing a topic which has to be managed entirely through language. When speakers talk about matters that relate directly to experiences that they mutually share at the moment, they can make use of gestures, demonstrations, and other nonverbal cues to get their message across. The learners, if they are at all observant, can make use of this kind of nonverbal embellishment and of contextual information which is available to them in order to figure out what is being talked about, even though they understand but little of the language being spoken. The learners, realizing that such talk concerns the present physical and social situation, will assume that it is possible to make use of situational cues to figure out the meanings of what has just been said. This kind of cognitive activity on the part of the learner is in my opinion an essential aspect of the language-learning process in all cases in which language is learned in a naturalistic setting.

A second characteristic of speech that successfully serves as input for second-language acquisition is that it is deliberately shaped with the learner's point of view in mind. As I have said, an important aspect of successful instructional language is that its level of difficulty is adjusted according to the age, experience, and ability of the students being addressed. This is the case here, too, except that when the students being addressed have limited comprehension of the language being used, much greater adjustments may need to be made, and far closer attention must be paid to their comprehension level than is necessary where language itself is not a factor. When the speaker keeps in mind the learners' limited comprehension, quite natural adjustments in the language used are made, and as a result, the language produced is much easier to understand. For example, language produced under these conditions tends to be structurally simpler than what one would ordinarily expect. This is not to say that only simple sentences are used, or that structures become "simplified" in any way that deforms them grammatically; however, people talking to language learners have a definite tendency to avoid complex sentences and to stick with simpler ones. Furthermore, utterances are likely to be repeated or paraphrased whenever the learners appear not to understand. Such repetitions or rephrasings are very useful to the language learners: they not only give the learners a greater chance of figuring out phonetically what is being said, but they also serve to teach the learners a variety of ways in which one can say the same thing in the new language.

An important point about adjustments that speakers make for the sake of language learners is that they are almost always triggered by cues provided by the learners themselves. In general, both form and content tend to be adjusted in response to feedback provided by the learners. When learners indicate noncomprehension, cooperative speakers will repeat, paraphrase, demonstrate, gesture, talk louder, or, in extreme cases, simply change the subject, to help the learner out. On the other hand, when learners respond appropriately to what the speaker has said, using whatever language they have learned up to that point, the speaker is encouraged to go on. Seeing that they are understood, speakers lessen the degree to which they adjust the form and content of their talk to the learners' comprehension level. In this way, as the learners make progress in the new language, they are continuously provided with input of just the appropriate level of difficulty, and this level increases as their control over the new language develops.

It is by this pattern of adjusting and readjusting that more accomplished speakers of a language give help to those who are learning it, either as a first or as a second language. The ability on the part of speakers to make the kinds of modifications I have been describing requires taking very close notice of the learners' needs and problems. Most people have the ability and the intuitions to do what is required on their part to provide such help. I found in my own study of second-language acquisition that young children are particularly good at providing this kind of help to learners. Even kindergarten-age children are quite aware of when others understand them or not, and they have a keen sense of what would be easy to understand and what would be hard.

Take, for example, this excerpt from the transcripts of recordings I made of the interaction between second-language learners and their English-speaking friends. This particular excerpt is from a session involving Jesús, a seven-year-old Spanish-speaking child who was in the process of learning English, and his English-speaking friend, Matthew. The session took place three months after Jesús had arrived from Mexico, so he had had only three months' exposure to English at this time. He was very smart, had a great ear, and a good memory for colorful expressions picked up from his buddies in the context of hours of play: "Shut up, stupid!", "So what?", "Oh, my gosh", "I goof", "Be quiet, you!", and "I'll beat 'em up after school." By using appropriately his actually very limited repertory of English expressions, Jesús was able to give the impression that he understood a lot of English. He played for hours on end with his English-speaking friends, and although he was constrained in what he could say, he was nevertheless able to get along quite nicely with what he had. I had the following conversation with Matthew, Jesús' English-speaking friend, after the boys had been playing together for close to an hour entirely in English. Matthew turned to me and asked:

Matthew: Hey, teacher got a TV, right?

Observer: Do I have a TV? Yes.

Matthew: Did you watch "The House without a Christmas Tree" last night?

Observer: No.

Matthew: Tell Jesús why he don't watch Channel 5. That program is going to be on again.

Observer: Why don't you tell him yourself?

Matthew: 'Cause he don't know what I'm saying.

Remember, Matthew had been talking and playing with Jesús in English for a full hour before this conversation took place. All of that talk, of course, related only to events and experiences the two were mutually involved in. Matthew had assured me many times that Jesús could understand anything; but in this conversation we realize that his intuitions told him, reliably, that for communicating with Jesús about a topic that was divorced from the immediate situation he needed help.

Now if the ability to adjust speech according to the needs of the language learners comes so naturally that even children have it, why, you may ask, am I making such a big deal of it? It turns out that doing what comes naturally is relatively easy when you are interacting on a one-to-one basis. It is easy, too, to limit your talk to contextually given topics if you are simply interacting socially, or if you are a child playing games with another child. The classroom teacher in the situations with which we are most familiar necessarily spends a good deal of time speaking to the class as a whole rather than to individuals, particularly when giving subject-matter instruction; and her interaction with the students necessarily goes beyond small talk and play.

In such instances it becomes more difficult to shape speech according to individual needs, since there are the needs of many individuals to consider. And when the objective of talk is the teaching of subject matter, it is impossible to limit topics to shared experiences, or to contextualize utterances adequately.

In spite of these complications, of course, we know that it is possible for instructional language to serve as input for language learning. The Montreal immersion programs have shown us that. There, children do learn a second language through having their school subjects taught in that language. The teachers in these classes have a certain advantage over teachers in American bilingual education classes, however. In the Montreal program, the children started out with no French at all, so for a while the degree and kind of language modification the teachers needed to make was essentially the same for all of their students. Because of this, it was easier for them than it could be for us to limit and modify what they actually said, and to contextualize their speech so the class could understand what was going on. And while they were teaching subject matter during the period before the children understood French very well, they regarded the actual communication of subject materials as a secondary goal, something that was possible simply because *all* of the children needed to learn the school language first; there weren't other children in the same school that they needed to keep up with.

In our own bilingual classrooms, the situation is far more complex. One almost always finds a huge range of language proficiency represented in the classroom. There are children who speak no English at all, those who speak nothing but English, and every conceivable combination of the two languages between these extremes.

It is going to be difficult for the teacher to decide how much to modify the language in which instruction is being given, or to know how much to limit what is talked about in the course of the instruction. If the language is set at too high a level, the language learners are not going to get much out of the lesson; if it is set too low, those who know the language are likely to be bored. What most reasonable people do in a situation such as this is to aim somewhere in the middle and hope for the best. Consequently, the system fails at both ends: the language being used for instructional purposes is not all that useful to the learners as language input data, and the information that is intended to be conveyed is not getting through to the students. Some teachers have tried to remedy the situation by offering the same instruction first in one language and then in the other, either back to back or in two different periods of the day. But such translational methods—and there are many variations on this theme—do not help the situation at all, at least as far as language learning is concerned. When this method is used the teacher is relieved of any responsibility to modify the instructional language for the sake of the language learners. The feeling is that the adjustments are unnecessary since those who don't understand will be able to learn what is being taught when it is offered in the other language. Thus the language is probably useless to the learners as input. Since the learner gets the same material at a separate time in a language he understands, he has little reason to figure out what is being said in the new language. Lastly, the amount of material that can be covered in a school day is cut roughly in half by this method.

The situation, of course, is not as hopelessly complicated as I have made it seem. It is complicated, to be sure, but it is resolvable. There *are* teachers—many perhaps sitting in this audience today—who have figured out how to handle the problems I have been discussing in this talk. I have seen a few in action, and I have marveled at their ability to facilitate both language learning and subject matter learning. Research is badly needed to identify and make teachable what such teachers have figured out on their own and are doing in their classrooms. Many master teachers cannot themselves articulate what it is that they know and do intuitively; we will have to watch closely to learn what sensitivities they have that the rest of us lack.

The point of such research is to discover what successful instructional performance in a bilingual classroom is like. What I have in mind is not to go into the classroom and pull out of it a teacher's guide that can be handed to other teachers to follow. What we can gain through such research is rather a map of a process, a blueprint that we might use for training teachers. Until we can adequately characterize what bilingual teachers must be able to do, we cannot adequately train them to do it. Until that time, teachers are pretty much left on their own with respect to this essential aspect of teaching.

Language Proficiency of Teachers

The skills and ability needed to use language in the ways I have said that it needs to be used in the classroom require a very high degree of facility with the language. The teacher must be able to deal with its subtleties and complexities in order to make all the necessary adjustments and still be clear, precise, and relevant. An important question needs to be raised in research: just how proficient in each language does a teacher need to be in order to handle the linguistic demands of serving a bilingual program? This will not be an easy question to answer, both because of the inherent problem of figuring out how to judge what a person must know in order to handle anything as complex as teaching, and then how to measure that knowledge; and because of the political issues involved. These problems notwithstanding, we must deal with this question. If we don't, we are avoiding a major problem in bilingual education. The results of this kind of research might help us not only to select teachers better, but also to provide the kind of language training needed by teachers and prospective teachers for bilingual programs.

Conclusion

These are just two of the questions I believe need to be investigated through research. Answers to them would help us know better how to improve the instructional process in our classrooms.

At present, much of our instructional practice is supported only by faith and goodwill. We need to exchange those temporary supports with a more permanent foundation in solid research. These are matters not just for researchers to be worried about; we all have to be involved: practitioners, parents, administrators, and researchers alike. The fate of bilingual education may well depend on whether the right research questions are asked and on how these questions are answered. Professional researchers will be needed in formulating these questions, but it takes the wisdom that comes from day-to-day familiarity with actual classroom practices to determine what questions most need asking. What is imperative, in other words, is that collaborative research efforts bring researchers and practitioners together to consider what needs to be studied and how to carry out the research so that the findings of such investigations prove most useful to practitioners. We really cannot afford to do it in any other way.

Reference

Mehan, Hugh D. "Accomplishing Classroom Lessons." In *Language Use and School Performance,* edited by A. Cicouril et al. New York: Academic Press, 1974.

How Bilingual Multicultural Education Can Save the World

Manuel Ramírez, III
Oakes College
University of California at Santa Cruz

The title of my talk this afternoon — "How Bilingual Multicultural Education Can Save the World" — implies that the world needs saving! And, indeed, a look at national and world events indicates that there is much distrust among peoples throughout the world. Witness our problems in international relations: there have been miscommunication and evidence of hurt feelings caused by blunders of our government (in its present monolingual, monocultural form) in dealing with other countries.

Closer to home, the gasoline and fuel shortages that we are experiencing provide direct evidence that we are dependent on the resources of other countries and that a crisis in any one country can affect all the countries of the world. In addition, it looks as if we were moving toward some serious confrontations between conservatives and liberals over affirmative action, taxes, and continued government support of social, health, and educational programs.

The gas crisis also leads us to ask such questions as "Can we trust the oil companies? our political leaders? the agencies of our government?" In fact, can we trust anyone in an inflation economy which appears to pit taxpayers against the government, tenants against landlords, unions against businesses, farmers against consumers, investors against spenders?

Given the existence of these problems and others, only strong leaders who are adaptable, sensitive to social cues, flexible, and not influenced by stereotypes and external characteristics such as appearance, accents, and clothing can save us. Leaders who are receptive to diversity in themselves and in others, leaders and advisors who are multicultural and multilingual can save us. Most of these people in the United States are members of minority groups—people who became multicultural and multilingual in order to survive in an exclusivist society. The majority of multiculturals are people who have experienced the feeling of being different in a conformist society and who, in coping with this feeling, have succeeded in finding their own unique qualities as well as appreciating uniqueness in others.

What does it mean to be multicultural?

How do people get to be multicultural?

Can bilingual, multicultural education really make a difference?

I'll address these questions in order.

For the past four years my colleagues, Barbara Goffigon Cox at the University of California at Santa Cruz, Ray Garza at the University of California at Riverside, Al Castañeda at Stanford, and I have been studying multicultural people, specifically multicultural Chicanos. The questions we have been trying to answer are, "How did these people become multicultural?" and "How do they differ in skills, lifestyle, and philosophy of life from those who are not multicultural?"

In particular, we have given special attention to flexibility of personality, ability to adapt to different tasks and environments, ability to transcend cultural and social rigidity, and ability to use various interethnic skills to resolve conflict situations in mixed ethnic groups. At this point I would like to review some of the findings we have obtained, and describe the current work which we are doing.

Focus on the Psychodynamics of Multiculturals

We have studied the development of multicultural dynamics in people from four years old through college age, and our results show that our multicultural Mexican American subjects exhibit the following characteristics:

• **Cognitive Flexibility.** Cognitive flexibility exhibited by elementary school children in our Follow Through Program led us to a model of bicognition or cognitive flexibility and to rejection of Witkin's model (1962) of psychological differentiation (Ramírez and Castañeda, 1974). More recently, we have been able to observe this cognitive flexibility in the four-year-old children who are participating in the field testing of our *Nuevas Fronteras de Aprendizaje* program, a bilingual bicultural program for Head Start children. For example, participating Chicano preschool children of poor families in Rio Grande City, Texas, scored higher on the Raven Progressive Matrices and the Preschool Children's Embedded Figures Test than middle-class Anglo children in an upper middle-class preschool.

• **Life Orientation Flexibility.** Data from the life histories of Mexican American college students and also from their scores on the

Bicognitive Orientation to Life Scale and the California Psychological Inventory (Ramírez, Cox, and Castañeda, 1977) demonstrate this flexibility.

• **Flexibility in Perception of the World.** This was evidenced by the variety of world views reported by our college subjects (Ramírez, Cox, Garza, and Castañeda, 1978).

• **Leadership Flexibility.** Experiences reported in life histories by Mexican American college students and scores obtained by these same subjects on a leadership potential and flexibility scale (Ramírez, Cox, and Castañeda, 1977) provide evidence of leadership flexibility in multiculturals.

• **Adaptability.** College students reported accepting and being accepted by people of different ages, sexes, backgrounds, and walks of life (Ramírez, Cox, Garza, and Castañeda, 1978).

• **Interethnic Skills.** The multicultural Chicano subjects exhibited the following interethnic skills:

1. Cultural facilitation: introducing others to one's own culture or to other groups with which one is familiar; serving as teachers of culture and history.

2. Intercultural mediation: helping people of different groups to communicate with each other and understand each other to prevent conflicts and misunderstandings and to foster cooperation (Ramírez, Cox, Garza, and Castañeda, 1978).

This area, intercultural leadership and mediation, is currently being addressed by our research, so I would like to give an overview of our research program in this area.

Flexibility, Unity, and Transcendence Model of Multiculturalism

The predictions we make in our study are based on a model of multiculturalism we have been developing entitled "Flexibility, Unity, and Transcendence." Basically, the model describes socialization and life experiences as determining degree of openness to diversity in self, others, and in sociocultural environments. This degree of openness, in turn, determines the size and richness (heterogeneity) of the person's perspective and behavioral repertoires, the richness of personality-building elements which determine how flexible and adaptable the person is to the demands of life. Flexibility and adaptability contribute to the degree to which a person is comfortable in sociocultural situations; that is, whether a person behaves as a "monocultural," as a "functional bicultural" with a preference for one culture or another, or as a "synthesized multicultural" who is identified with several sociocultural groups. The size and richness of the perspective and behavioral repertoires also determine a person's orientation toward developing knowledge of self and self-growth.

Our hypothesis is that multicultural persons will use more effective behaviors to get a group composed of members of different ethnic groups to reach consensus of opinion (under conditions of conflict) and will be more flexible in the kinds of leadership behaviors they use than persons who are not multicultural. Effective behaviors and a flexible leadership style have been described as including the following:

1. Permitting all the group members to express their opinions

2. Giving equal status to opinions expressed by each member

3. Clarifying opinions expressed by individual group members as necessary

4. Providing direction without being authoritarian

5. Attempting to mediate between members

6. Remaining neutral; that is, not "taking sides" with any of the members of the group.

Group Work Sessions

Three students, a Black, an Anglo, and a Chicano, were selected and trained to assume each of three roles: a pro, a con, and a fence-sitting position on a controversial problem dealing with preservation of the cultural integrity of a hypothetical nonindustrialized society. The subjects were Chicano male college students from either Texas or California; some were multicultural and some were not. The subjects were assigned to be coordinators for the four-person groups, although it appeared as if they were selected by chance. The procedure is as follows:

1. The coordinator is instructed to try to get his group to achieve consensus on the controversial problem.

2. Each member of the group reads a summary of the problem. The group has twenty minutes to discuss the problem; the discussion between the confederates holding the con and pro positions is heated.

3. Fifteen minutes into the discussion the student playing the fence-sitter role switches to either the pro or con position, leaving one member of the group who is in disagreement. This member maintains his opinion, so the group never achieves consensus.

4. Then the coordinator reports the results to the experimenter who asks him to rate the three members of his group on various indices (how cooperative, capable, open, etc). The group sessions are tape-recorded as well as observed in order to rate the coordinator on leadership behaviors.

We have barely completed collecting our data, but preliminary findings indicate that multiculturals are more effective as leaders in many of the criterion behaviors: they are assertive but democratic in their style; they use more mediation in attempting to get members of their group to see the value of each other's point of view; they are more successful in remaining neutral during the discussion and they make fewer errors of communication. They do not misinterpret one member's position to another member, and they help clarify issues over which there is a difference of opinion. Finally, they are less critical and express less hostility toward the dissenting member.

Our ultimate objectives are to train people to use effective interethnic leadership skills which lead to less alienation and greater understanding in conflict situations in mixed groups. However, training in multiculturalism or bilingualism is extremely difficult; thus the great need for bilingual multicultural educational programs.

Bilingual Multicultural Education Encourages Development of Multiculturalism

Our life history research has established that early socialization and life experiences are of great importance in encouraging development of multiculturalism. Also important are parental and teacher attitudes toward diversity in people and in sociocultural environments (Ramírez and Cox, in press). It is important to give children the message that they can learn from everybody.

Our findings show that education experiences are crucial: meeting and interacting with people of different ethnic groups and socioeconomic backgrounds while at the same time maintaining close ties with people of your original group leads to a multicultural orientation. Also important are being in a position to teach others about your culture and language, and having an early opportunity to interact with adults and peers of different backgrounds and ethnic groups under conditions of cooperation and equality of status. Our data also point to the importance of "true bilingualism" in the development of multicultural orientations to life (Ramírez, Cox, and Castañeda, 1977). "True bilingualism" is more than knowing lexicon and syntax of two languages: it is knowing diversity through the experience that represents the two or more linguistic and cultural realities. Developing bilingualism through early experience fosters understanding and communication, not just at superficial levels. The potential for internalization of cultural diversity is nowhere greater than in our bilingual multicultural education programs.

In order to ensure that we can provide multicultural leaders, we must concentrate on fighting to save bilingual multicultural education. We must hold the line against opposition until the current political tide of retrenchment dissipates.

In his most recent newsletter (1979), Congressman Leon Panetta told his constituents "We live in a world that is rapidly shrinking as the technologies of communications and transportation grow more advanced, and as the role of international economics in our everyday lives becomes increasingly important. Unless this nation finds ways of improving its knowledge and understanding of foreign language and foreign cultures, we will be placing a severe handicap on our ability to understand, influence, and react to world events."

James Baldwin, the Black writer, in a recent speech at the University of California at Berkeley (*Los Angeles Times,* 1979), echoed Panetta's views but emphasized the importance of recognizing the diversity that is reflected in members of minority groups in our own country. He said, "I suggest that what the rulers of this country don't know about the world which surrounds them is the price they pay for not knowing me. If they couldn't deal with my father, how are they going to deal with the people in the streets of Tehran? I could have told them if they had asked."

Our mission as bilingual multicultural educators is clear: we must train multiculturals to be our future leaders.

References

Los Angeles Times, 27 April 1979.

Panetta, Leon. *Report to the Sixteenth District.* Winter 1979.

Ramírez, M., and Cox, B. "Parenting for Multiculturalism." In *Parenting in Modern Society,* edited by M. Fantini. Longman, in press.

Ramírez, M.; Cox, B.; Castañeda, A. "The Psychodynamics of Biculturalism." Unpublished research report, 1977.

Ramírez, M., and Castañeda, A. *Cultural Democracy, Bicognitive Development, and Education.* New York: Academic Press, 1974.

Ramírez, M.; Cox, B.; Garza, R.; Castañeda, A. "Dimensions of Biculturalism in Mexican American College Students." Unpublished research report, 1978.

Witkin, H.; Dyls, R. B.; Fatersen, H. F.; Goodenough, D. R.; and Karp, S.A. *Psychological Differentiation.* New York: John Wiley, 1962.

Some Personal Reflections on the Bilingual Education Movement and the Challenge Ahead

Tomás A. Arciniega
San Diego State University

Although genuinely honored and pleased to have been invited as one of the keynote speakers, I face you this afternoon with mixed emotions. In fact, let me put it stronger than that. Given the status of bilingual education today, before you stands a man who is simultaneously *proud, troubled,* and *angry.*

I want to discuss the things driving those developments and share some thoughts about the why and the implications, and most important of all, the where to from here — *porque ahora es cuando.* The next two years are *the* critical ones, and we had better face that full square. And incidentally, it may well be that Hispanics, as the largest of the language-minority groups, will have to play the principal role and carry the major responsibility in that struggle.

As so many of you in this audience have noted in your speeches and in some of the things you write and talk about, it is always a beautifully reinforcing and self-renewing experience to participate in this kind of conference. Perhaps the most satisfying aspect to me is the opportunity to listen to, interact with, and marvel at the caliber of the new wave of — *la nueva ola de* — bilingual educators. My chest and soul fill with pride to note the strength, vigor, and intellectual power which that new wave represents. For in the fullest sense of the word that is what the fight for bilingual education has always been about and is now : the right to seek the best way to ensure *que los nuestros* grow up proud and confident about

21

themselves and their abilities. And equally important is that they become imbued with a sincere commitment, nay an eagerness, to jump into the fray—*la lucha continua*—as we push to improve conditions for minority peoples in U.S. society. That new wave exemplifies in living form what that expectation is all about. There is no question in my mind that the bilingual education movement in the United States has been the major force that enables you and me—us—to rejoice and take heart in the rise of that *nueva ola*. More than any other development in the history of bilingual minorities in the United States, bilingual education, as a concept as well as an action agenda, provides the means to shatter the normative structure within groups as well as in the general society, the structure which in the past spurred our *abuelos y nuestros padres* to believe and act in ways which demonstrated unequivocally that they knew well that in order to succeed and progress economically—to make it in U.S. society—one had to trade in his or her ethnic soul. For Mexicans we had to become de-Mexicanized. For all language minorities that message was dreadfully similar. And as we all know, it wasn't that those *viejos* lacked courage or didn't want to buck the system, it simply was the way it was. Given the oppressive nature of the limited opportunity in the United States for ethnics, there was no other practical way, short of open rebellion. We have seen significant changes in that regard.

Bilingual education as part and parcel of the civil rights movement has enabled us to make operational the noble concept so positively embraced by our society in the late sixties and early seventies. I'm referring to cultural pluralism, which rejected assimilation and promoted the importance of the right to be different, and most important of all, the need to provide an education which honored and responded to cultural differences. Bilingual education, as no other single program extension of that commitment, has challenged the U.S. public education status quo to demonstrate in actual form and practice that the United States is sincere in its commitment to equality of educational opportunity for all.

The rise and spread of bilingual education in the past few years have been spectacular. The strength and power of the program have been especially dramatic when one stops to consider that it is a pedagogical movement conceived and born outside the mainstream of the Anglo American way in a conventional sense.

The establishment of hundreds of school district bilingual programs; the network of training resource centers, materials development centers, and dissemination centers; the bilingual clearinghouse; and shortly an NIE-funded national bilingual research and development center, too—all represent truly remarkable accomplishments. I am firmly convinced that our having come so far is living testimony both to the courage and tenacity of people like yourselves and your counterparts across the land and to the educational soundness of our cause.

I am particularly encouraged, too, by the solid research and pilot-study evidence on bilingual education and in a broader sense on bilingualism viewed from a cross-cultural perspective. Efforts in as diverse settings as Israel, Canada, New York, and the Southwest are beginning to show consistently that children who achieve bilingualism through formal bilingual schooling are scoring higher on achievement *and* IQ tests compared to their peers (Lambert, 1977). This is holding true consistently for both majority kids as well as minority-culture kids. Significantly, the key strengths appear to be in problem solving and creativity, which are areas deemed particularly critical to succeeding in a highly technological society. These are welcome developments with important implications.

When one stops to reflect, we have come a way, haven't we? Yes, there is much to be proud of regarding what we've been about these past six or seven years especially. But, as we all know only too well, we've got a tremendously long way still to go. The struggle is far from over.

Of Things to Be Troubled and Angry About

As I implied in the first part of my discussion on the importance of the bilingual movement, what concerns me about the public educational systems we're trying to reform through bilingual education is not that they aren't functioning well enough, but rather that they are functioning only too well and too consistently with the type of societal structure they were designed to promote and maintain. School systems serve an important "maintenance" function in the way they socialize individuals to the roles they are "supposed" to play in the greater society. They accomplish this macrosocial function in the typical school in the United States with devastating effectiveness.

Thus, my quarrel with the prevailing state of things is with the outcomes or benefits derived from the school system by its various clienteles. I am appalled that the basic legitimacy of a system which distributes its educational benefits in a grossly unequal manner is so seldom really questioned. From my perspective, it is sad and personally painful to note the efficiency of those organizational mechanisms which transform the schooling process into a sham game of losers and winners with the cards stacked against minorities and the lower classes. The ultimate tribute to the finesse with which the game is played is that so often the "losers" graduate convinced of the fairness of the process. In blunt terms, then, my critique is aimed at the structure of schools that promote the interests of the dominant powers who control economic wealth at the expense of excluded minorities—and specifically at the expense of the linguistically different.

The problem of such domination in our schools is tied inextricably to the broader social system. As I have noted elsewhere:

> The organizational problem of how to change schools to meet more adequately the needs of bicultural clients can appear deceptively simple. In reality, it is tremendously complex because educational systems reflect quite accurately the existent socioeconomic stratification makeup of the communities they serve. (Arciniega, 1971)

The reforms needed in public education to bring about genuine improvements will not come easily. They require time, great sacrifice and effort, and a long-range commitment to changing the real "meaning" of schools.

Perhaps the most important message is that in most places school organizations provide fantastically powerful learning environments about life, who and what is important, and how best to get ahead. Schools as human organizations seldom fail to teach certain important lessons about the worth of education, the dynamics of authority and status, and honesty, reality, and relevance of education as these have been defined by the majority society.

Let me give you a specific example or two of the effects of those school organizational games. An important finding reported in the fifth report of the U.S. Commission on Civil Rights Mexican American Education Study (1973) was that teachers of the Southwest are failing to meet their most basic responsibility—that of providing each bicultural child the opportunity to gain maximum benefits from school and to develop his or her capabilities to the fullest. Directly pertinent to our discussion here, the commission concluded that "Changes are needed in the way teachers are trained and in the standards by which they are judged, and changes are needed in educational programs and curriculums so that all children may be reached."

Of central importance is that the commission found that the amount of praise given to Mexican American and Anglo students varied with the ethnicity of the teacher. Significantly, they found, even in the case of minority teachers, that:

> . . . Mexican American and Anglo teachers give similar amounts of praise and encouragement to Chicano pupils. However, Mexican American teachers praise Anglo pupils considerably more than their Anglo colleagues. This results in a larger disparity in praise or encouragement from the Mexican American teachers in favor of Anglo students.

> . . . Mexican American teachers may tend to use relatively few Anglos in their classrooms to emphasize the middle-class Anglo culture and values to the Chicano pupils. It is possible that, to a large extent, many Mexican American teachers operate under the philosophy that success for Chicano pupils lies in acquiring Anglo traits.

> As a result of having gone through an educational system dominated by the Anglo culture and working in a school system directed by Anglo administrators, it is possible that many Mexican American teachers seek to identify with the culture and values of the dominant society.

Thus, even minority-group teachers have been socialized by norm, authority-status, and reward structure pressures to become imparters of majority-culture values and norms as defined by the prevailing order, even at the expense of the bicultural student. As a result of primarily the power and status-prestige rules inherent in the school "game," many Chicano teachers and administrators (and to a lesser extent, even parents) seek so strongly to identify with Anglo cultural values and norms that their behaviors begin to reflect a pejorative view of their own background and cultural heritage. Many insist that Chicano students acquire Anglo traits, for they have decided that only in this way can bicultural students succeed in U.S. society. It should perhaps be stressed that this is done in an effort to "help" the child and to find what is best for him or her. Sadly, even some minority-group educators in the system seem to have concluded, sometimes more strongly than their Anglo counterparts, that the best way—perhaps the only way—for bicultural students to succeed in this country is to rid themselves of all vestiges of minority-group identity. It is particularly pathetic to see brown faces line up with those fighting bilingual education.

This example is presented not to make a case against the hiring of bicultural or minority personnel, but rather to begin to sketch the organizational complexities involved in achieving meaningful reform and to stress the importance of the bilingual education movement. It is a harsh but true reality of school and university life that all too often those best in a position to provide an authentic, culturally pluralistic learning environment have been coerced into behaving in ways completely at cross-purposes with their own best interests and at variance with democratic principles and ideals which should be the guiding axioms of our schools and universities.

The issue of pushing changes for the better through bilingual education is indeed a social and most political matter. The backlash we're experiencing at the local, state, and federal levels is actually a positive sign when viewed from a long-range organizational perspective. I think the very strength of that negative tide indicates that only now are the full reform implications of what it means for schools and school personnel to implement bilingual programs beginning to be recognized. And the fact that this push is backed by federal and state bucks and a sound, fast-developing research and theoretical base has scared the hell out of some pretty perceptive folks in too many high places. The growing possibility of the pedagogical viability of bilingual education as a better schooling alternative for all children and the shift of power implications of such a development has not gone unnoticed, either. Of importance also is the fact that bilingual education leaders, as a potent new force on the scene, have made it abundantly clear—and the message has been received loud and clear—that we are no longer talking about a few scattered projects to keep this particular category of ethnics placated. When you think about it, what is really surprising is that the backlash didn't get mounted sooner.

It is precisely during these difficult times that unity and concerted efforts by bilingual educators are so necessary to press this nation to deliver on the promise of recently won court and legislative commitments. Incidentally, the most troublesome and difficult part of that task may well be in how to hold ourselves accountable measured in the simple terms of the greatest good for the greatest number of bilingual kids in school. In order to accomplish this we need to insist on unity and a desire to help,

Figure 1
Schematic Outline of the Principal Forces
Working For and Against Bilingual Education at Present

Mexican oil forcing more positive U.S. posture ———→ 1 ←—	Economic crunch spurring national conservative mood

Population growth of Hispanics, the largest bilingual group ————→ 2 ←—	Declining enrollments forcing loss of jobs, closing schools, etc.

Continuing court victories (school finance, *Lau*) ————→ 3 ←—	White backlash sparking national pullback on equal employment opportunity and civil rights programs at federal, state, and local levels

Federal bilingual program $ increased ————→ 4 ←—	Attempts to repeal and gut bilingual legislation at federal, state, and local levels

Growth in power, competence and numbers of bilingual educators ————→ 5 ←—	Teacher organizations lining up against bilingual education

Growing commitment to bilingual education in colleges and universities ————→ 6 ←—	Severe budget cuts which have drastically reduced the ability of SEAs to mount bilingual programs on their own

Greater self-awareness and pride in culture and language among bilingual ethnics, which bilingual education has promoted ————→ 7 ←—	Backlash causing too many bilingual educators and supporters to compromise too far, too easily, and too early

certainly; but, perhaps most important of all, we need to press ourselves to face, each on his or her own terms, the reality of the Hispanic or Asian American or American Indian in the United States which binds us in common cause.

This is the first step *y quizás el más importante y profundo. Porque, queridos hermanos y hermanas, la verdad es que sólo nosotros conocemos bien y verdaderamente nuestra realidad. Por eso mismo es que estoy tan convencido que soluciones para los problemas que enfrentamos tienen que venir principalmente de las mentes, manos, y acciones de los nuestros. Y éso es lo que obliga a gente como nosotros —como paso imprescindible —*

el no rechazar la riqueza de nuestra realidad, de nuestros antecedentes, nuestros idiomas, y el tesoro de nuestro biculturalismo.

Unity with a commitment to action among all who proclaim themselves to be bilingual educators is absolutely essential in these troubled times. The crosscurrent of pressures is fierce with the battle lines clearly drawn. But there are forces working for as well as against our cause.

My analysis of the prevailing state of things points to seven principal cross-pressures (Figure 1). On the plus side, or what we've got going which can work for us, are the following:

1. Mexican oil and the rise of Mexico, which are forcing a more positive view and posture toward bilingual concerns

2. The population growth of Hispanics, soon to become the largest minority group in the United States

3. The continuing trend of court victories, particularly in school finance and *Lau*

4. Federal bilingual program budget increases

5. Growth in competence, numbers, and power of bilingual educators

6. Growing commitment to and investment in bilingual education at colleges and universities

7. The greater self-awareness and pride in bilingual ethnic America which has been promoted by bilingual education.

On the negative side are the following:

1. The economic crunch, spurring a conservative national mood

2. Declining school enrollments, which are forcing a loss of teaching jobs, the closing of schools, etc.

3. White backlash, producing a pullback from equal employment opportunity and civil rights programs

4. Very apparent attempts aimed at gutting bilingual legislation at federal, state, and local levels

5. Teacher organizations that are lining up against bilingual education

6. Severe budget cuts which have drastically reduced the ability of state education agencies (SEAs) to mount bilingual programs

7. The backlash that has caused too many bilingual educators and supporters to compromise too far, too easily, and too early.

The critical and necessary first step, then, involves ensuring a united front regarding the need to push actively for changes in the public educational status quo. That unity has to be based on full acceptance of a pluralistic rather than an assimilationist model of change. As we do so, whether at the school-district level or with individual teachers, principals, deans, or *lo que sea,* we have to recognize that the thrust toward achieving cultural pluralism in educational form and practice strikes directly to the heart of some of this country's most hallowed traditional beliefs, involving the distribution of educational benefits. Massive reorientation and program changes will be required if schools no longer are to be allowed to melt away differences. Instead, as bilingual education does so well, we have to insist that schools openly affirm and promote cultural, ethnic, and linguistic differences as good and positive national resources worthy of preservation and enhancement. The new models must require schools to reorganize programs and reorient staffs to capitalize and build upon precisely those basic differences which heretofore they have been so committed to wiping out in children.

Facing up to and promoting that bold new ideal and reality with courage and conviction is the basic first step. That is the backdrop, *hermanos,* against which we need to ponder our position at a crucial juncture in public education's response to the linguistically different in this country. We face a tremendous challenge to which we must respond with professional facts, theories, and overt actions, not political ethnic rhetoric.

Another way of saying this is that it isn't enough to know and care and to hurt *as* or *for* Chicanos or Puerto Ricans or Filipinos: we've got to go beyond. We've got to be able to assess where we are and, most important, specify carefully where we want to go even as we continue to confront obvious obstacles to progress.

What this implies can be seen as a three-dimensional obligation that each of us has in the months ahead. First, we've got to carry out the most technically and professionally sound program effort we know how to design and implement whatever our respective roles. Second, we've got to become a part of efforts to energetically promote, in a politics-of-education sense, the worth and importance of bilingual education for our children and our peoples. And third, we've got to actively fashion and support ways and means to *reach all segments of our population who have the most at stake, to convince them of the seriousness of where we are and of the obligation they have to become involved and mobilized in the fight for bilingual education.*

In closing, let me state my message very straightforwardly. I implore you — us — to recognize, as bilingual educators, how important each is and to continue to be proud of that fact. *La imploración que les hago es que como educadores bilingües tenemos que reconocer cuán tan importante somos en estos tiempos. Y hay que tener orgullo del hecho.* But recognize also the very real obligation that this entails. *Pero reconozcamos también la verdadera obligación que esto conlleva.*

And recognize, too, that diversity always creates opportunities. Today and the immediate tomorrows, if nothing else, present us with the opportunity to stand and fight together for the most just of causes. It is beautiful to demonstrate with courage and conviction *juntos y unidos,* in a Burkian sense, how to be true to our character — how to be worthy of the title *Bilingual Educator.*

References

Arciniega, Tomás A. *Public Education Response to the Mexican American Student*. Innovative Resources, Inc., 1971. (Available through author only.)

Lambert, Wallace E. "The Effect of Bilingualism on the Individual: Cognitive and Sociocultural Consequences." In *Bilingualism: Psychological, Social, and Education Implications*. Edited by Peter A. Hornby. New York: Academic Press, 1977.

U.S., Commission on Civil Rights. *Teachers and Students: Differences in Teacher Interaction with Mexican American and Anglo Students*. Mexican-American Education Study, vol. 5. Washington, D.C.: U.S. Government Printing Office, 1973.

Toward Understanding Cultural Difference in Public Education

Gene T. Chávez
Arizona State University

Because American public education has traditionally emphasized cultural assimilation, children who are different from the mainstream have suffered alienation, discrimination, and, for the most part, a poorer quality of education (Ramírez and Castañeda, 1974). Although much progress has been made in the last fifteen years toward providing education geared for culturally different children, there still exists much misunderstanding about the needs of these children. When one suggests that a problem exists in such a respected institution as the public school, one runs the risk of being misinterpreted and misunderstood, especially if one advocates changing institutionalized attitudes about how children are to be treated.

Yet the fact remains that just because some individuals are culturally different in our society, they experience frustration, underachievement, and sometimes mental and physical abuse at the hands of those who wish that they would conform, assimilate, or acculturate.

After the smoke cleared from the sixties and certain basic human rights were gained, a growing desire for cultural democracy was articulated by more and more culturally different individuals (Belok, 1978). For the racially or ethnically different individual, this desire has been developed into an alternative ideology which has emerged in reaction to the conformist view of assimilation and acculturation into mainstream, middle-class Anglo culture and values (Epstein, 1977). This is not to say that wholesale rejection of mainstream culture is advocated, but rather that it is the right of every individual to maintain whatever aspects of culture(s) he or she holds valuable. As a matter of fact, culturally different persons would find it in their favor to be able to participate in mainstream U.S. culture as well as in their own. Thus, these individuals may have the "best of two (or more) worlds" as long as the two are compatible and cognitive dissonance does not result (Paulston, 1978).

One of the dilemmas in U.S. education is really understanding what cultural difference means and how it should be interpreted into meaningful learning experiences for ethnically and culturally different students (Appleton, Jordan, and Papen-Jordan, 1978). The understanding of cultural difference must eventually concern itself with the need for providing culturally different students with the educational experiences that enhance their right to feel positive toward their native cultures, as well as to feel that they know the world of the Anglo mainstream culture well enough to make a contribution to it if they so choose.

In many ways, U.S. schools have propagated Anglo conformist views of acculturation, or at best, certain interpretations of cultural pluralism. Usually variations of the "American melting pot" have failed to fully appreciate the psychological and sociological needs of culturally different students (Gordon, 1964). The failure has been the oversight in recognizing differences in such areas as cognitive styles, social values, and individual preferences. Within the melting-pot ideal, these children have often been forced to make a series of decisions about cultural values for which they are not prepared (Banks, 1975). For example, a child from a traditional Chicano family may be considered by the teacher to be uninterested because the child does not stay after school to work on a project with other fellow students. The fact is that the father, whose values are different from the school's, requires that all his children accomplish assigned tasks by the time he gets home and won't listen to any excuses. Regardless of the child's interest in "getting involved," he or she is labeled "uninterested" by teacher and peers.

An understanding of the child's home value system, which is often based on an ethnic subculture, can eliminate much of such labeling of culturally different children with its resulting pain (Rivlin and Fraser, 1977). As a child matures and reaches the age when rational decisions are possible, he or she should be allowed to know the various options. Whether the child remains within the boundaries of thinking created by birth or branches out into mainstream thinking is made possible by the efforts of the school to help the child appreciate the values of both the native culture and that held by the majority. In order for the culturally different child to learn these appreciations, it is important that educators first recognize cultural difference; second, that they know how to appreciate cultural difference; and third, that they know when to appreciate cultural difference.

Analysis of Cultural Difference

Cultural difference is still a vague and abstract term to most people and bears further analysis. To begin, it may be asked "What is culture?" Consider the following uses of the word *culture* :

1. She is a very cultured lady.

2. The culture of the Apache is different from that of the Navajo.

3. He was inoculated with a virus culture.

4. Cultured pearls are relatively inexpensive.

In the first use of the word *culture*, training, development, and refinement of mind, morals, or taste are implied. The process of education or refining may also be called culturing. Culture used in this sense is the kind in which teachers are most often involved as they endeavor to train, develop, and refine the minds, morals, and taste of their students.

The second example looks at culture in an anthropological sense. In this way, *culture* is defined as the sum of the attainments and learned behavior patterns of any specific period, race, or people. It may be regarded as expressing a traditional way of life which is subject to gradual but continuous modification by succeeding generations. Attainments of a people include art and literary forms, as well as technological innovations. Behavior patterns are general and enduring ways that a given people respond to stimuli within their environment. It is in this sense that the person who studies cultural difference considers culture. He or she is interested in legitimizing the preservation of some cultural differences of the nation's various ethnic groups. This view justifies the results of such preservation as providing a more democratic, more interesting, and more dynamically fruitful culture for all, rather than one in which uniformity is the norm. I will discuss this meaning of culture later in relation to appreciating cultural difference.

The third example uses the word in a strictly biological sense which means the development of a microorganism in an artificial medium for medical purposes.

The last use of the word *culture* is very much like the third, except that it is used in an active sense. That is, the pearls produced by human intervention in a natural process can be considered as having been acted upon. A synonomous term would be *cultivated* as used in the following example : *The farmer cultivated his field early in the spring of the year.*

When the term *cultural difference* is used, *culture* carries the meaning of at least examples 1, 2, and 4. Understanding and appreciating cultural differences in the public school setting means that a person may be considered cultured even though his or her training, development, and refinement may consist of experiences and values that differ markedly from those of the mainstream. It certainly reflects the anthropological meaning of the word and recognizes the contributions of past attainments and learned behavior patterns as important factors in which a group of people are or are not allowed to be. In the last sense, culturally different children who are allowed to experience their inherited "culturing" and who are encouraged by the schools to believe that their birthright cultures are good will feel that they have contributions to make to society. The children feel that they have the potential for succeeding in interactions within their own ethnic communities as well as within the mainstream culture.

This, then, is the basic educational issue as it is interpreted in this paper: the need for providing culturally different children with the educational experience necessary to enhance their right to be able to participate in more than one culture, if only because some children are called upon to do so. Of course, it is realized that culture is dynamic and changing, so that it becomes important for individuals (1) to be able to take part in the culture in which they find themselves and in the modes that are appropriate *al día* and (2) to feel that they are contributing to the enrichment and continued development of their own cultures.

The Mexican American child provides an example of how public education has failed to meet the educational needs of culturally diverse children. If a Mexican American child is raised during the preschool years in the sociocultural system characteristic of the traditional Mexican American community, the socialization practices pertaining to language, cultural values, and learning style are unique to the Mexican American heritage. The child will have developed communication, learning, and motivational styles and skills that are appropriate to the native culture. When this child begins to experience public education which emphasizes Anglo conformity, his progress toward feeling good about himself and the contribution he has to make is impeded — impeded because the new cultural world, which he has come to explore and to understand for his own advantage, fails to take into account the reality that he must continue to function effectively in and contribute to the Mexican American cultural community.

Hence, an appreciation of cultural difference is proposed for public schools. The reality is that many students in the United States who are culturally different are taught the mainstream Anglo culture, too often to the exclusion and sometimes to the prohibition of their own language, heritage, cultural values, learning, and motivational styles. Under a system of education where cultural difference is recognized, appreciated, and taught, the phrase *equal educational opportunity* becomes meaningful. Acquiring the skills that are necessary for effective participation in and significant contribution to one's native cultural community and to the mainstream society becomes possible.

Such a system of public education would also provide the opportunity for any student (culturally or ethnically different, or not) who lives in an area in which an ethnic minority group predominates (e.g., the Southwest) to learn to participate effectively in, or contribute to, the development of a culture different from his or her own. For example, in the southwestern part of the United States, many students who eventually become members of the helping professions in ethnic minority areas do not learn in schools the skills that would help them understand and work better with Mexican American or Native American populations.

Appreciating Cultural Difference

The concept of appreciation is not a new one to educational curricula. In fact, many schools offer courses such as Music Appreciation or Art Appreciation. Designing curricula which would appreciate cultural difference as earlier defined becomes the next step toward understanding cultural difference in public education.

Although appreciation as a concept is complex and may call for a sophisticated analysis of theories of aesthetics, we can find meaning and applicability to the understanding of cultural differences by examining the following interrelated usages found in our everyday language (Appleton, 1978):

1. Appreciation as pleasure. Example: "I really appreciate a cold glass of Carta Blanca after a hard day at work." At this level, appreciation is an unanalyzed expression of feelings or value placed on an object of enjoyment. It does not demand justification, but rather is a straightforward expression of pleasure.

When we consider the immense quantity of pleasurable aspects of different cultures (e.g., Mexican folk music, Indian art forms, Japanese food), the significance of appreciation at this level becomes immediately apparent. Unfortunately, appreciation of cultural difference often stops at this level. There is so much more.

2. Appreciation as gratitude. Example: "I really appreciate all the hard work you did for me on this project." To appreciate in this sense is to recognize the contribution of the efforts of others to one's personal well-being. Another aspect of appreciation at this level is the ability to see the applicability or usefulness of others' contributions to our own needs.

Students cannot appreciate in this sense what they do not "see." That is, if students are not given the opportunity to recognize the positive contributions made by the many culturally diverse minorities, they may never come to appreciate or have gratitude toward the contributions of these fellow Americans.

3. Intellectual appreciation. Examples:
a.1. "He has gained an appreciation of the Navajo culture by living on the reservation for two years." Appreciation in this sense implies a level of understanding acquired through actual experience.

a.2. "She has learned to appreciate Hopi religious beliefs by seeing a film about how Hopi leaders work together with Anglo recreational developers to preserve sacred grounds." In this example, appreciation is learned vicariously. Nevertheless, it is learned as well, perhaps, as if she were the Anglo recreational developer in a.1.

Learning about the culturally different is a good start toward understanding their value system. Experiencing how cultural difference feels can lead to an even closer intellectual appreciation of the culturally different person's world view.

b. "He has gained an appreciation for the factors leading to the urbanization of Blacks in Northern cities after the Civil War." In this case we recognize an ordering of the knowledge of events assembled in such a way that the student creates a thesis of causality, a hypothesis testing of sorts which can eventually lead to a profound appreciation of the predicament in which many inner-city, poor Blacks presently find themselves. With this kind of appreciation, the student is more likely to make more meaningful generalizations about Blacks and perhaps even other minority groups.

c. "I have learned to appreciate the Chicano point of view on the matter of retaining some aspects of Mexican heritage." To have learned another point of view by (1) understanding ("seeing") the difference and by (2) understanding the reasons for that difference, whether or not we agree, brings us to another level of intellectual appreciation. It is like appreciating the differences in styles among painters. The individual who appreciates variance in painters' styles knows something about painting techniques and also understands something about how each style uses these techniques to achieve a visual and psychological effect. The educational implication here is that students don't just come to appreciate cultural difference, they must *learn* to appreciate it.

From examples *a*, *b*, and *c*, it becomes apparent that facts alone are not enough to bring about intellectual appreciation of cultural difference. Students must be taught to be able to order facts in such a way that they come to see their effects. Hence, they learn to appreciate factors involved in cultural difference, which enables them eventually to develop theoretical positions based on a profound grasp of facts about cultural difference which are more generalizable.

4. Aesthetic Appreciation. Example: "She appreciates fine Navajo rugs." This brings us back to the affective domain and combines intellectual appreciation with appreciation as pleasure.

For our purposes it may be useful to consider aesthetic appreciation on a continuum:

Aesthetic Appreciation

"I just like it!"   "I recognize these elements of
                                                     style, detail, and imagination!"

Affective Appreciation   Intellectual Appreciation

As we move up the continuum, our appreciation is more refined. It becomes fuller and more laden with meaning. We enjoy because we appreciate; we appreciate because we understand. The tremendous pedagogical implications of bringing students to an aesthetic appreciation of cultural difference challenge us to get out of our ethnocentric shells and help students know what the real world is all about.

References

Appleton, Nicholas. "Appreciation: Another Look." Unpublished article, Arizona State University, 1978.

Appleton, Nicholas; Jordan, Daniel; and Papen-Jordan, Michele. *Cultural Pluralism and the Social Structure: A Systems View*. Bilingual Education Paper Series. Los Angeles: National Dissemination and Assessment Center, 1978.

Banks, James A. *Teaching Strategies for Ethnic Studies*. Boston: Allyn and Bacon, 1975.

Belok, Michael V. "Minorities and Ethnicity." In *Social Control for the 1980's*. Edited by Joseph S. Roucek. Westport, Greenwood Press Conn.: 1978. Belok summarizes his chapter in his concluding remarks: "The discrepancies between the American ideal and practice result in tension in the social order as more and more individuals become conscious of the frustrations inherent in their positions. Ethnicity has become a vehicle for pushing group demands."

Epstein, Noel. *Language, Ethnicity, and the Schools*. Washington, D.C.: Institute for Educational Leadership, 1977. Epstein explores the educational implications of the policy alternatives suggested by those who advocate the alternative idealogies of bilingual bicultural education.

Gordon, Milton M. *Assimilation in American Life: The Role of Race, Religion, and National Origins*. New York: Oxford University Press, 1964. "Anglo-conformity received its fullest expression in the so-called Americanization movement, which gripped the nation like a fever during World War I. Whole Americanization in its various stages had more than one emphasis; essentially it was a consciously articulated movement to strip the immigrant of his native culture and attachments and make him over into an American along Anglo-

Saxon lines—all this to be accomplished with great rapidity" (pp. 98-99).

Paulston, Christina Bratt. "Biculturalism: Some Reflections and Speculations," *TESOL Quarterly* 12, no. 4 (December 1978). An excellent paper which explores in speculative fashion the process and characteristics of becoming bicultural. The basic argument is that becoming bicultural is an eclectic process which results in an idiosyncratic mixture of the two (C_1 and C_2) cultures, with one basic "cultural competence" but with two sets of "sociocultural performance"—R. Keesing, "Theories of Culture." In *Annual Review of Anthropology* 3 (1974): 73-97.

Ramírez, Manuel III, and Castañeda, Alfredo. *Cultural Democracy, Bicognitive Development, and Education.* New York: Academic Press, 1974. In chapter 1, pp. 1-20, Ramírez and Castañeda point out the history of neglect that is associated with the Mexican American educational experience in this country.

Rivlin, Harry, and Fraser, Dorothy M. "Ethnic Labeling and Mislabeling." In *In Praise of Diversity: A Resource Book for Multicultural Education,* edited by Milton J. Gold, Carl A. Grant, and Harry Rivlin. Washington, D.C.: Teacher Corps, Association of Teacher Educators, 1977. An excellent article on the misuse of ethnic labeling. "Everyone knows that there are laws and regulations against mislabeling canned goods. The weight of the contents of the can of food and the ingredients the can contains must be stated on its label. Don't we also need ethnic laws against mislabeling people? Especially the children in our schools?" (p. 6).

Special Populations

Cultural Pluralism in Japan:
A Sociolinguistic Outline

Nobuyuki Honna
Kinjo Gakuin University
Nagoya, Japan

Japan is generally said to be a mono-ethnic, monocultural, and monolingual society both at home and abroad. But this is not true. In this paper, I would like to speak for a small number of people in Japan who have started to reconsider the Japanese social structure in terms of linguistic and cultural pluralism. Our observation will be, then, from a worm's-eye view rather than from a bird's-eye view, because a localized down-to-earth point of view is essential when we try to understand human struggles for self-identity.

I will choose six sociolinguistic topics from the fields in which I have been working in Japan: (1) bimodalism of the deaf between sign language and spoken language, (2) bidialectalism in a multidialectal society, (3) significant differences in the way language is used between urban and rural children, (4) the Ainu and (5) Korean minorities, and (6) foreign language education.

Talking about deaf people and their language and education problems, one can easily allude analogically and allegorically to almost all that is happening in the discussion of linguistic, cultural, and cognitive pluralism in the world. Therefore, I think that it is an appropriate topic to start with in the discussion of the whole theme.

Sign Language and Spoken Language of the Deaf

There are 250,000 deaf persons in Japan out of a total population of 120 million. This amounts to a deaf-to-hearing ratio of one to five hundred, which is a slightly high proportion, considering the fact that one out of every thousand people in the world is said to be deaf.

A few ethnographical studies available in Japan of the social relationship between deaf and hearing persons indicate very similar domination patterns to those between minority groups and majority groups in any human society. Deaf people are socially ostracized and educationally mishandled.

Specifically, the language of the deaf, their native sign language, is regarded as a simple collection of animal-like gestures, and not as a natural human language. Their syntax is considered to be merely an underdeveloped and rudimentary subsystem of the spoken version of a language.

In deaf education, the use of native sign language is usually discarded, and instead the use of speech is almost categorically imposed upon deaf students. Teaching speech to deaf students (generally called oralism) has been unsuccessful, and this has led some of the public to wrongly believe that deaf students are not intelligent enough to acquire language.

Deaf students would tell a lot of stories a few years ago about how severely they were punished by their teachers when they were caught signing in class or at school. Students trying to communicate with teachers by sign were ignored at best, and their hands were tied at worst, which was not unusual. Teachers willing to sign for communicative rapproachement with students were reprimanded by principals. Teachers trying to learn how to sign were advised against doing so. Few people were interested, it would appear, in listening to the message deaf persons were trying to bring from their world of silence.

However, current studies of Japanese sign language[1*]–particularly in the field of sociolinguistics, which highlights language use in social contexts—clearly indicate that Japanese sign language, or generally any sign language in the world, is a natural human language as complex and well organized as any spoken language in terms of phonology (or kinesics, more precisely), syntax, semantics, and socio-psychological style-shifting. The only difference of a significant nature between sign language and spoken language is in articulatory modes: manual for sign language and oral for spoken language.

Sociolinguistic studies[2] reveal how ignorant most speakers-hearers are of the natural language systems that the deaf communities have developed over the centuries. The deaf have established by themselves an effective system of thinking and communicating which is quite appropriate to their physical characteristics. Those studies also suggest how presumptuous hearing persons tend to be about the necessity of speaking and hearing. They consider it abnormal not to be able to speak and hear. Actually, however, deaf persons are living a complex life without the use of speech

---

*See notes on pages 53-54.

and hearing, but with the use of their natural sign language. Treating the use of sign language as some form of deviance, deficiency, or pathology, therefore, stems from ignorance of the nature of sign language on the part of the hearing population.

If language is the most important manifestation of the self, as is often argued in the theory of bilingual education, and if sign language is a natural human language, as is suggested in current sociolinguistic surveys, then a deaf person should not be deprived of his or her mother language in any way.

Of course, there is no need to dwell upon the fact that speech is the door to a wider society in which a deaf person is encouraged to participate through the acquisition of appropriate forms of spoken language. But oral language acquisition will be more comfortably facilitated if it is based on sign language than if it is not, as any second-language acquisition is more naturally facilitated if it is based on the native language than if it is not. Spoken language acquisition in deaf education should not be the practice of speech pathology, but the exercise of second-language teaching.

Because the difference between sign language and spoken language is in modes of communication, I call a deaf person who acquires Japanese sign language as the mother language and who also acquires Japanese spoken language as the second language as "bimodal." Although this "bimodalism" is far from the reality in Japan's deaf education, I am optimistic that this will be accepted in due course. Scientific investigations have started coming out in favor of this form of bilingualism.

The crux of the matter is the recognition that it is psychologically most natural that a person should grow in and then maintain the native language. If a person is socially required to learn another form of language, the most natural process is not to force him to abandon the native language for the sake of a politically, socially, or demographically more important or dominant language, but to encourage him to develop bimodalism or bilingualism, an ability to switch back and forth between the plural languages and cultures of the society.

Obviously, these arguments apply to the children of various minority groups who speak unofficial dialects or languages. I would now like to turn to the dialectal situation, particularly multidialectalism, which is beginning to gain popular support in Japan.

Bidialectalism in a Multidialectal Society

Japan is a small and populous country. It has only half of the space Texas has and ten times more people living in it. The arability of the land is only 18 percent. Yet, because of its long history of social change, there are hundreds of different dialects in Japan. The dialects spoken by a million people in Ryukyu Islands, a chain of islands in Japan's southernmost territory, are almost totally unintelligible to speakers of any dialect of modern Japanese. Actually, Ryukyu dialects are mostly the remnants of

Japanese believed to have been spoken in the sixth or seventh century. Because of the geographical distance and the political, social, and cultural isolation of those southernmost isles from the four central islands of Japan, the varieties of Japanese spoken there evolved in very different directions. Moreover, each island in the Ryukyus has its own dialect which is in many cases seldom comprehensible to people living in another island in the same area.

Even on the four main islands of Japan, a large number of dialectal varieties exist which are mutually unintelligible. For example, people from the northern part and people from the southern part of Honshu, the main island of Japan, have tremendous difficulties with mutual communication if they speak their own dialects of Japanese.

Aware of this extraordinary variety in the Japanese language, which is more of the phonological, morphological, and lexical nature than of the syntactic nature, the Japanese government, the mass communication media, and educational circles did their best to establish standard Japanese about one hundred years ago, when Japan was unifying and strengthening itself against the threats of advancing Western powers. As a basis of standard Japanese, authorities selected parts of the Tokyo dialect which was becoming the most popular and effective source of spoken and written communication throughout the country. Tokyo was then emerging as the center of modern Japanese culture and civilization from which a new value system was to be transmitted throughout the nation. Authorities generalized the Tokyo usage and spread it across the nation through centralized mass communication and education networks. These efforts have apparently been totally successful. The majority of the population now can read, write, and comprehend the standard form of Japanese, although there are many who cannot, or do not necessarily speak it.

The primary emphasis on teaching of and in standard Japanese, however, produced many problems for the whole nation, particularly for those who lived outside Tokyo and who spoke nonstandard dialects. Speakers of nonstandard dialects were laughed at, humiliated, and despised. Many cases of self-abandonment and some cases of suicide were reported among those young people who came to Tokyo to work or to study.

Quite recently, however, linguistic studies have demonstrated that even Tokyo residents speak a nonstandard dialect, as much as those who live outside Tokyo. These studies have revealed that the most common linguistic way of life in Japan is actually bidialectalism with diglossia, a linguistic practice of switching from a certain form of standard Japanese to other dialectal varieties in a person's repertory as dictated by the social situation or the psychological state of mind in communicative interaction. Influenced by these studies, people have at least intellectually recognized that it is a shame to debase people just because they speak nonstandard Japanese. In education, special care has begun to be taken with pupils who speak nonstandard dialects. Teachers have become very discreet and careful not to hurt their pupils' pride while teaching of and in standard Japanese.

At the same time, the criterion of acceptability concerning the varieties of standard Japanese spoken by its nonnative speakers has been moderated. Many different varieties of standard Japanese have been tolerated and accepted just as many different ways of life. As people have begun to appreciate linguistic and cultural diversity in a country rich with various regional traditions, folk bidialectalism will probably receive more popularity and reinforcement as a desirable national aspect of life in Japan. I am not trying to say that this bidialectalism is here to stay everywhere in Japan. But the trend now seems to indicate this favorable direction.

Again, the underlying philosophy here is that if the situation demands that some groups of people acquire another form of language, it should not be imposed upon them at the cost of depriving them of their native tongues. Rather, societal efforts must be made to create the situation in which second-form learning is most naturally facilitated socio-psychologically.

Different Modes of Communication of Urban and Rural Children

In connection with this bidialectalism in Japanese society, I would like to discuss another problem which is more difficult to define and solve. I have elsewhere[3] pointed out that there are significant differences in the way language is used as a means of social communication and intellectual operation between urban children and rural children in Japan. Syntactically and semantically, urban children use a more elaborate fashion, while rural children employ a more rudimentary manner of expressing their everyday experiences in classroom situations. In other words, urban children are more explicit, while rural children are more implicit in linguistic operation.

This difference is surprising in a sense, since the national goal of education for 100 years in Japan has been to eliminate regional discrepancies and to attain national standardization of student achievement. This national educational goal should have been successful in view of the fact that the Education Ministry, with its strong centralized power, has enforced mandatory national educational policies throughout the country. The ministry controls almost every aspect of school education including textbooks and curricula. There is little room left for local substandardization. The only freedom local teachers are allowed to exercise is when they consider how to attain the national standard for their students in specific local situations.

How, then, can we account for the regional differences in children's use of language? I assume that children's acquisition of the mode of language use is determined by patterns of social relationships in the community in general and in the family in particular. This process of determination is so strong that any outside force, such as education, will not usually be able to intervene in it without proper programs. As biological beings, normal children are gifted with the universal propensity to develop any type of language and language use, but as social beings, they are generally restricted to the types of language and language use which prevail in the social structure in which they find themselves.

In an urban community, people are more heterogeneous and less likely to share communal presuppositions. In a rural community, people are more homogeneous and more apt to share communal assumptions. If the social relationships in two types of communities are different, modes of language use are expected to be different, too. In urban communities where chances are that people do not know each other and little is taken for granted, people have to be explicit in communicative interactions. This will result in internalizing more elaborate syntactic and semantic structures. I hasten to add that these two different linguistic systems could not be the object of value judgment. They are just the reflections of two different social structures.

The problem is that the mode of language used in school education is based on the more fully developed version of syntax and semantics of the Japanese language, because it is more appropriate and effective for complex symbolic and conceptual operation. Serious problems arise here. While the school language is the mother language for many urban children who acquire it early in their social settings, it is almost a foreign language for many rural children who first begin to learn it at school. The gap between family language and school language is narrower for urban children than for rural children. For urban children, school life is a constant continuation of their sociolinguistic experience, while for rural children it is a series of new encounters.

Indications are that this gap partly explains why urban children achieve better than rural children at school and why urban children are able to pass college entrance examinations more frequently than rural children. It is not because urban children are more motivated, more encouraged, and better guided by their parents than rural children. In Japan, the education of children is a national fad. In a sense, rural parents may encourage their children to work hard and go to institutions of higher education more eagerly than urban parents, because rural parents know from experience what it means to lack education.

The problem is more sociolinguistic than psychological. The crux of the matter lies in the failure to recognize this sociolinguistic gap on the part of those concerned with education.

Probably, the division of labor has created an unequal distribution of the linguistic means of knowledge. It has differentiated the sociolinguistic systems between the two major segments of the modern industrial society. This is a great epistemological problem in a democratic society, where every member is equally entitled to the linguistic means of acquisition and transmission of a complex system of knowledge. Unfortunately, we have little understanding of the nature of the problem. More systematic research is in order to define and explore the problem.[4]

I would now like to turn to the ethnically based discussion of possible linguistic and cultural pluralism in Japan. Although there are several ethnic minorities living in Japanese society, I will have to restrict myself in this paper to the explanation of the current states of two more visible groups—the Ainu and the Koreans.

The Ainu: To Melt or Not to Melt?

The origin of the present-day Ainu is still difficult to determine with certainty.[5] Their language, for example, is unrelated to any other known language of the world. However, archeological and anthropological evidence indicates that they were the aboriginal settlers of the northeastern part of the Japanese islands. Their presence there was recorded as early as the seventh century by Japanese imperial historians. Their highest estimated population was 25,000 in the early nineteenth century.

In the late nineteenth century, partly threatened by the Russians who were escalating their activities in the south, the *deshogunated* Japanese government began intensive maneuvers to explore and colonize the northern part of Japan. Due to the loose-knit nature of their traditional social structure, common to their hunting and fishing economy, the Ainu could not put up successful resistance to the invading Japanese.

Soon, assimilation of the Ainu into the formal structure of Japanese society became a principal object of national policy. In mapping out the strategy, the Japanese government sought the assistance of other countries who had similar experiences with minority groups. Thus, the United States sent consultants to demonstrate their experiences with the American Indians. In the end, the Japanese government rejected the reservation policy, choosing instead the complete detribalization and assimilation under the principle of civil equality.

What actually happened, however, is the history of Ainu subjugation to a colonial power. The experience of the Ainu was exactly the same as that of any people overwhelmed by a technically advanced and territorially expanding power. In spite of *de jure* equality as Japanese citizens, most of the Ainu are still suffering from poverty, lack of education, and various forms of social injustice such as job discrimination.

The Japanese assimilation of the Ainu was so quick and powerful that contemporary scholars conclude that there remain very few "pure" Ainu. According to one study, there are possibly 300 persons who might be considered to be pure Ainu if one counted those who claimed Ainu ancestry as far back as the great-grandparent generation.

However, the Ainu Association today claims a membership of 70,000. This phenomenon can be explained by a relatively high proportion of Ainu families adopting children of Japanese parentage. The Ainu account for the practice of adoption by citing their traditional love of children. Some Japanese officials add that the Ainu's desire to develop strong biological and social linkages with Japanese society has accelerated the traditional practice of adoption—an indication of the severe assimilative pressures exerted upon them.

The most important sociological consequence of this intermixing process is that children adopted by Ainu families are, thereafter, treated as being Ainu by the general community and by themselves. When such a child marries a person of Japanese blood, the new family may be considered Ainu, since one spouse is known as Ainu. This amalgamation trend would explain the Ainu Association's relatively large membership. But most of them are only nominally, or sociologically, Ainu.

Currently, there are certain groups of people who wish to reestablish the Ainu world by restoring and maintaining their ethnic language and culture. Politically, their wish will not be materialized, because they are demanding the return to some portion of Hokkaido, one of the four main islands of Japan which is becoming more and more important economically and territorially nowadays to their self-government. This is a demand which unfortunately is unlikely to ever be met.

Linguistically and culturally, however, their ethnic assertiveness can possibly be realized if carried out in a politically appropriate way. There is an indication that the Japanese general public is beginning to acknowledge that the Ainu have a right to be Ainu, although within the framework of overall Japanese society. Ainu restoration and maintenance programs are now at an incipient stage, and we cannot predict where and how far they are going, if anywhere. Although their ethnic efforts will not be innovations from the top, but developments from the grassroots, the Ainu will need some degree of endorsement and encouragement from the national government and the general public if they are to be successful. And how far the people are willing to accept ethnic and cultural differences in their society will be really tested when actual programs are proposed.

As to the restoration of linguistic practices, tremendous difficulties might present themselves to those Ainu who would wish to maintain their ethnic language. First, there are fewer than ten native speakers of the language left. They are all old people whose memory is not very clear in all aspects of the language. Second, Ainu has no written form, and the data that have been collected and phonetically transcribed by Japanese linguists and anthropologists would not be sufficient for the reconstruction of the dying language. In spite of all these stumbling blocks, however, the Ainu language salvation efforts should be encouraged. They are significant not for practical purposes of social communication, but as symbolic manifestations of the whole Ainu maintenance endeavor.

As to the restoration of their cultural heritage, the folkloric literature will be reinterpreted from an Ainu point of view. The history of the Ainu and the history of Japanese-Ainu interactions, as now understood generally in Japan, will also be reconsidered from an Ainu point of view. Consequently, an entirely different picture of the situation will certainly emerge, which will provide a multidimensional view of the interesting historical dramas staged on the islands of Japan. This form of multicognitivity will be a necessary step toward our synthetized understanding of human experience.

It should be pointed out here that an increasing number of young scholars in Japan agree that social scientists should not study people as anatomical objects, but as human beings. They think that their job is not only to gather scientific information but also to work for the benefit of the people who cooperate with them. Thus, young linguists, anthropologists, and sociologists are more and more concerned with, and committed to, the well-being of the people whom they try to understand. Those young scholars also believe that Japanese people could have enriched themselves culturally if they learned more from their encounters with the Ainu or with any other culturally different groups who surrounded them. They warn that Japan should not repeat this history of ethnocentric ignorance and parochialism. It is to be hoped that these efforts at awareness will culminate in a totally new outlook on various multicultural problems in Japanese society.

The Koreans: A New Problem, Two Thousand Years Old

The most visible ethnic minority in Japan is Korean. There are about 600,000 Koreans, who amount to 90 percent of all the foreigners living in Japan. Today, domestically and internationally, the relationship between the Japanese and the Koreans is *new* — about two thousand years old.

The current problems originated in 1910 when Japan, with its "Greater East Asia Coprosperity Sphere" version of Manifest Destiny, incorporated the Korean peninsula and deprived the farming population of their lands. Just to survive, many Koreans in the northern part went to Manchuria and many in the southern part came to Japan. During the war, the Japanese military brought back as many Koreans as it could find for forced labor and military services.

During its administration of Korea, Japan attempted to "Japanize" the Koreans in various ways. Japanese authorities banned the use of Korean and required the learning of Japanese, disregarded the Korean version of Buddhism and imposed Shintoism, stripped Koreans of their traditional costumes, and forced them to adopt Japanese names. Japanese officials promised Koreans equal treatment as children of the Japanese emperor. But this promise was never kept, and Koreans were almost always treated as second-class citizens.

At the end of the war, there were 2 million Koreans in Japan. When Korea gained independence, many went home, but a considerable number remained in Japan for various reasons. The political and ideological division of their homeland was the most serious one. Today, 75 percent of the 600,000 Koreans living in Japan were Japanese-born; serious identity problems stem from this generational change. Their future depends largely upon the feasibility of unification of their homeland. Their strong wish for unification is evident from the fact that, of all those who are eligible, only 5 percent have applied for permanent residence in Japan.

There are two major organizations of Koreans in Japan. One supports (and is supported by) North Korea and the other supports South Korea. North-affiliated Koreans explicitly express their desire to return home and devote themselves to the reconstruction of their homeland under the "eternally faultless" guidance of their "great comrade-leader-father," Kim Il Sung. South-related Koreans fluctuate concerning their final destination. Many seem to be inclined toward assimilation and naturalization in Japan, if they are well accepted. And because their present situation in Japanese society is not comfortable, they have more serious identity problems over whether they should stay Korean or become Japanese.

There are about 150,000 Korean children learning in Japan, and two-thirds of them go to Japanese schools. Among those going to Korean schools, 80 percent go to 145 North Korean-affiliated schools, which can accommodate about 38 percent of the North Korean-affiliated children. Ten percent go to eight South Korean-related schools; and the remaining 10 percent go to three neutral schools.

North Korean schools, which are financially supported by the North Korean government, provide ethnic education in Korean in an attempt to maintain their readiness for the exodus when the situation ripens. South Korean schools, inclined toward the policy of smooth assimilation of children into Japanese society, teach most of the subjects in Japanese and provide special lessons on Korean. Japanese schools teach only in Japanese and offer no bilingual education.

Today, many Koreans are socially functional bilinguals, but they are not happy about their bilingual situation. Here, let me digress briefly, and explain my distinction of "happy bilingualism" and "sad bilingualism."

An individual is a happy bilingual if he becomes a bilingual because of his desire to be so. An individual is a sad bilingual if he becomes a bilingual in spite of his desire not to be so.

For a potentially happy bilingual, the motivation to learn the language is integrative rather than instrumental,[6] because he feels that it enriches his personality to learn the language. Upon becoming a bilingual, or while striving to be a bilingual, he is happy about himself, and he is proud of himself.

On the other hand, for a sad bilingual, the motivation to master the language is instrumental rather than integrative, because survival is the primary reason for the efforts. He is socially compelled to acquire the other tongue because his language is so stigmatized and his culture so denigrated that he has no choice but to learn the dominant language simply in order to make a living. Upon becoming a bilingual, or while picking up the language, he is neither happy about himself nor proud of himself. His self-respect is damaged and his integrity destroyed.

In the process of becoming a bilingual, a person is very likely to experience a certain period of insecurity, or "anomie" in Durkheimian sociological terms. For a certain period of time, he becomes a victim of the disharmony between the norm of his native culture and that of the culture in which his target language is embedded. He experiences a period in which he has no constant and definite norm on which to base his behavior, judgment, and identification. He has left his native culture far behind yet he is far away from the second culture to which he aspires or he is destined to internalize, fluctuating back and forth between the two frames of reference. This feeling of not belonging is experienced whether a person becomes a bilingual willingly or unwillingly.

However, given the assumption just outlined, the magnitude of this anomic mentality is greater for sad bilinguals than for happy bilinguals. If bilingualism is a coercively imposed social condition, the burden a potential bilingual will have to bear will be much heavier than if bilingualism is a sociopsychologically natural development.

Koreans living in Japan are discriminated against in many ways, and they are forced to learn Japanese in order to get along well in Japanese society. Naturally, they are not happy about their bilingualism. They frequently ask themselves, "What makes us have to speak Japanese?" Bilingualism is an institutional disgrace to their integrity.

Returning from the digression, let me explain what is being done about the Korean situation in Japan. The Japanese government and its educational agents have done nothing so far to support the language and culture maintenance efforts of Korean people. This is partly because the Koreans have not expressed an interest in ethnic education publicly to Japanese authorities. Korean parents are so confident that their request for, say, bilingual education will be immediately rejected by Japanese school systems that they have never dreamed of making such a request public. More regrettably, Japanese authorities have not recognized their historical, moral obligations to advance the educational opportunities of Korean children in every possible way.[7]

Koreans will have to go a long way before it becomes possible for them to live a sociolinguistically comfortable existence in Japanese society. Currently, however, desirable developments are occurring. The traditional Japanese-Korean suspiciousness toward each other is evidently disappearing, although gradually and sporadically, among the younger generations in both groups. On the Japanese side, generational change is obviously erasing their demagogically concocted superiority complex toward their closest neighboring people. The Korean language is gaining popularity, although slowly, as an object of intellectual inquiry as well as practical mastery. Influential opinion leaders have organized a public pressure group to demand that the Japan Broadcasting Corporation, the nation's only public radio and television network, add Korean to its present foreign-language education programs of English, French, German, Spanish, Russian, and Chinese. All these pro-Korean efforts reflect the

Japanese people's increased interest in rectifying their centuries-old misunderstanding of the Korean people, who have been nearest to them physically, but farthest from them mentally.[8]

For stable bilingualism and biculturalism to take place among minority members, majority individuals do not have to be bilingual and bicultural themselves. But they have to be "bicognitive"[9] enough to allow linguistically, culturally, and ethnically different groups of people to exist along with them. And this state of mind will have to be attained by both mainstreamers and those outside the mainstream. When people of the core culture become bicognitive, they are more likely to approve and support the linguistic, cultural, and cognitive diglossia of minority members of the society. They will be less afraid of and more interested in variety as a fact of life. Xenophobia or superiority complexes will be less likely to occur in this state of mind. Therefore, it is indispensable that Japanese people achieve drastic attitudinal changes in order to become sensitive and compassionate toward minority groups. This objective needs priority attention in Japanese education, because the social conditions of most of the core-culture Japanese are more inclined to make them ethnocentric, rather than linguistically, culturally, and cognitively flexible and adaptable. From this point of view, the existence of Ainu and Korean "problems" here is extremely significant for Japanese people. In an effort to solve these problems, we hope that the Japanese people will be able to learn that difference is beautiful because it is what life is all about.

In the formative process as a cultural entity and as a nation, Japan integrated many aspects of Chinese and Korean traditions into its ethnic character. However, in its subsequent history of long insulation, Japan developed a particularly strong national, cultural, and spiritual identity of its own. This self-identity was so monolithic that everything foreign had greater chance of rejection than acceptance at the deep psychological level. Japan's experience with other cultures was almost always in the form of conquest and seldom in the form of intercultural understanding.

Although quite recently, however, partly for intellectual but mostly for economic reasons, increasing numbers of people have recognized that cultural parochialism is Japan's primary enemy, and they have begun to search for a new philosophy of human coexistence. But ethnocentrism is so deeply rooted in history that it is perhaps the most difficult awareness to rectify in the evolution of human nature. I believe that foreign language education is one of the most effective means to realize this socio-psychological evolution. Finally, let me touch on some of the problems of Japan's foreign language education defined as a means of enhancing intercultural communication and understanding.

Foreign Language Education

A glance at the history of European language teaching in Japan might be revealing in this respect. When Japan knew that Western powers were advancing to its territory more than a hundred years ago, it chose to modernize by learning their technology and industry. Japanese leaders encouraged the nation's young elite to learn European languages, but this was only for the purpose of acquiring scientific information, not for the purpose of starting intercultural communication. There were several reasons for this priority, but I will state only one of them briefly.

Japanese leaders thought that Western cultural forces with powerful technological gimmicks were dismantling the national integrity of India and China, and took exceedingly cautious measures not to repeat the destinies of these countries in Japan. They pursued the policy of strengthening the nation's history-nurtured cultural and spiritual identity as a symbol of unity to defend its independent sovereignty from Western intervention. Japan opened its front door to usher in Western civilization, but kept its back door shut to keep out Western culture. When self-defense was a primary preoccupation, intercultural understanding was a luxury which they could not afford.

Many people are persistently suspicious about learning other languages as a means of attaining intercultural understanding. They are afraid that their children's sense of national identity will be diluted, weakened, or destroyed by their exposure to influential foreign culture. Therefore, Japan now confronts great difficulties in introducing intercultural aspects into its foreign language education programs.[10]

Notes

This is a revised version of the paper presented at the Symposium on Cultural Perspectives for Educators at Texas Christian University, February 24-25, 1978. I would like to thank Dr. Marjorie Herrmann, Dr. Andrew Miracle, and Dr. James Williamson for their valuable comments and their encouragement.

1. For example, see Honna, 1977b, and some other articles in Peng and Tanokami, eds., 1977.

2. For example, see Cicourel and Boese, 1972.

3. Honna, 1975, 1977a.

4. In my earlier papers, I followed the Bernstein (1971, 1973) hypothesis. It will be necessary to examine his theory again in order to obtain a clear picture of the situation. For further comment, see Honna, 1979a.

5. Perhaps, the best available anthropological information on the present-day Ainu is Peng and Geiser, 1977. I owe some of the information presented in this paper to them.

6. For the definition and implications of these terms, see Lambert, 1972.

7. For further description of the situation, see Honna, 1979b.

8. For further information, see Honna, 1979c.

9. An interesting theory fully described by Ramírez and Castañeda, 1974.

10. What is being done now in bilingual education in the United States will be of particular interest. However, there are some problems in this field. As far as I can see, most of the programs are directed toward *intra*group solidification of a certain ethnic population, but not toward *inter*group unification of the ethnically plural U.S. society. Bilingual education in the United States could not be achieved effectively and meaningfully without the mutual understanding and support of both majority and minority members of the society. And within-group-oriented bilingual education would not only decrease the opportunities for majority support, but also increase the chances for majority resistance. What would remain might be a "you-get-more-if-you-ask-than-if-you-don't" type of schism. There seems to be an indication of this possibility already, which might eventually put into question the justice and wisdom of bilingual education itself. If one knows the history of minorities in U.S. society, one will understand the reasons for current priority on in-group ethnic maintenance efforts. But still I believe that if it incorporates an essential extent of intergroup understanding programs, bilingual/bicultural/bicognitive education will more successfully facilitate majority cooperation. Then bilingual education in the United States will stand a better chance of promoting a more desirable degree of intercultural understanding in an ethnically diverse society. For further comment, see Honna, 1978a,b.

References

Bernstein, Basil. *Class, Codes and Control, Volume 1: Theoretical Studies toward a Sociology of Language.* London: Routledge and Kegan Paul, 1971.

———, ed. *Class, Codes and Control, Volume 2: Applied Studies toward a Sociology of Language.* London: Routledge and Kegan Paul, 1973.

Cicourel, Aaron V., and Boese, Robert J. "Sign Language Acquisition and the Teaching of Deaf Children." In *Functions of Language in the Classroom,* edited by Courtney B. Cazden, Vera P. John, and Dell Hymes. New York: Teachers College Press, 1972.

Honna, Nobuyuki. "A Note on Social Structure and Linguistic Behavior: A Case Study of a Japanese Community." In *Language in Japanese Society: Current Issues in Sociolinguistics,* edited by Fred C.C. Peng. Tokyo: University of Tokyo Press, 1975.

————. "Bilingual Education in the United States: From a Melting Pot to a Culturally Pluralistic Society?" Lecture in the seminar on multicultural education at Pan American University, 20 June 1978a.

————. "Bilingual, Bicultural, and Bicognitive Education: An American Experiment." Paper read at the First International Congress for the Study of Child Language. Tokyo, Japan, 7-12 August 1978b. In *Language Sciences,* edited by Fred C.C. Peng. Tokyo: International Christina University, forthcoming.

————. "On the Word Order of Japanese Sign Language." In *Aspects of Sign Language,* edited by Fred C.C. Peng and Ryuji Tanokami. Hiroshima: Bunka Hyoron Publishing Company, 1977a.

————. "On the Modes of Communication of Urban and Rural Children." In *Language and Context,* edited by Fred C.C. Peng. Hiroshima: Bunka Hyoron Publishing Company, 1977b.

————. "On the Modes of Communication of Urban and Rural Children: A Sociolinguistic Analysis with Educational Implications." Report for the Japanese Ministry of Education. In preparation, 1979a.

————. "Some Problems of English Teaching in Japan." In preparation, 1979b.

————. "The Bilingualism of Koreans in Japan." In preparation, 1979c.

Lambert, Wallace. *Language, Psychology, and Culture.* Stanford, California: Stanford University Press, 1972.

Peng, Fred C.C., and Geiser, Peter. *The Ainu: The Past in the Present.* Hiroshima: Bunka Hyoron Publishing Company, 1977.

Peng, Fred C.C., and Tanokami, Ryuji, eds. *Aspects of Sign Language.* Hiroshima: Bunka Hyoron Publishing Company, 1977.

Ramírez, Manuel III, and Castañeda, Alfredo. *Cultural Democracy, Bicognitive Development, and Education.* New York: Academic Press, 1974.

A Comparison of
Peruvian and United States
Bilingual Education Programs

Liliana Minaya-Portella
Ministry of Education, Peru
University of Texas

and

Mary Sanches
Austin, Texas

Although in the history of the societies of the world, multilingualism has been a frequent occurrence in social life, in modern national states the idea of publicly sponsored bilingual education is relatively new (Zirkel, 1978). It has been motivated by diverse political and ideological considerations in different countries, has been received in various ways, and has produced different outcomes in the societies involved.

While it is not our intention to provide a thorough cross-cultural review of bilingual education policies and programs here, we would like to present a comparison of the bilingual education programs and the sociocultural circumstances surrounding bilingual education in two countries, the United States and Peru. Both programs were established approximately contemporaneously, but as they emerge from radically different sociocultural-political circumstances, we think that an interesting comparison can be made.

We will begin by looking at the legal frameworks of the Peruvian and the United States bilingual education programs, the processes of their establishment, and their implementation. Since these two programs do not exist in a vacuum (i.e., unrelated to any sociocultural matters) and since this review will show increasing divergence between the two programs the further we proceed from purely legal frameworks, we will then provide a look at the sociocultural (including historical) contexts out of which each program grew and which each, of course, reflects. Finally, we will consider some of the differential effects each is having in light of its stated aims and inferable long-term goals.

Legal Frameworks and the Establishment of Bilingual Education Programs

The legal frameworks of the Peruvian and the United States programs look quite similar on the surface. In the United States the current national Bilingual Education Act, in the words of Parker (1978, p. 26), "gives official federal and/or state sanction or recognition to providing special educational services to limited-English-speaking (LES) or non-English-speaking (NES) students." Likewise, the Peruvian legal framework for bilingual education, which was set in place in 1972, instructed the Ministry of Education to initiate programs to "provide instruction in their own language to students who come to school speaking little or no Spanish."

However, if one looks at the processes — the means by which these laws came to be in the two countries — we begin to see the tip of the iceberg of sociocultural differences involved.

In the United States, while there have been scattered historical instances, usually private but occasionally public, of bilingual education programs in bilingual communities (Andersson and Boyer, 1978), the initial national sanction for such programs came through the Bilingual Education Acts of 1968 and 1974. These had been stimulated by the court challenges brought by citizens or citizen groups claiming discrimination on the basis of the 1964 Civil Rights Act. The 1964 Civil Rights Act, in turn, had been engendered by court decisions brought by plaintiffs claiming discrimination on the basis of violations of their rights to equal educational opportunity as guaranteed by the Fourteenth Amendment to the Constitution.

In other words, there would be no bilingual education acts and probably only private programs or minuscule numbers of public programs in the United States were it not for the individual efforts of private citizens challenging an existing state of social affairs in relation to an abstract principle voiced in the Constitution. Furthermore, it is evident that not just one challenge and one precedent-setting decision have been sufficient to establish bilingual education programs nationally in the United States: this process has had to be repeated in the various localities where bilingualism or non-English monolingualism (e.g., Spanish monolinguals) is present. The first court decisions led Congress to pass the education act which directed the establishment of bilingual education programs.

However, even with this law on the books, subsequent actions have been necessary to get programs started in specific localities or challenge the validity of the program of a specific school district as conforming to the aims of the court-directed mandate. Currently, we can see a secondary process with the incorporation of state policies for implementation of the acts. In some states, state education agencies have taken responsibility for identifying target populations for bilingual education programs.

Thus, the establishment of bilingual education programs has taken several stages, as depicted in Figure 1.

The conditions surrounding and the factors motivating the inception of current bilingual education programs in Peru have been quite different from those just outlined for the United States. The first major difference is that the initiative for establishing the present program came solely from the central government and not from court actions initiated by individual citizens on the basis of violated civil rights. Prior to the Peruvian Education Act of 1972, there were no legal suits brought by citizens claiming that their basic rights to equal educational opportunity had been violated by the failure of the school to teach in their native language. There is, in fact, no law in Peru comparable to the United States Civil Rights Act of 1964. Nor is there anything equivalent to the United States Constitution's Fourteenth Amendment.

While there has been a tradition of positive government policy toward bilingual education programs in Peru, in order to account for the current motivation to establish comprehensive bilingual education and the innovative form those programs are taking, we must look solely at the sociopolitical ideology of the Peruvian government of the seventies, which included the following as goals for the society:

1. The achievement of political, economic, and cultural independence in the international community

2. The sociopolitical integration of the heretofore unintegrated nonmestizo populations as a necessary means to achieving the first goal.

Figure 1

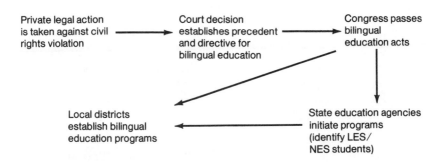

Private legal action is taken against civil rights violation → Court decision establishes precedent and directive for bilingual education → Congress passes bilingual education acts

Local districts establish bilingual education programs ← State education agencies initiate programs (identify LES/ NES students)

In other words, to become an economically developed, technologically advanced nation, the current Peruvian government feels it cannot do without having a polity, i.e., a national citizenry, which includes all sectors of the population. In order to achieve this second goal, it was thought necessary to better integrate the populations linguistically and, consequently, to establish a new bilingual education program through a bilingual education act.

Thus, we can visualize the process of institutionalization of the current bilingual education programs in Peru, in contrast to that of the United States, as shown in Figure 2:

Figure 2

Central government administration establishes social ideology

↓

Central government administration establishes bilingual education policy and act

↓

Ministry of Education:
1. formulates bilingual education programs
2. researches local community needs
3. establishes bilingual education programs at local level

Not only is there a tremendous difference between the United States and Peru in the way bilingual education acts and programs were initiated, but these differences can also be seen in the implementation and administration of the programs in the following ways:

1. In the United States the responsibility for initiating bilingual education programs rests with the state education agencies and local school boards. However, in Peru the decision to establish a bilingual education program in any given community is made by the central government after it has undertaken research and reconnaissance to determine the needs of the local communities.

2. Related to this fact is the way in which the federal government and local school districts participate in programs already underway. In the United States, the major objective of the federal government is funding, as both Molina (1978, p. 18) and González (1978, p. 16) have mentioned. Funding is provided, of course, only at the initiative of a school district or individual (e.g., for a research project on bilingual education). But in Peru, the responsibility of the central government, through the Ministry of Education, extends to planning and administering the entire program; the government does not give funds to local school districts and individuals to administer; it administers the funds.

In Peru, there is a curriculum of bilingual education established centrally by the ministry of education. This situation differs in two ways from the situation in the United States. First, in the United States the curriculum for bilingual education consists of the same courses as the regular curriculum, but it is taught in the students' native language, *and* as such, it is an adjunct program. In Peru, however, the bilingual education is at the *core* of the curriculum. Second, in the United States the bilingual education program is thought of as *remedial*, much like the Head Start Programs, for children who are linguistically disadvantaged and in some way culturally "lacking." In Peru, the program is thought of as *augmenting* the set of language skills which children already have from their native community.

Thus, in the United States, there is a wide range of variation in the kinds and the quality of bilingual education programs from one state to another, because the initiative in both establishing and planning the programs is left in the hands of local school district officials. Within the United States system this has also meant that room is left for further litigation if the program does not meet the minority language community's satisfaction.

It might seem from this description that the Peruvian case is totally centralized, and might produce a program which is relatively inflexible in response to local needs. But when we compare the criteria for qualifying teachers and selecting materials in the two programs, it appears otherwise. In the Peruvian system a teacher in the bilingual education program (e.g., Quechua-Spanish) must (1) be a native speaker of Quechua; (2) have been born and raised in the region; (3) be a fluent Spanish speaker, graduated from college, and accredited as a teacher; and (4) have taught at least five years in rural areas of the region. In addition, in Peru, the creation and selection of instructional materials in the different localities are responsibilities of the local bilingual program teachers. This allows for teaching flexibility which can correspond to the area dialects.

In order to see the difference in the meaning of bilingual education programs in the two societies, we need to examine the relative status of the languages involved. In the United States there is, of course, just one official national language — English — and a lot of nonofficial languages. In Peru in 1975, Quechua was made a national language, equal with Spanish. In concrete terms, this meant the following:

- An official alphabetic writing system was adopted for Quechua and a commitment was made to incorporate a Quechua literacy program as part of the bilingual education program. This part of the program necessitated researching and preparing six reference grammars and dictionaries for the six major dialect areas of Quechua spoken in the country.

- Newspapers have been made bilingual in Quechua and Spanish. That is, there are articles in Quechua in the areas of national interest — ideology, education, agriculture, industry, and commerce.

- Daily and weekly radio programs in Quechua are available on news, music, festivities, and local accomplishments of a cooperative government-community effort. There are also programs sponsored by the National Institute of Culture — daily TV shows presenting dramas, ritual dances, and music of Quechua culture.

An initial response to the two bilingual education programs might be to say that, of course, the programs are different because they grew out of the totally different circumstances surrounding bilingualism in the two countries. That is, one might say that because the contact situation in Peru has been predominantly between two languages only, Spanish and Quechua, it is more easily resolved than in a situation like that of the United States. In the latter, there have been only small pockets of monolingual and bilingual minorities speaking a wide range of languages in addition to English, while the vast majority of the polity is English monolingual. Thus, we could not reasonably expect that an official status equal to English could be given to any of the multitude of minority languages spoken in the United States.

However, the differences in the formal structure involving the bilingual education programs and their operation in Peru and the United States, the differences in the status of the languages involved, and the differences in the relative distribution of the monolingual and bilingual populations is not all. If we look more closely at the sociocultural differences in the two socieites, we will see how the history of the languages and their speakers produced *both* the situations toward which bilingual education programs now respond *and* the thinking behind the programs.

Cultural-Historical Background of Language Contact and Attitudes

The United States. If we had a motion-picture map of the language distribution and contact in North America corresponding roughly to the geographical boundaries of the United States from the initial stages of European immigration through the present, something like the following would be revealed:

1. We would see a stage of intrusive European language commu- nities — English, Spanish, French, Dutch, etc. — during the seventeenth and eighteenth centuries in contact with American Indian languages in various, often widely separate locations.

2. We would later see a stage from the eighteenth through the nineteenth centuries, during the first part of which English is the official national language of the newly formed political entity occupying the eastern seaboard and extending increasingly inland. During this period we can see three important processes occurring:

    a. The American Indian languages in contact with English continue to disappear from an ever-expanding area. Most simply cease to be spoken, though a few, like Cherokee, move westward to escape the inevitable results of the contact.

b. Formation continues on a large scale of what is to become the only other major variant of English, Black English. The emergence of Black English can be observed throughout the southern half of the United States.

c. A third process taking place during this time is the gradual yielding of other European language communities to the pervasiveness of English as those communities become increasingly incorporated into the United States polity. This process can be seen in areas like Florida, the southern parts of the Louisiana Purchase, and the Dutch-speaking portions of New York.

3. A new kind of contact situation intensifies during the late nineteenth and early twentieth centuries between established communities of English speakers and groups of newly arrived speakers of other languages — Norwegian, Italian, German, Swedish, Polish, Yiddish, Chinese, Japanese, etc. In these cases, we can see initially non-English monolingualism usually shifting to one-and-a-half generational bilingualism and finally to English monolingualism. However, the languages of certain groups of immigrants (for example, Chinese speakers and some Yiddish speakers), who had continuous immigration and a localized community, remain in a stage of rather more stable bilingualism.

4. The final westward expansion of the late nineteenth century continues the eradicatory contact with American Indian languages and brings new contact with older, established communities of non-English speakers, most notably the Spanish speakers of the West and Southwest.

Thus, currently, we have not one, but a large number of different social processes reflected in the various bilingual situations extant in the United States: the English-Black English contact situation; contact with the remaining, though numerically attenuated, American Indian language communities; and, those situations like the English-Spanish or English-Chinese contact where the nonofficial language is represented by a long history within the United States and where there is a wide range of dialects in which it is spoken.

In understanding the reshaping of processes of change in the United States language-contact scene over the last 300 years, we must understand the attitudes about language that reflect social concepts of "humanness" on the part of members of, especially, the sociopolitically dominant English-speaking community.

We have seen in United States society overall an almost entirely one-way dominance of English in language use. This may be due to three factors: (1) There is a great sensitivity toward language use. That is, there is no casualness toward which language one uses in the United States. It is very important to speak the "proper" language. (2) This attitude is supported by the feeling that there is only *one* acceptable language — English. Monolingualism is accepted as a normal situation in the United States. Being a non-English speaker in the United States society has meant being socially not quite as acceptable as the native English speakers. (3) There is, and has been historically, almost no structural effect on English of the various languages involved in the different kinds of contact situations.

Peru. In contrast to the situation in the United States, in Peru both the nature of the bilingual situation and the conditions of contact relations between the language communities have been different.

Although the indigenous populations of the area which is now Peru represent a number of culturally distinct groups, speaking about forty-two languages of ten linguistic families (in a population of 4 million, 3.5 million speak Quechua and approximately 500,000 speak other languages), two historical factors have served to reduce the present situation to one of contact between two major languages. They are:

1. Quechua was the native language spoken by the largest number of people indigenous to the Andean area before European contact.

2. Quechua was the official language of the Inca Empire. By virtue of this fact Quechua developed as a lingua franca over the entire area of what is now Ecuador, Peru, Colombia, Bolivia, Chile, and Argentina. Thus, the bilingualism of Peruvian contact has involved, ideologically, only two languages: Spanish and Quechua.

This second fact has had important results. Although Spanish is currently monolingually spoken by a majority of the 16 million Peruvians, they represent only a slim majority of 54 percent. Quechua, on the other hand, is monolingually spoken by a large minority of 25 percent. An additional 21 percent of the population are bilingual Quechua-Spanish speakers. However, these figures, which are for the entire country, are somewhat misleading, because of the geographical distribution of the languages. Most of the monolingual Spanish speakers are concentrated in the coastal areas. If we look at the southern highlands districts, the percentage of monolingual Quechua speakers rises to between 87 and 95 percent and the number of bilingual Quechua-Spanish speakers correspondingly drops to between 5 and 13 percent. This contrasts dramatically with the distribution of bilingualism in the United States.

In order to further understand the current situation and attitudes toward bilingualism in Peru, we must also look at the historical development of relationships between the different social groups involved. The current situation of both language distribution and bilingual education programs in Peru arises from the historical development of social ideology and attitudes toward other languages prevailing in the contact situation.

First of all, the Spanish colonizers of Peru did consider the native inhabitants of the area. While from our contemporary perspective, we would not applaud the Spanish colonists' aim of subjugating the native population, it produced a different kind of outcome from that occurring in the North American case. It meant, first of all, that some degree of relationship was possible between the two populations. It also meant that the native populations were accorded a degree of human identity. This situation was augmented, of course, by the proselytizing aims of the Catholic Church. Furthermore, the fact that Quechua was the language of a socially complex, stratified, expansive theocratic state allowed the Iberian colonists to accord it a degree of prestige which the North American colonists did not give to any of the native languages they encountered.

If we had a graphic historical representation of the Peruvian situation over time parallel to that we have outlined for the United States, something like the following would be identified:

1. A stage of intrusive European colonization occurs during the sixteenth and seventeenth centuries between a group of Iberian-Spanish speakers (socially *españoles*) and speakers of Quechua and other indigenous languages (socially *nativos*).

2. During the period from the sixteenth through the eighteenth centuries a gradual, though expanding, social merging of the two original populations, *españoles* and *nativos,* takes place and a new social-ethnic category emerges: *mestizo.*

3. The political revolutions of the nineteenth century bring about the establishment of a national identity, *peruano*, which is distinct from that of the inhabitants of the Iberian peninsula. This period also marks the continued emergence of a cultural dominance by the social-ethnic category of *mestizo.* This is accompanied by the parallel development of a national language which becomes increasingly distinct from Iberian Spanish. This process continues and intensifies during the twentieth century.

Figures 3 and 4 present ethnic categories of the two societies and the language identities corresponding to those categories; the figures demonstrate the differences in thinking about the relation of language to the nature of social-person.

Figures 3 and 4 exemplify, in the first columns, some of the terms for socioethnic categories of persons in the United States and Peru and, in the second columns, the way in which these correspond to language identities. In the United States the term "American" has two meanings: (1) one of national identity and (2) that ethnic category of citizens who are tokens par

Figure 3
Taxonomy of Ethnic Categories of Social-Person
in the United States in Conjunction with Language Identities

Ethnic Identity	Language
1. American (National Identity)	English
1.1 American	English
1.2 Mexican American	Spanish ($\pm$English)
1.3 Chinese American	Chinese ($\pm$English)
1.4 Italian American	Italian ($\pm$ English)
1.5 Japanese American	Japanese ($\pm$English)
1.6 -etc.-	
1.8 American Indians	Navajo ($\pm$English)
1.8.1 Navajo	Apache ($\pm$English)
1.8.2 Apache	
1.8.3 -etc.-	

Figure 4
Taxonomy of Ethnic Categories of Social-Person
in Peru in Conjunction with Language Identities

Ethnic Identity	Language
1. Peruano (National Identity)	Spanish and/or Quechua
1.1 mestizo	Spanish and/or Quechua
1.2 nativo/campesino	
1.2.1 Quechua	Quechua
1.2.2 Aymara	Aymara
1.2.3 Campa	Campa
1.2.4 Aguaruna	Aguaruna
1.2.5 -etc.-	

excellence of the identity, i.e., not members of any other of the many "foreign" groups. The national language, English, is the language identity of this group. In Peru, on the other hand, the inclusive term for national identity, *peruano,* does not correspond to any of the terms designating the narrower ethnic identities. Also, the language identities for national identity are multiple. That is, both Spanish *and* Quechua speakers are *peruanos.*

The existence in Peru of the socioethnic category *mestizo,* the social product of *españoles* (a category which no longer is present in Peruvian society) and *nativos,* contrasts with the situation in the United States. In the United States, there is no socioethnic category of person that is the "social product" of two or more categories. Although the word *mestizo* does occur in English, it is a term for a "racial" category with no socioethnic implications. That is, in the United States, a person who is racially mestizo has the ethnic identity of one or the other parent.

Implications for Long-Term Effects or
Results of Bilingual Programs

We will consider these results in terms of two dimensions: (1) the final linguistic state of the societies, in terms of whether they are to be bilingual or monolingual, and (2) the degree of mutual versus unidirectional influence of the languages involved.

In the United States, bilingual education programs have as their aim facilitating a transition from monolingualism in a non-English language through bilingualism on an individual level to ultimate English monolingualism on the community level. Bilingualism is seen as transitional, with the ideal goal being English monolingualism for the entire population.

In Peru, the aim of the bilingual education program, as officially stated, is not to produce a nation of monolingual Spanish speakers, but rather one of bilingual Spanish-Quechua speakers. Given that (1) a significant minority of the population in Peru is currently Quechua monolingual and another large minority is Quechua-Spanish bilingual, (2) the contexts in which Spanish is learned and used for most bilingual speakers are public ones (Quechua remains for "private" situations), and (3) there is no derogation of Quechua usage, it seems reasonable to expect that bilingual usage on the basis of different social functions for each code may continue for a long time. Comparative figures from the 1961 and 1972 census in Peru present striking evidence that current language shifts are not in the direction of increasing Spanish monolingualism.

In the United States, the non-English languages in the various contact situations have had almost no influence on English. This has been because of the attitudes toward language use in conjunction with the direction of bilingualism, i.e, monolingual English speakers in contact with bilingual speakers of a native language plus English.

In Peru, bilingualism has proceeded in both directions. That is, there is both native-Spanish-plus-Quechua-as-a-second-language bilingualism and native-Quechua-plus-Spanish-as-a-second-language bilingualism. The result has been that a distinctive national language has emerged—Peruvian Spanish. Peruvian Spanish, a national variant of a more universal Spanish, consists of a range of styles, each manifesting different syntactic, phonological, and lexical influences from Quechua.

In conclusion, the aim of the bilingual education programs in both the United States and Peru is the social integration of members of ethnic groups who have been in the past at least partially socially disenfranchised. However, the differences in the bilingual education programs in the two societies, growing out of attitudes toward bilingualism versus monolingualism on the part of the socially dominant group in each society, reveals what each feels is required in order to achieve that integration. In Peru, social integration is being achieved by extending higher status to the culturally second language, a process which simultaneously broadens the societal definition of each person. In the United States, on the other hand, the establishment and operation of bilingual education programs have largely proceeded on the assumption that one can only be a "real" member of society by becoming a monolingual English speaker, thus giving up one's native language and ethnic identity.

We can see even from this comparison the historical determinants of the attitudes in the United States toward non-English speakers. Since this attitude does not occur in all other societies, we know that it is not a necessary adjunct to bilingual education programs. What would happen in the United States bilingual education programs if the monolingual and bilingual non-English speakers in our communities were not seen as "lesser Americans" and "linguistically disadvantaged"? What expansion in thinking about ourselves as members of a national community would take place if we saw the native speakers of other languages in our communities as bringing a valuable resource to be shared in realizing the potential for the next generation to become multilingual in the other important languages of the world?

References

Andersson, Theodore, and Boyer, Mildred. *Bilingual Schooling in the United States.* Austin, Tex.: National Education Laboratory Publishers, 1978.

González, Josué. "Bilingual Education: Ideologies of the Past Decade." In *Bilingual Education,* edited by Hernán Lafontaine, Barry Persky, and Leonard Golubchick, pp. 24-32. Wayne, N.J.: Avery Publishing Group, 1978.

Molina, John C. "National Policy on Bilingual Education: An Historical View of the Federal Role." In *Bilingual Education,* edited by Hernán Lafontaine, Barry Persky, and Leonard Golubchick, pp. 16-23. Wayne, N.J.: Avery Publishing Group, 1978.

Parker, Leann L. "Current Perspectives." In *Bilingual Education: Current Perspectives,* pp. 1-62. Arlington, Va.: Center for Applied Linguistics, 1978.

Presidencia de la República del Perú. *Indicadores demográficos, sociales, económicos y geográficos del Perú,* Vol. 2, Lima, 1974.

Quinta Región de Educación. *Proyecto de Educación Bilingüe.* Cuzco: Unidad Regional de Educación Bilingüe, 1975.

República del Perú. *Ley General de Educación.* Lima, 1972.

Sexta Región de Educación. *Proyecto de Educación Bilingüe.* Puno: Unidad Regional de Educación Bilingüe, 1976.

Zirkel, Perry A. "The Legal Vicissitudes of Bilingual Education." In *Bilingual Education,* edited by Hernán Lafontaine, Barry Persky, and Leonard Golubchick, pp. 48-51. Wayne, N.J.: Avery Publishing Group, 1978.

The National Impact of Multicultural Education: A Renaissance of Native American Indian Culture through Tribal Self-Determination and Indian Control of Indian Education

Joseph C. Dupris
Coalition of Indian Controlled School Boards, Inc.
Denver, Colorado

We know you highly esteem the kind of learning taught in these colleges, and the maintenance of our young men, while with you, would be very expensive to you. We are convinced, therefore, that you mean to do us good by your proposal; and we thank you heartily. But you who are so wise must know that different Nations have different conceptions of things; and you will not therefore take it amiss if our ideas of this kind of education happen not to be the same with yours. We have had some experience of it. Several of our young people were formerly brought up in the Colleges of the Northern Provinces, they were instructed in all your sciences; but when they came back to us, they were bad runners; ignorant of every means of living in the woods, unable to bear either cold or hunger, knew neither how to build a cabin, take a deer, or kill an enemy, spoke our language imperfectly, were therefore neither fit for hunters, warriors, nor counsellors; they were totally good for nothing. We are, however, not in the less and to show our grateful sense of it, if the gentlemen of Virginia shall send us a dozen of their sons, we will take great care of their education, instruct them in all we know, and make men of them.[1]*

---

*See notes on page 78.

69

Multicultural education is a rather ambiguous term as it relates to Native American Indians—not so much in the practical application by knowledgeable practitioners and Native American tribes and communities but often in the multiple interpretations by administrative bodies of the federal, state, and local education agencies. As currently analyzed by the educational community, multicultural education has the dubious distinction of being, on the one hand, a valuable striving towards the goal of cultural pluralism and cultural diversity and, on the other hand, a direct threat to the traditional cultural values of both ethnically and racially diverse communities and to the traditional U.S. education system, which has promoted the "melting pot" theory of American life and the competitive race towards the "American Dream."

Multicultural education has an origin in the first contacts of individuals and tribes much before the advent of written languages and formal institutions for acculturating the different groups to each other. The goal of multicultural education can be characterized as learning a second, third, or more cultures, in addition to one's own. Multicultural education is an adaptation to or a survival technique for situations different from one's native culture, the first and usually only culture taught in the normal process of growing up. A main purpose of understanding other cultures is acquiring the benefits to be derived from the different cultures. These benefits can be placed on a continuum, ranging from a treaty of mutual protection and trade to the recognition of irreconcilable differences and cultural taboos. The educational institutions of the United States have yet to comprehend the extent and essence of multicultural education. The history of education provided by the United States government and educational institutions to Native American Indians is a prime example of a failure in multicultural education which reaches the proportion of national tragedy.

The mandate of the federal government to educate Indians is well documented in federal laws, treaties, and the U.S. Constitution. The consortium of institutions delegated by the government to educate Indians has achieved astonishing success for the United States and astounding failure for the Indians. The most remarkable feature of this failure is that, from the wide range of philosophies and ideas of the various institutions concerned with their task of educating Indians, no definite policy on Indian education has ever been spelled out in terms understandable and acceptable to the Indians.

Once the legal status of the Native American Indian was revised by the government from a citizen of an Indian Nation within the boundaries of the United States to a "ward" of the United States government, the value of the American Indians' culture was designated as "dysfunctional" and was, therefore, to be eliminated. This elimination process is exemplified by the experience of the Cherokee Nations.

According to the *Harvard Journal of Legislation* (Vol. 9, 1972, p. 265), in the nineteenth century when the Cherokee had control over their own bilingual schools, they were 90 percent literate in their own language and Oklahoma Cherokees had a higher English literacy level than native English speakers in either Texas or Arkansas[2]. Today, after almost seventy years of White control of the schools, the Cherokee Nation presents an entirely different picture. Cherokee dropout rates in public school run as high as 75 percent. The median number of school years completed by the adult Cherokee is only 5.5; 40 percent of adult Cherokees are functionally illiterate; and 90 percent of the Cherokee families living in Adair County, Oklahoma, are on welfare.

This loss of parental and tribal control over the education of their children by the Cherokee Nation was not an isolated incident. The following quotation from the Annual Report of the Commissioner of Indian Affairs of 1903 typifies the philosophy of federal agencies with respect to Indian education:

> To educate the Indian to ways of civilized life, therefore, is to preserve him from extinction, not as an Indian, but as a human being. As a separate entity, he cannot exist encysted, as it were, in the body of this great Nation. The pressure for land must diminish his reservations to areas within which he can utilize the acres allotted to him; so that the balance may become homes for White farmers who require them. To educate the Indian is to prepare him for the abolishment of tribal relations, to take his land in severalty, and in the sweat of his brow and by the toil of his hands, to carry out, as his White brother has done, a home for himself and his family.[3]

This is one philosophy of Indian education that has permeated the Department of Interior, the Bureau of Indian Affairs (BIA), and other state and federal agencies. Other public and private institutions are also imbued with similar ideas, couched in different esoteric ramblings but advancing the same philosophy.

As one reads and interprets the voluminous records and reports of these various local, state, and federal agencies involved in Indian education, one definite concept unequivocally manifests itself above all others in the education of the Indian and symbolizes the reality of Indian education throughout the history of the United States:

> "Baptize him, anglicize him, disfranchise him, steal his land in the process, and eulogize him for not complaining about it too much." (Testimony of Birgil Kills Straight before the Indian Policy Review Commission on Indian Education)[4]

When the educational systems of the Native American Nations were finally abolished, a main feature of the many-faceted "education" endeavors was the total destruction of the native languages. This point was illustrated by the former policy of the BIA schools which reprimanded those Native American students who chose to communicate in their native tongues. Although this was not the only method employed to suppress the language usage of the Native American students, the tenacity and pervasiveness of this practice underscores the fact that many native languages are today almost extinct.

Therefore, the interpretation of the terms "multicultural" and "bilingual education" should, for Native American Indians, be rejuvenation and preservation of the Native American cultures and languages.

Self-Determination and Multicultural Education

Governmental and institutional intervention has denied the Native American Indians the right to control the enculturation of their children—the process of growing up within the family and tribal environment, learning the tribal language, involvement within the social structure, and clear transmittal of a common tribal "world view." The denial of controlling access to the fundamental mechanisms for transmittal of culture, native language, and tribal social structure precludes multicultural education. To be multicultural, the learner must first have a firm foundation in his or her own culture and share the common world view. Without reinforcing the base culture, the imposition of another culture through schooling will result in coercive assimilation. This leads to anomie or alienation, the inability to integrate one's self into either culture. Governmental structure and educational institutions must incorporate controls to ensure the cultural and linguistic viability of the Native American Indian.

There must also be a change from the concept of Indian education based on Anglo Christian models to one founded on ideals articulated for Indians by Indians. The principle of incorporating these required changes is self-determination, the right and ability to control direction and purpose; for Native American Indians equal educational opportunity is defined as self-determination. The desired direction is to establish a sound educational policy on a foundation of Indian ideals and significant concepts relevant to the Indians' future as a race, as a people, and as a culture.

In January 1975, the U.S. Congress enacted the Indian Self-Determination and Education Assistance Act, P.L. 93-638. This legislation validated the Indian Nations' right to assume responsibility for and control of the most important services provided for them by the federal government without risking "termination," the withdrawal of Indian Nation Status—which has been a disastrous experience for the Indian tribe. P.L. 93-638 is in part a recognition of the destructive effect of termination and a strengthening of self-government and control of Indian education by Indian people. This statute has been augmented by passage of the Basic Indian Education Act, commonly referred to as H.R. 15 or P.L. 95-561, which defines for the first time a clear and undeniable federal education policy for the Bureau of Indian Affairs and the executive departments of the U.S. government:

> Section 1130. It shall be the policy of the Bureau, in carrying out the functions of the Bureau, to facilitate Indian control of Indian Affairs in all matters relating to education.[5]

This policy statement has no "report language" attached to it in the legislative report; therefore, interpretation of the policy must be based on the exact meaning of the legislative language as written and approved. The impact of the combined legislative intent of P.L. 93-638 and P.L. 95-561 is to continue to validate the right of Indian tribes and people both to govern themselves and to control the education of their children. Thus, multicultural education has a new meaning for American Indians. Through the direct efforts of the tribe, the cultural identity and language can be a legitimate and funded activity of the U.S. government within the context of Indian-controlled and -operated school systems. If the public or Bureau of Indian Affairs schools are not meeting the needs of the Indian Nation, that Indian tribe may contract directly with the U.S. government for a school system of its own.

Thus, through the efforts of multicultural education and bilingual education, Native American Indian tribes and people can open the doors to a rediscovery and strengthening of tribal and individual identities. The results of these efforts will, in turn, enrich other cultural entities and place the Indian peoples in a social and political position to responsibly contribute to and share in society.

Overview of Bilingual Education as Related to Native American Indians

Traditional bilingual education has encouraged the philosophy of eventual assimilation while recognizing the value and importance of different cultures and languages. The essence of this approach is born of the fact that only standard languages that are written or spoken are given educational credence. This is emphasized by the HEW Title VII ESEA Rules and Regulations, subpart A 123.4 [20 U.S.C. 3223(a)(2)](1), which read as follows:

> There is instruction given in, and study of English and (to the extent necessary to allow children to achieve competence in the English language) the native language of the children of limited English proficiency. (*Federal Register* 45, no. 67 [4 April 1980])

This paragraph sets the tone insofar as the federal commitment is concerned and the interpretation it lends to bilingual education in general. Upon preliminary examination, reliance upon standard written languages in bilingual education appears to limit participation by a great many Native Americans. Although there are 275,000 Indian students enrolled in the U.S. educational system from kindergarten through Grade 12 (H.E.W. *Bulletin,* "The American Indian in School," Number 13, January, 1973), there are only approximately twenty-five formal bilingual education programs. To bring this situation into even more understandable terms: There are 30,000 Native American students in Oklahoma and only three formal bilingual education programs.

Pragmatic approaches to bilingual education as it exists presently hinge upon a written standard or "proficiency" spoken language.

There are a number of Title IV (P.L. 93-638, The Indian Education Act of 1972) Indian education programs addressing culture to some extent and language to a limited degree. The limitation of these programs in addressing language instruction lies in federal stipulations regarding segregation and HEW regulations.

Johnson O'Malley (P.L. 93-638 Section II) monies are also available to a varying degree, but those tribes in a position to use these funds in linguistic, educational projects (usually in those public schools on or adjacent to reservations) are under constraints, also. These constraints usually are embodied within "state plan" regulations. For those operating without state plans, the result is a parasitical effect on these funds. In essence, programmatic and fiscal limitations dictate that other avenues for approaching bilingual education be explored.

In the natural progression of bilingual educational endeavors, staff training and the availability of those trained personnel become an ever-increasing concern of local and state education agencies, not to mention parents, local advisory groups, tribal education committees, etc. More and more, when these various groups ask us to recommend personnel and especially those institutions that train such personnel, we are forced to explain that there are virtually no Native Americans available to train such personnel. The inappropriateness of this situation is magnified when the number of Native American students enrolled in institutions of higher education, approximately 30,000, is taken into consideration.

Another facet of bilingual education is materials development. There are a number of materials development centers dealing with Spanish-speaking people and programs; however, there are only two centers dealing with materials development for Native Americans. One is the Native American Materials Development Center, located in Albuquerque, New Mexico, funded under Title VII-ESEA, and the other is the Northwest Regional Education Laboratory in Portland, Oregon, funded by the National Institute of Education. The scope of their efforts is dictated by need and geographical location. The output and impact of these two centers is laudable, yet their scope in terms of the number of tribes benefitting leaves much to be desired. In the case of the Albuquerque center 90 percent of the materials are Navajo oriented, and in the case of the Northwest Lab Center twelve tribes benefit. How many tribes remain unserved? Approximately 300. There simply are not enough Native American materials development centers. Multicultural education that validates the differing cultures and strengthens the native language and world view is essential, and the need must be made clear through the Office of Bilingual Education (OBE), BIA, and the state education agencies (SEAs). In providing technical assistance (TA) to Indian groups, tribes, and local education agencies (LEAs) with Native American students enrolled, such agencies must make a coordinated effort in planning, training, and implementing bilingual education programs to fuse them into a predictable, cohesive educational process. As the situation stands, the Equal Employment Opportunity Commission and the Office for Civil Rights appear to be the only two agencies that coordinate their efforts. Once coordination has taken place, however, there is a need to define the specific areas needing attention. The catalyst for both of these situations appears to be the lack of understanding of the requirements under *Lau* v. *Nichols* and of awareness that all tribes and languages are significantly different.

Specific Problems

As has been stated, the number of Indian students enrolled in public schools and the number of bilingual programs is disproportionate. This is a basic problem. Given the number of tribes and students, there is an absence of relevant assessment tools by which proficiency in a specific native language can be measured. The overriding factors in this case are that educational agencies do not take into consideration (1) the student's first acquired language, (2) the language most often spoken in the home, and (3) the language most often spoken by the student. These factors must be weighed together and not as separate entities. This is not being done.

Another area of concern is the problem of disassociating the school and home. Most public schools are structured according to White middle-class mores and virtues. As Indian students come into the public school systems the mores and virtues they have learned and practiced at home are more or less dismissed. This is a practice often found in the classrooms of teachers with lower middle-class or middle-class background. The value of associating the classroom and home is succinctly illustrated by Clyde Kluckhohn, late professor of anthropology at Harvard in a chapter entitled "Queer Customs" in his book *Mirror for Man*. Kluckhohn discusses the concept of culture in the context of biology and individual variation. All people are born with certain basic biological drives and problems, but how these drives are satisfied shows tremendous variation between and within communities. The teacher of the culturally different child must learn that differences among people in the same group are idiosyncratic and the subject of psychology, but that different cultural groups are the subject of anthropology.

One important aspect of culture discussed by Kluckhohn is the interrelatedness of different culture traits. If people change their economic activities they will have to make some adjustment in their social life to allow for the new schedule; or if people change their religious beliefs they will in all likelihood need to adjust their child-training practices to accommodate the new ethical ideas.

For example, serious problems can result for Indian young people who have our Indian value system emphasizing contributions to the community when the only jobs available rely on a desire for personal gain to motivate work performance. The basic message for teachers in Kluckhohn's essay should be that cultural differences are real and legitimate, and cannot be divorced from the language influence of any particular culture. Further, while this may be a general philosophy of LEAs, it is not filtering down to the individual classroom teachers whose students reflect different cultural and linguistic traits.

This pervasive lack of understanding of Native American cultures and languages has perpetuated a belief that under such conditions nothing can be done to arrest the miserable academic statistics of Native Americans. Undeniably, this is consistent with the constrictive philosophy and regulations regarding bilingual education which have been discussed.

An associated problem is the virtual absence of maintenance and restoration programs. This situation is easier to perceive when scrutinized using the 1969 Department of Labor study, conducted under the auspices of then Attorney General Robert Kennedy. The results of the study were published in a report entitled "Indian Education: A National Tragedy; A National Challenge."

The four major points brought out in this report are:

1. Twenty-five percent of teachers surveyed stated that they would rather not teach Indian students at all.

2. There is a high academic failure rate for Indian students.

3. The dropout rate is horrendous — 40 percent average and 100 percent in some areas.

4. The looking-glass attitudes of those children interviewed were in most cases poor, expressing very little sense of self-worth.[6]

The report notes that coercive assimilation has been the main culprit. It further notes that "Indian community and parental involvement in the development and operation of public education programs for Indian children" is one remedy. However, connected with this push is the fear among Indian parents that they, because of their inability to verbalize with school personnel, will be looked upon as a source of amusement rather than as a resource. It would seem from a rational standpoint that maintenance and restoration of languages would, if nothing else, circumvent the negative assimilation repercussions plus involve the parents in the educational process, as sound educational practice dictates. This gives rise to the notion that if sound education is enhanced by bilingual education, then maintenance and restoration models serve to fortify this practice.

In the area of staffing, certain glaring insufficiencies are evident:

1. The number of certified teachers in school districts with large Native American enrollments is not commensurate with the percentage of Indian students, particularly in such metropolitan areas as Billings, Montana, and Tulsa, Oklahoma. (Source: Center for Cross Cultural Education data, Coalition of Indian Controlled School Boards.)[7]

2. There is lack of training for teachers in Indian bilingual education. The following are noted:

    a. There are no undergraduate programs leading to a bachelor's degree in Indian bilingual education.

    b. Colleges which serve large Indian populations, such as the University of South Dakota, only have Indian studies courses.

    c. Only one university offers a postgraduate degree in bilingual education: the University of Oklahoma, with five doctoral candidates.

3. Most of the programs in Lau Center Federal Region VIII service area have limited cultural components.

4. There are no language maintenance or restoration programs.

5. There are no teacher training programs at the district level. In these situations there is a two-pronged effort by the resource centers such as the Lau Center and school districts, usually in the form of inservice workshops.

6. Random assessments have indicated that Native American teacher training is virtually nonexistent. This, coupled with the large enrollment of Native American students, suggests a dire need for the training of Native American bilingual teachers.

The extent of bilingual teacher training is at best piecemeal. The need exists and the development of resources must be addressed. In looking at the situation for facilitating the training of personnel to maintain and restore languages, the prospects are even more bleak. At present, land grant institutions of higher education that have received large grants to teach Native American students are even less aware of the need for LEAs, but it is obvious that they must give priority to this need if the training of bilingual personnel in maintenance and restoration is to be realized.

As far as materials development is concerned, there are two main pitfalls. One is that there are simply not enough materials development centers, as discussed earlier. Another is that, once a bilingual program is funded, there is not enough money in the budget for materials development. The tragedy is compounded because the limited monies that are available are being used not for basic content materials but for supplementary ones which are limited in scope and content and which often run the risk of duplication among programs within a region. How does one teach without proper tools? It is akin to asking a carpenter to build a house without hammer and nails. A teacher has equal need of appropriate materials.

The practices of isolation and cultural destruction, which have traditionally characterized educational policy at the national level, must be discarded. New definitions need to be adopted, based on the reality of the Native American Indian. The term *bilingual education,* for example, requires a necessary expansion. It needs to incorporate the language and culture of the Indian, viewing these as integral components of any effort to upgrade Indian education.

With the commitment of the federal government to promote Indian control of Indian education and the subsequent realignment of terms and interpretations for Indian people, the future direction for multicultural education for Indian tribes and people has to be viewed as one of innovation and renaissance. With this in mind, there should be major expenditures of energy and funds in the restoration and maintenance of Native American Indian languages. In order to achieve this goal, emphasis should be on teacher training centers to serve the educational needs of the Indian Nations.

Notes

1. Speech by Canassetego in reply to the Virginia state legislature, as cited in the *Coalition News,* Coalition of Indian Controlled School Boards (Denver, Colo.), Nos. 10-12 (October-December 1978), p. 8.
2. Kobrick, Jeffrey W., "A Model Act Providing for Transitional Bilingual Education Programs in Public Schools," *Harvard Journal on Legislation* 9, No. 2 (January 1972), pp. 260-300.
3. "Report of the Commissioner of Indian Affairs," *Annual Reports of the Department of the Interior* for Fiscal Year ending 30 June 1903, Part I (Washington, D.C.: U.S. Government Printing Office, 1904).
4. Birgil Kills Straight, testimony in unpublished hearings before the Indian Policy Review Commission, Task Force Five: Indian Education (January 1977).
5. U.S. Congress, Public Law 95-561, 92 Stat 2143-2380, Title XI, Indian Education (1 November 1978).
6. U.S. Senate, *Indian Education: A National Tragedy—A National Challenge,* report by the Special Subcommittee on Indian Education, Committee on Labor and Public Welfare, pursuant to Senate Resolution 80 (Washington, D.C.: U.S. Government Printing Office, 1969).
7. Unpublished data gathered by the Center for Cross Cultural Education, Coalition of Indian Controlled School Boards, Denver, Colo.

Motivation Based on
a Chicano Value System

James A. Vásquez
University of Washington
Seattle, Washington

A growing body of literature suggests that differences in achievement levels between minority and nonminority students can be explained in terms of cultural and socioeconomic background, areas quite apart from any supposed inherent intellectual differences. Such areas as cognitive style (Ramírez and Castañeda, 1974; Lesser, Fifer, and Clark, 1964), locus of control (Coleman et al., 1966; Gurin et al., 1969) and language (Cole and Bruner, 1972; Williams ed., 1971) are frequently cited as evidence that differences in culture and social class contribute considerably to the educational disadvantage of minority children in our schools.

Motivational factors is another major area of difference that ought to be added to this list when comparing minority and mainstream youth. Motivation is closely linked to learning in school-related activities. Were it not, teachers would not spend as much time as they do identifying ways to motivate students to higher levels of interest and attainment. Yet Maehr (1974) has recently pointed out the need to understand motivational factors "in terms of the sociocultural context in which they are found" in order to avoid making observations about student behavior that are biased because of middle-class performance settings.

It is our contention that minority students are not less motivated to achieve at high levels in school, but that in many cases they are motivated by different factors than the Anglo. Consequently, when the teacher (who is usually Anglo) is effective in motivating Anglo students but not minority students, she or he may erroneously conclude that minority students are less motivated to achieve than Anglo students.

Since motivation is related to the values one holds, motivational factors will differ between groups to the same degree that their socioeconomic backgrounds and cultures — and value systems within them — differ.

According to Atkinson (1957), motivation to achieve may be expressed as follows:

$$Ta = f (Ms \times Ps \times Is)$$

where Ta = Tendency to achieve
    f   = Function of
    Ms = Motive to succeed at a task
    Ps = Probability of success at the task
    Is = Incentive value of success.

Incentive is of considerable importance in this model, since incentive directly influences the amount of motivation one has for any given task. But if teachers do not know what is meaningful to students, they will never be able to provide the necessary incentive to motivate them in learning activities.

The Need for Social Reinforcements

Various studies have recently reported data that suggest Mexican American students are highly motivated by reinforcements that are social in nature.

Ramírez and Price-Williams (n.d.), for example, showed pictures to Anglo and Mexican American youth in a study conducted in Texas. Students were asked to describe what was happening in the pictures and received no prompting. While Anglo students gave responses that were reasonable, there appeared to be no patterns for responses among students from this ethnic group. Mexican American students, however, repeatedly indicated by their responses that individuals shown in the pictures were motivated by a desire for some form of social reinforcement. A typical answer was, "The little girl is trying to read the book so she can read it to her blind grandfather."

Various researchers have found that when content is presented in a way that involves people interacting in some way with one another or with factual information, learning among Chicanos is increased. Yet another of their findings that appears to substantiate the highly social orientation of these students is that they appear to be more sensitive to and influenced by the opinion of adults than are their Anglo peers.

These findings suggest that teachers urgently need to be aware of and make use of reinforcements that are meaningful to the Chicano child, instead of relying upon those that may be effective only with Anglo youth.

The minority child's high sensitivity to social reinforcements was observed in yet another manner by Hilgard (1956) when he stated "[these] pupils experience satisfactions when they realize that they are needed . . . when they can help others in meaningful ways." This trait suggests that minority children, including Chicanos, must perceive a clear relationship between school activities and helping other people. They are looking for some humanitarian end result that is a direct outcome of the effort spent in learning activities. Whether the outcome, or opportunity actually to be of assistance to others, is immediate or more remotely in the future may not matter. What does appear to matter is that the teacher take care to point out to these children (and why not to all other children?) that activities chosen for the classroom often do prepare students in some way to be in positions where they can help others.

This particular trait is almost certainly traceable to the experiences of early childhood in a low socioeconomic status environment. People's activities in subsistence-level communities tend to be highly geared toward conserving resources, whether they be financial, food related, or material, since virtually everyone in such communities is aware that survival may well depend on full utilization of whatever resources are to be found. Thus, when they enter school (and for as long as their communities play a role in their socialization), these children will be more motivated to participate and achieve when the teacher is able to demonstrate a relationship between classroom activities and eventual assistance to other people in need.

The efficacy of models in the classroom is additional evidence of the Chicano child's high sensitivity to social reinforcements. It is indeed difficult for minority children to aspire to enter professions when they seldom see members of their own ethnic groups in those professions. Once Chicanos are able to make a breakthrough in a specific high-prestige profession, however, and thus serve as models for other, younger minorities, a steady stream of individuals often follows. Some teachers sense the motivational force accompanying the use of ethnic models and invite them to make "guest appearances" regularly in the classroom. What is needed are not only models representing the high-salaried professions, as in the case of a professional athlete or entertainer, but also those from the many other professions that are equally honorable (if lower paying), to which most children may aspire.

Finally, the existence of strong family loyalties (Ramírez and Castañeda, 1974) suggests another method for motivating Chicano youth in learning activities. Countless teachers admittedly have failed in their attempts to motivate these children because they assumed teacher reinforcement would be sufficiently satisfying, as it often is with Anglo youth. However, when the teacher says "Carlos, you did well on this test. I commend you," the statement may mean nothing to Carlos if the teacher has not yet been accorded status by Carlos and his peers. The teacher can effectively reinforce and thus motivate Carlos by resorting to points of reference that are highly meaningful to him in his motivational system. With much greater frequency teachers ought to say such things as "Carlos, you did well on this test. Your family will be proud of you!"

The Need for Cooperative Tasks

Researchers have reported that cultures may differ substantially from one another in the tendency to achieve depending on whether achievement is mediated through cooperative or competitive tasks (Mead, 1961; Romney and Romney, 1963). Kagan and Madsen (1971), for example, found that Chicano children were clearly more able to achieve through activities perceived as cooperative in nature, while Anglo American children exhibited a significantly higher competitive tendency in the same activities. Similarly, Nelson and Kagan (1972) found that Anglo American children were willing to achieve on cooperative types of tasks far less frequently than were Chicano children (10 percent as compared with 33 percent of the time on specific tasks). However, they also found that Anglo American children were superior at tasks requiring a competitive spirit for achieving.

Whether a competitive or a cooperative approach to achievement is superior is a value judgment and not within the purpose of our discussion. What is important, however, is that many Chicano children differ from their Anglo peers in that they come to school with a readiness to achieve through the medium of cooperative, or group, effort instead of through competitive activities. To the degree that the classroom stresses activities that pit one child against another, then, an advantage is being offered to children of one specific cultural background at the expense of children from another. And it is hardly contestable that many of our classrooms contain a high number of activities that require a competitive spirit on the part of students. Teachers who grade on the curve, who offer special privileges that are only available to a restricted percentage of students, or who allow activities in which some students, no matter how hard they try, are destined to fail or come out second best, inevitably cater to the competitively oriented student.

Teachers, therefore, must be encouraged to provide learning opportunities that more fairly meet the respective needs of these two types of students. If our society requires that children learn the game of competition for survival purposes, surely an equally weighty argument can be adduced to support the notion that competitive children should learn how to achieve through cooperative endeavors. From an international perspective, this is clearly the more pressing need of the two.

A teacher once told the author, "I am totally democratic in the way I teach my class; I treat all my students the same." Perhaps this teacher's intent was commendable, but she neither was democratic nor was she offering her students equal educational opportunity. All students are not the same, therefore we cannot teach them as if no differences existed among them. Students differ markedly from one ethnocultural group to another in various critical areas, including the ways in which they are motivated to achieve in classroom activities. As we continue to learn more about cultural distinctions that strongly impinge on how different students learn, and as we take these differences into account in the instructional procedures we use in the classroom, we begin to offer equality of educational opportunity to the different types of students constituting our schools in today's society. Equally important, we should begin to close the achievement gap between ethnically different students and mainstream students.

References

Atkinson, J.W. "Motivational Determinants of Risk-Taking Behavior." *Psychological Review* 64 (1957): 359-372.

Cole, M., and Bruner, J. "Preliminaries to a Theory of Cultural Differences." In *National Society for the Study of Education Yearbook, 1972.* Chicago: University of Chicago Press, 1978.

Coleman, J.S.; Campbell, E.Q.; Hubson, L.J.; McPortland, J.; Modal, A.M.; Weinteld, F.D.; and York, R.L. *Equality of Educational Opportunity.* Washington, D.C.: U.S. Government Printing Office, 1966.

Dewey, J. *Experiences and Education.* New York: The Macmillan Co., 1938.

Gallimore, R.; Weiss, L.B.; and Finney, R. "Cultural Differences in Delay of Gratification: A Problem of Behavior Classification." *Journal of Personality and Social Psychology* 30, no. 1 (1974): 72-80.

Gurin, P.; Gurin, G.; Lao, R.; and Beattie, R. "Internal-External Control in the Motivational Dynamics of Negro Youth." *Journal of Social Issues* 25, no. 3 (1969): 29-53.

Hilgard, E. *Theories of Learning.* New York: Appleton-Crofts, 1956.

Kagan, S., and Madsen, M. "Cooperation and Competition of Mexican, Mexican American and Anglo American Children of Two Ages under Four Instructional Sets." *Developmental Psychology* 5, no. 1 (1971): 32-39.

Lesser, G.; Fifer, G.; and Clark, D. *Mental Ability of Children in Different Social and Cultural Groups.* Chicago: University of Chicago Press, 1964.

Maehr, M.L. "Culture and Achievement Motivation." *American Psychologist* 29 (1974): 887-895.

Mead, M. *Cooperation and Competition among Primitive Peoples.* Boston: Beacon Press, 1961.

Nelson, L., and Kagan, S. "Competition: The Star-Spangled Scramble." *Psychology Today* 6, no. 4 (September 1972).

Ramírez, M., and Castañeda, A. *Cultural Democracy, Bicognitive Development, and Education.* New York: Academic Press, 1974.

Ramírez, M., and Price-Williams, D.R. "Achievement Motivation in Children of Three Ethnic Groups in the United States." Houston, Texas: Center for Research in Social Change and Economic Development, Rice University, n.d.

Romney, K., and Romney, R. "The Mixtecans of Juxtlahuaca, Mexico." In *Six Cultures,* edited by B. Whiting. New York: Wiley, 1963.

Williams, F., ed. *Language and Poverty.* Chicago: Markham Publishing Company, 1971.

Language Renewal: Strategies for Native Americans

Robert St. Clair
University of Louisville
Louisville, Kentucky

and

Rosalie Bassett
Toppenish, Washington

What Is Language Renewal?

The loss of a language and its culture appears to be a common socio-political experience in the Pacific Northwest. Time after time, various native groups have gone through this process. Characteristically, it consists of three stages: First, there is contact with the language of colonial administrators and their representatives, and this leads to the acquisition of a European language for commerce. Next, the foreign language begins to dominate in proportion to the power exercised by the colonials. Finally, the native languages begin to attenuate in importance, become limited, and approach extinction. This demise of a language and its culture represents a sad commentary on bilingual and bicultural education. Many of the members of the Sahaptian and Salishan tribes have experienced this firsthand. They have seen their language go from stability to termination with the death of their elders. When the language has been documented, it has been done by those with a repository mentality who prefer to display the grandeur that was in the shiny cases of museums or the dusty shelves of unused archives. Language renewal is an attempt to halt this process of erosion. It is concerned with reversing the processes of time and space. It is, in essence, affirmative Indian education.

Having discussed the structure of despair that accompanies language loss, it is now time to ask a more basic question: How did this come about? The answer can be found in the literature of education and colonialism, for American Indians are victims of internal colonialism. Theirs is a conquest culture that has been forced to supplant its rich language with English. They are a people who have been coerced into denying their own values and belief systems for an alien epistemology. They have been politically socialized by all that was foreign to them. The stories they read are not of their past. The system of government in which they participate has no link with their former practices. The god that they worship does not speak of the sacredness of the land or the freedom of the sky; there is no mention of mother earth and father sky. Time has been replaced by the moving hands of a mechanical clock and space has been apportioned for commercial gain. Such is the verdict of political socialization. This is why many have argued that to lose one's language and the values that accompany it is tantamount to ethnocide. There no longer is a sense of community. People no longer share the same values or experience the same emotions. They no longer hold the same things sacred. They have become disenfranchised.

The most effective instrument of political socialization is language education. When teachers claim to be merely practicing grammar drills or checking for punctuation, they are unknowingly doing much more. The language that they use is not neutral. It is armed with a value system that permeates its very existence and manifests itself in metaphor and other forms of rhetorical expression. The readers before them are not neutral, either. The image of the Indian continues to be a pejorative one. When these stories are transplanted into the complexity of the industrialized United States, the Manichaean dichotomy of good versus bad still exists. Those who are minorities are depicted in menial tasks and continue to act as servants for the needs of the corporate interests. They are patronized and dealt with as little children who continue to need supervision and guidance from the Great White Father. Their very existence has been devalued by social distance and personal alienation. Hence, the curriculum can socialize, and language can set an agenda of social expectations. If language renewal is to be successful, it must take these factors into consideration.

Is Language Renewal Possible?

The classical paradigm of language renewal can be found in the revival of Hebrew in Israel: Aaron Bar-Adon notes in *The Rise and Decline of a Dialect: A Study in the Revival of Modern Hebrew* (Hawthorne, N.Y.: Mouton Publications, 1975) that the language was renewed after 1,900 years of dormancy. Ben Yehuda, the Father of Modern Hebrew, is noted for his attempts to nativize modern Hebrew when the first immigrants settled in the area in 1882-1903. At first, there was no centralized system of education and no program of language teaching; each school followed its own policy and methods. Currently, the revival of Hebrew has come under serious discussion. It is argued by some that Yiddish is the lingua franca of Israel because it is spoken at home by both Russian and German Jews and hence should be the official dialect of the land. These social and historical factors in the development of Hebrew can provide valuable insight into language renewal in the Pacific Northwest.

Unlike the sporadic attempts of Ben Yehuda and others, the nature of language planning among American Indians is more scientific. There is now an abundance of literature on bilingual and bicultural education. Furthermore, the sociopolitical situation in the United States is rather different. It reflects a state of internal colonialism for the reservation Indian and one of neocolonialism for the urban Indian. Hence, any sense of tribalism is contrained by a network of dependency relationships which virtually dictate the interests of federalism. Given this context, one must continue to ask the question of whether or not language renewal is possible in the United States.

Language Planning Strategies

Where does one begin to renew a language? From a very practical point of view, this can be done by developing a language arts program with its textbooks on grammar, its pedagogical dictionary, its readers on history and culture, and its inservice workshops for teachers. If this program were unwisely implemented, it could lead to failure in a tribal nation that continues to associate literacy with an oral tradition which may not look kindly upon the intrusion of the print media. In addition, the population that one addresses must also be carefully examined. The elders know the language, but they are against teaching it by the more technological methods which conflict with the personal imparting of knowledge through apprenticeship. The sons, daughters, and grandchildren of these elders are against learning the language because they have become alienated from it and can no longer cherish the values of the old ways. Finally, there are the children. Here one finds a ray of hope. Children have a natural ability to acquire language. They are still open to alternatives in life and have not summarily dismissed the social worlds of their ancestors. Hence, one possible strategy for language planning is to first teach the children the language. Once they have embarked on a language arts program, have them converse with their grandparents. They can both learn from each other. The children know the alphabet, the elders know the language and can reconstruct its social reality for them. What about those in the middle who have been alienated by the effects of time and the pressures of socialization? It appears that when they are ready to participate, they could be easily incorporated into parenting programs. In this way, the whole community becomes linked across generations.

There is another problem that must be faced in language planning: What dialect is to be taught? The solution is not an easy one. As a working strategy, several groups of speakers have resorted to teaching a common alphabet which can be readily employed by all. The advantage to this approach is that it enhances the development of language programs and short-circuits controversy over elitism and political dominance.

Curriculum

Alternative Approaches in Bilingual Education Teacher Training

Atilano A. Valencia
New Mexico State University
Las Cruces, New Mexico

With bilingual education teacher training being implemented in school districts and universities throughout the nation, the question now is "What should programs emphasize?" Where federal funding is involved, the principal curricular components include language, linguistics, culture, methodology, and field experience. In universities, the degree of focus on any given component is often relative to the philosophical-psychological perspectives of the program designers. In some instances, humanists have influenced the curricular structure and instructional emphasis—this usually takes a cultural awareness approach. Closely related is the influence of ethnic studies programs, with courses primarily related to the social sciences. In other cases, cognitive-oriented educators, whose approaches are based on Piagetian and Brunerian theoretical constructs, have taken the lead. Specialists in languages and linguistics have promoted curricular offerings with specific reference to their fields of specialization.

State department accreditation committees also have affected curricular emphasis in bilingual education teacher training. Where any one of the above-mentioned approaches is overrepresented on a committee, the nature of accreditation requirements often reflects the committee's predominant frame of reference. In turn, institutions desiring to maintain bilingual education teacher-training programs are obliged to follow the accreditation guidelines. Where guidelines are based on a sound educational rationale for promoting the overall growth and development of children through effective teaching, results may be noteworthy and beneficial. Where guidelines tend to be oriented toward a given discipline, a similar orientation will very likely occur in the field, while the overall educational advancement of bilingual children remains questionable.

The Language/Linguistics Approach

The involvement of a target population's native language in the educational process has taken at least two approaches in bilingual education teacher training. In teacher-training institutions where the program designers represent the foreign languages or linguistics, the teacher-training program carries a particular emphasis on either or both of these disciplines. In these instances, the emphasis is to develop among participating students proficiency in all of the communication arts of the target language. This type of program for Spanish/English bilinguals may include any number of courses in grammar, composition, and peninsular and Latin American literature. Additionally, various courses in Spanish linguistics may also be included. There are at least two shortcomings in this type of emphasis. First, in the majority of cases, language courses in departments of foreign languages were initially intended to prepare persons to speak a second language or to teach a foreign language in a secondary school, college, or university; the courses have little or no relationship to the content that bilingual education elementary teachers need. A second shortcoming is that little or no attention is given to the integration of the native language in other courses in the bilingual education program; i.e., courses dealing with methodology, history, and culture. Thus, the trainees often leave the program with little knowledge of techniques for applying the target language as a medium of instruction. A teacher with this type of orientation often becomes preoccupied with furthering the child's bilingual ability, often in favor of the native language, rather than with enhancing the child's overall cognitive and affective development. In bilingual education programs where this emphasis especially is found, research may reveal that program children will show relatively smaller gains in English compared with nonprogram children from the same ethnic group.

A second approach for incorporating the target language is found where bilingual education curriculum specialists view a background in languages and linguistics for teachers as facilitating the development of instructional media for students in kindergarten through grade 12, with bilingual development occurring as one of the products in the total educational process. In this respect, languages and linguistics courses are designed with content and activities that offer greater utility for prospective bilingual education teachers, in comparison with courses traditionally designed on a foreign language basis. The content essentially

contains features that serve as ready reference.
understanding and furthering the communication proc
with different levels of bilingualism. Moreover, this appr
trainees with opportunities to use the target language in in
strategies and techniques for furthering the cognitive developn.
bilingual students.

The Cultural-Historical Awareness Approach

A teacher-training program, with a particular emphasis on the culture and history of a given target population, can provide the students with a broad and indepth knowledge of the anthropological, sociological, and historical aspects of a given cultural group. Teacher-training programs with this emphasis provide the student with research methodologies and specific strategies for establishing and furthering school and community relations. Research methodologies related to these social science fields often employ survey, interview, and case study techniques. In turn, the field experience component provides opportunities for student interns to apply the knowledge and research techniques that are emphasized in their coursework.

One of the shortcomings in relying solely on this type of program is that students often fail to acquire knowledge and skills in applying bilingual methodologies, arrangements, and activities in actual classroom situations. In essence, exiting students may incorrectly envision themselves as well-prepared bilingual bicultural teachers, when in reality they are trained more specifically as social science researchers and community or social workers.

However, the foregoing type of training can play a significant role in the preparation of bilingual education teachers, for it provides a dimension that is often neglected in United States school systems. School administrators, teachers, and members of school boards need more knowledge about ethnographic factors in communities; moreover, they need knowledge about effective strategies for increasing parental and community involvement in the education of their children. This training component is unavailable in many bilingual education teacher-training programs. Yet, in programs where it is found, other training components, i.e., bilingual methodologies, are relatively weak or absent.

Another approach related to the sociocultural is the cultural awareness or cultural sensitivity type, which incorporates a combination of sociocultural concepts and psychological principles. Usually, it is designed to advance the learner's knowledge of a particular culture or cultures. But it also proposes to change negative attitudes or enhance favorable attitudes among participants with respect to one or more minority groups.

The principal shortcomings in this approach are similar to those of the former in that it often disregards bilingual methodologies related to cognitive processes. Another shortcoming is the assumption that attitudinal changes among participants can be dramatically affected through short-term workshops. In a psychological perspective, it is questionable that a brief and intensive cultural sensitivity session will suddenly generate positive and long-lasting attitudinal changes among participants toward children with different cultural backgrounds, for the effects are heavily dependent on the nature and intensity of the internalized attitudes (McDonald, 1975).

The foregoing analysis does not imply that short-term cultural sensitivity workshops are ineffective and should be dismissed as a training approach. However, this author proposes that the degree of effectiveness is dependent on the existing attitudes, the nature of the activities, and provisions for follow-up processes beyond the duration of the particular workshop.

The "one-shot" approach may have an impact on individuals who are psychologically ready for this type of information. These individuals may be searching for practical ideas and techniques to apply in classroom situations. On the other hand, the one-shot approach will arouse a passive awareness among participants who are attending the workshop for other reasons, e.g., to fulfill a district inservice training requirement, or to acquire credits for salary advancement or a credential endorsement. The short-term workshop must have a specific purpose, and all of the participants must recognize that their participation is related to the stated objectives.

One may expect that teachers and administrators who are in most need of training will frequently fail to enroll in this type of workshop. Yet, one may also predict that the short-term workshop will fail to make a significant impact on persons who are not psychologically ready for this type of training; therefore, it is preferable that another approach be envisaged for affecting an attitudinal change among this type of personnel in an educational system.

It is extremely difficult to ascertain changes in negative perceptions or gains in favorable attitudes in a short-term workshop. Well-designed questionnaires and interview techniques may draw responses that reflect attitudinal changes or gains; however, the carry-over of behaviors to actual situations remains a variable. For this reason, the degree of effectiveness can be most appropriately ascertained in reference to actual behavioral modification in the field setting, and a follow-up process in the field is essential. First, the trainers must note teacher behaviors in bilingual classrooms; second, the trainers must provide feedback and additional interactive sessions with teachers on a one-to-one or small-group basis. For the purpose of promoting attitudinal changes, this author proposes a continuous and progressive system, compared with a one-shot workshop approach.

Psychological Orientations in Bilingual Teacher Training

One or more psychological orientations also are found in teacher training programs. While bilingual education students and teachers in the field often claim to follow an eclectic frame of reference in the application of learning theories, the content and training activities provided by institutions of higher education for bilingual education trainees do not always reflect a balanced orientation.

The behaviorist's approach is frequently found in second-language techniques and programmed instruction. English-as-a-second-language (ESL) and Spanish-as-a-second-language (SSL) approaches usually incorporate stimulus-response-reinforcement instructional techniques. Materials for second-language development often include techniques for modeling and shaping of sounds, ways for correcting responses, approaches for reinforcing correct responses, formats for manipulating puppets in a stimulus-response type of dialogue, and techniques for applying a chain dialogue (Valencia, 1970). The behaviorist's approach in second-language development need not be completely discarded in teacher training; however, it should be viewed as one of several alternative instructional modes, for research has revealed robot-like responses among children involved in this type of learning process (Valencia, 1969). Moreover, the indiscriminate application of token reinforcement, without consideration of the dignity of the individual or of its compatibility with the cultural values of the target group, is a question that must be given serious attention in this type of training approach.

Where a teacher chooses to begin with the achievement level of the learners and allow them to progress at their individual rates, programmed instruction offers a viable alternative. The principal shortcoming in highly structured programs is the absence of opportunities for spontaneous exploration and creativeness. Moreover, these types of programs limit the opportunities for learning through small-group interaction.

However, instructional approaches based on behaviorist principles may prove advantageous in certain situations; in this regard, dynamic bilingual education teachers may consider it as one feature in their repertoire of instructional strategies.

Among the various instructional modes related to learning theories are the cognitive-oriented approaches. Cognitive-oriented instruction tends to be associated with at least two types of psychological perspectives: cognitive learning styles per se and cognitive development based on cognitive-field psychology. Contemporary authors on the theme of cognitive styles give particular reference to researchers such as Witkins, Miller, Woodworth, and Albrech (Witkins, 1967), while authors on cognitive field psychology frequently cite scholars such as Tolman, Lewin, Bruner, and Piaget (Biggs, 1971).

Further research is needed on variables related to cognitive learning styles of distinct ethnic groups in the United States. Particular attention must be given to the validity of existing instruments and the composition of sampling groups in these research efforts. This is an important consideration, for the erroneous classification of children from any ethnic group in terms of specific learning style can, in essence, generate negative psychological effects of a self-fulfilling nature. Variations in environmental conditions, socioeconomic status, age and sex factors, etc., make it extremely difficult to generalize in terms of an entire ethnic group. A careful review of recent research on learning styles and cognitive development reveals the danger of such generalizations (DeAvila, 1974). At best, the teaching approach may well be that of observing and allowing children, irrespective of ethnic groups, to enhance their cognitive development through learning styles most congruent with their immediate dispositions, while they also are given opportunities to explore and acquire alternative cognitive skills.

The rationale of providing goal-oriented instruction, associating the perceptual-experiential world of the learner with concepts given in the curriculum, and extending the learner's cognitive repertoire through the exploration of new concepts and processes, is directly related to cognitive-field psychology (Biggs, 1971). It includes the creation and relationship of cultural-based materials, the association of languages with cognitive development, the analysis and integration of ideas with environmental phenomena, and the opportunity for the learner to apply cognitive processes in the acquisition of new concepts.

In this approach, it is envisaged that cognitive development means more than the learning of concepts through a singular instructional mode, e.g., memorization via the rote method. The cognitive approach provides teachers with a repertoire of strategies for creating a variety of learning conditions that are natural and meaningful for children at their respective levels of development. It provides teachers with a communication system and a set of cultural references to facilitate the identifying, labeling, and classifying of perceived concepts. And it provides teachers with instructional strategies that will open opportunities for children to acquire and apply a variety of cognitive processes, i.e., identifying, classifying, comparing, analyzing, hypothesizing, inferring, and evaluating. Thus, the cognitive development of children refers to the acquisition of concepts and application of cognitive processes that are carried bilingually—they need not be limited to an English communication mode. This is a significant feature in bilingual education, for any concepts and cognitive processes that are learned in one language can be readily transferred and applied via a second language. This approach explicitly shows that languages in bilingual education offer the media for facilitating cognitive development—they represent one of the means for enhancing the educational processes of bilingual students.

A Relative and Flexible Approach

While it may be difficult to develop a teacher-training program with a completely balanced structure in terms of all of the above-mentioned components, program designers must, nevertheless, strive for sufficient scope in a curriculum. Curriculum designers must hypothesize about the educational effects that a program will have on the prospective teacher and, in turn, on the growth and development of youngsters in the public schools. In this sense, too, the content across the disciplines must be relevant to the type of professional person being prepared for service in the field.

Language, culture, and cognitive concepts are relative factors. Conceivably, references to the learner's language and culture facilitate the acquisition of new concepts and application of cognitive skills. In turn, new perceptions and experiences will facilitate bilingual development and relationships with others. In the final analysis, the bilingual education teacher, equipped with multiple and alternative approaches to learning, can effectively interrelate the aforementioned elements in the advancement of the learner. Thus, rather than overemphasizing one discipline, today's teacher-training programs must provide a sufficiently broad curriculum and a variety of activities to enable trainees to acquire meaningful knowledge and applicable professional skills.

References

DeAvila, Edward; Havassy, Barbara et al. "Intelligence of the Mexican American: A Field Study Comparing Neo-Piagetian and Traditional Capacity and Achievement Measures." Stockton, Calif.: The Multicultural Assessment Program, ESEA, Title VII Project, January 1974.

Biggs, Morris L. *Learning Theories for Teachers.* New York: Harper and Row Publishers, 1971.

McDonald, Frederick J. *Educational Psychology.* 2nd ed. Belmont, Calif.: Wadsworth Publishing Company, 1965.

Valencia, Atilano A. "An Innovative Language Program for Non-English Speaking Children." Albuquerque: Southwestern Cooperative Educational Laboratory, Inc., 1970.

_____ . "Identification and Assessment of Educational and Community Programs for Spanish Speaking People." A study prepared for the Southwest Council of La Raza. Albuquerque: Southwestern Cooperative Educational Laboratory, Inc., 1969.

Witkins, H.A. "Cognitive Styles Across Cultures." *International Journal of Psychology,* 1976, pp. 233-250. Cited by J.W. Berry and P.R. Dosen in *Culture and Cognition: Readings in Cross-Cultural Psychology.* New York: Harper and Row Publishers, 1974.

Guidelines for Program Development in Teacher Education for Multilingual Settings

Frank X. Sutman
MERIT Center
Temple University
Philadelphia, Pennsylvania

Basic Premises

Bilingual education is a reality, despite its recency. Thousands of children are enrolled who, because of familial and cultural background and consequent limited ability to use the English language, find themselves unable to participate fully in the learning activities of their classes. Many qualified and devoted teachers are meeting the challenge of educating these children. In addition to the personal initiative of these teachers, federal and state legislative actions have led some school systems in forty-two states to introduce system-wide programs to meet the basic language and cultural needs of this special school-age population.

At the same time, the high probability that increasing numbers of people, for whom English is not a first language and U.S. culture is essentially foreign, will enter the United States calls for extensive efforts to prepare personnel to administer multicultural multilingual programs. Further, institutions of higher education, conventionally the sole source of preservice education and inservice graduate education, will assume major responsibility for preparing these administrators and supplying teachers who are professionally equipped to teach in bicultural bilingual situations.

There will be no royal road to any single, ideal professional preparation pattern. We may expect that school systems, colleges, and universities (and such centers as MERIT) will multiply with alternative undergraduate, graduate, and inservice designs. This is the genius of United States education. At the same time, it is reasonable to anticipate that most programs will move forward from common, basic premises. Six such premises appear to be fundamental:

Premise 1: It is unrealistic to think that the conventional undergraduate four-year curriculum will include all of the experience essential to the many competencies expected of the beginning teacher in any classroom, much less in the bilingual classroom. This means, of course, that it is not to be anticipated that every teacher fluent in even two of the languages to be used in the classroom will be able to teach specialized disciplines in those languages. Conversely, it is not to be expected that the teacher who has in four years completed a major in science, math, or art, will acquire sufficient mastery of additional languages to be able to teach in a medium other than his or her mother tongue. It follows, then, that when changes within the four-year, prebaccalaureate curriculum are proposed, priorities need to be considered by each prospective teacher, and varieties of preparations must be allowed for.

Premise 2: A mature and effective approach to teaching evolves only over a period of several years. Premise two is corollary to the first. Effective teaching comes with professional preparation and experience. There is greater probability that effective teaching strategies will be introduced by teachers who come through their professional preparation under the guidance of faculty who themselves are maturing in their understanding of the teaching process. Yet, even under the most adroit instruction, it would be less than realistic to expect effective teaching strategies to be fully developed during the prebaccalaureate years.

Premise 3: To develop effective teacher education programs, it is essential to distinguish among different levels of competencies. Some basic competencies can be developed within a relatively short period. The related skills of administering and scoring a language proficiency test are examples. These are what we might call lower-level competencies, and they can be acquired in one or two lessons or perhaps the teacher develops them quickly to meet an on-the-job crisis. In contrast, choosing an appropriate evaluation strategy, understanding the significance of the range of language proficiency and pretest scores, and the ability to take appropriate actions to improve instruction based on high test results, is a higher-order competency that develops through synthesis of a number of lower-order competencies. Very few higher-order competencies are developed during the preteaching college experience, while lower-order competencies can be developed during the initial instructional period. Experience coupled with inservice education activities are the major vehicle through which lower-level competencies gel into the higher-order competencies needed for effective bilingual teaching. Accepting this premise requires a cautious examination of existing checklists of generic competencies to be met during the early years of prebaccalaureate education. Caution is essential, since many of these lists are ineffective because they call for an unrealistic level of professional development during this relatively short period of collegiate education.

Premise 4: Competencies generally considered essential for outstanding teaching in most academic areas are also essential for the bilingual teacher. Additional competencies, however, are needed for effective performance in bilingual situations. These added competencies are similar to those underlying excellence in second-language or foreign-language teaching. The first is basic for all teachers in bilingual situations: reasonable ability to communicate with children and their parents in their own language. Second, somewhere in the faculty line-up there need to be teachers professionally prepared to teach the language or languages familiar to the children. The capacity for teaching the language is an added professional competence not necessarily possessed by even the most fluent speaker of the language. Third, somewhere in the faculty of the multilingual school there must be teachers sufficiently bilingual themselves to teach other academic subjects such as science, math, art, etc., in both English and a second language — and know when it is appropriate to invoke which language.

Premise 5: In any bilingual program the teaching of English is an important and integral part of helping students to be able to use English as well as their mother tongue. The fields of English for Speakers of Other Languages (ESOL) and Teaching English to Speakers of Other Languages (TESOL) have long dealt systematically with bilingualism. Their very titles mandate it. Both fields antedate governmental funding for bilingual education in the United States, though they have received extensive support for the teaching of English overseas. The important concept to be underscored here is that bilingual education, specifically so called, and ESOL and TESOL are all fundamentally committed to the development of bilingual competence. And where funds permit and where parents who understand the multicultural nature of modern society embrace the opportunity, bilingual education can extend bilingual competence to otherwise monolingual children in the United States.

Premise 6: Quality teaching is sustained and burn-out is minimized by teachers who maintain a reasonable balance between the art of teaching and the science of education. Teaching has an artistic and a scientific component. Beginning teachers reveal a larger emphasis on the artistic aspect of their work. Maturity in teaching comes gradually as increasing concern for the scientific component establishes an equation between these two inescapably essential elements.

Running through these six premises is an intended note of flexibility. The rate of development of competencies, the degree of excellence to be anticipated, the almost infinite range of alternate combinations of specialization called for in meeting the needs of children in a school system — all are variables to be kept in mind as we move now to closer consideration of curricular provisions for the education of teachers in multilingual schools.

Curriculum in Bilingual Teacher Education

Bilingual education is an area of professional education in teacher education. It is not an area of instruction in elementary and secondary schools. It focuses specifically on preparation of teachers to work in bilingual situations, much as the special education teacher works with young people in situations involving the exceptional child. The bilingual teacher education curriculum presented here is spelled out in terms of studies and experiences designed to meet specified objectives. The spectrum of activities proposed suggests the wide range of skills and competencies needed for effective instruction in bilingual education settings. But specifically, what skills and competencies are called for?

One approach to a comprehensive listing is found in the *Federal Register* of 11 June 1976. This document spells out competencies essential for applicants for "Fellowships for Preparation of Teacher Trainers." These competencies include the ability to:

1. Teach various subjects or courses of study in elementary or secondary schools using English and a language other than English

2. Provide instruction in elementary or secondary schools in the history and culture of the United States and of geographical areas associated with a language other than English

3. Select and use appropriate instruments for measuring the educational performance of children of limited English-speaking ability

4. Involve parents and community organizations in programs of bilingual education, and incorporate into such programs the use of appropriate available cultural and educational resources.

These four higher-level competencies appear to be central to carrying out the legal mandates of bilingual education. They are deemed necessary for educators who prepare bilingual teachers. Because teacher educators should minimally have the same competencies they expect their students to develop, it seems reasonable to assert that these are competencies eventually to be developed by those who would teach bilingually at all school levels. It must be kept in mind that these broad competencies usually do not emerge until the teacher has been involved in advanced inservice professional experiences. Perhaps this level of competency development does not occur until the teacher advances to professional study at the doctoral level or its equivalent.

How does the curriculum planner map out the sequences of educational experiences for the future bilingual teacher? First, it is reasonable to assume that different levels of competency are developed at different stages of professional progress — preservice, upper preservice, early inservice, experienced inservice. Second, recognizing these four stages of advancement, the skills and competencies to be developed at each stage are determined. Third, within institutions of higher education, the nature of the curriculum (studies, experiences, and activities) that can facilitate the acquisition of these skills and competencies is defined.

This sequence may become clearer in graphic form. Figure 1 lists the competencies and the experiences and activities contributing to each competency, plus a time line proposing the optimum point in progress at which the experiences can be provided. The time periods, of course, are not absolute, since students may begin their preparation with widely varying levels of competence.

The brevity of listing in the graphic form of Figure 1 calls for some clarifying detail. Five of the items merit such special consideration: the teaching of English, the use of tests and measurements, historic contributions, cultural awareness, and community involvement.

Teaching of English. Competency 3 (Figure 1) considers teaching English to speakers of other languages as a professional specialization related to but clearly distinct from teaching English to persons speaking English as the mother tongue. The bilingual curriculum must not only contain the special theoretical bases and methodology for teaching ESOL, but it must also supply ample opportunity, through well-planned field experiences, for the bilingual teacher trainee to teach ESOL under the supervision of knowledgeable professional personnel. The course work and field experiences should be woven together and extend over a considerable period of time.

The training experiences must be planned to prepare teachers of ESOL for bilingual classrooms, where the goal is development of a usable level of English, especially in listening to and speaking English. The heard and spoken utterances in English will be the child's first and probably major contact with English on his or her way to bilingual competence.

Many critics of bilingual education have been especially concerned about school districts that receive federal funds to implement bilingual programs but ignore this important ESOL component. At the same time bilingual specialists at both state and federal levels indicate that in many instances local educational agencies having student populations with limited competence in English provide only ESOL instruction while ignoring other components of a quality bilingual program. These

Figure 1
Skills and Competencies to be Planned for in Designing a
Curriculum for Bilingual Teachers*

Competencies to Be Achieved	Enabling Studies, Experiences, and Activities	Timing
1. Ability to organize subject matter to meet the psychological readiness of children from varying backgrounds and of varying abilities	Specially designed courses which "professionalize" the approach to subject matter; i.e., which exemplify organization and methods appropriate to school level	Preservice, continuing well into inservice level
2. Ability to organize an effective academic and social classroom which individualizes instruction	Supervised student or intern teaching experiences in bilingual school settings	Preservice, continuing into inservice level
3. Ability to communicate (listen and speak) in two languages, including English; to teach English as a second language; and to understand how this differs from teaching English as a first language or from merely being fluent in English	Courses emphasizing oral facility in these languages, with opportunities to listen and speak in bilingual contexts	Preservice
4. Ability to select appropriate diagnostic testing procedures and tests, and to administer tests that are appropriate both to conventional and bilingual instruction	Involvement with a variety of tests and measurements and evaluating procedures as used in classes and field work in working toward competency #1, 3, 5	Early inservice
5. Ability to read in two languages, including English	Courses involving a wide range of readings appropriate for elementary and secondary school age children	Preservice
6. Awareness of the differences of cultures and their traditional values, behaviors, mores, etc.	Optimally, opportunity to visit, live, or work in a second culture, including work in community services in a developing country	Summers, preservice, and inservice
7. Consciousness of the value structure and customs of at least one culture other than that of the United States	Specially designed assignments demanding sustained work with a professional and knowledgeable leader in a second culture	Summers, preservice

*Condensed from a broader listing prepared by Francis X. Sutman and Annette López.

Competencies to Be Achieved	Enabling Studies, Experiences, and Activities	Timing
8. Linguistic and social grace to enter into co-operative planning and work with parents and community leaders in educational activities	Intern field work in multilingual communities	Inservice
9. Work within professional organizations dedicated to improving bilingual and multicultural education	Report formally to fellow students and colleagues on central issues dealt with in professional meetings, professional journals, and the like	Early inservice and continuing
10. Knowledge of the history of the United States	Course work focused on contributions of people from other cultures, possibly employing languages of those cultures in the courses	Preservice and continuing
11. Familiarity with location of and use of instructional materials, including remedial materials appropriate for use in bilingual teaching situations	Supervised assignments requiring location and use of instructional materials	Upper preservice and continuing throughout inservice

components include a strong impetus for improving the child's use of his mother tongue and enriching his understanding of the history and culture of his familial background. When this is combined with the history and culture of the United States, which is conventionally included in ESOL programs, an entire school population may be on its way to developing a positive self-image.

Test and Measurements. Competency 4 (Figure 1) calls for ability to select appropriate diagnostic testing procedures and tests. This competency, related to the evaluation of normal academic and social concerns, is lacking from many preservice teacher education programs. There has been relatively little emphasis on the development of this competency even at the early inservice level of teacher education. The situation is particularly acute in relation to teacher-prepared tests for classroom use. This vacuum is reflected in comments made by teachers at all levels of instruction. How often, for example, do we hear teachers' comments reflect the erroneous notion that true-false questions test for different understanding than do multiple-choice or matching questions? Very little understanding is required to realize that true-false questions are simply a special class of the multiple-choice question. Beyond this concern, teachers too seldom understand that appropriate formulation of questions may be the most difficult, certainly the most important, skill the teacher exercises.

Ignorance in the area is even more serious in relation to bilingual needs. Here analysis of language competence is an essential part of needs assessment. Bilingual teachers should have ample opportunity to deal rigorously with the contents of such publications as *Oral Language Tests for Bilingual Students: An Evaluation of Language Dominance and Proficiency Instruments,* published by the Northwest Regional Educational Laboratory in Portland, Oregon (1976), and *The Politics of Speaking: An Approach to Evaluating Bilingual-Bicultural Schools,* one of the "Bilingual Education Paper Series" published by the National Dissemination and Assessment Center at California State University, Los Angeles (1978). In this latter publication, Frederick Erickson of Harvard University recognizes the trauma for foreign students in taking standardized tests. He proposes a sociolinguistic approach to assessment, utilizing interaction schemes and observers in the classroom.

It would be comforting to believe that the low priority given to adequate evaluation techniques in teacher education programs results from the fact that guidance personnel have become more and more responsible for diagnostic testing. Unfortunately, the general lack of sophistication regarding use of appropriate testing techniques and the notable near-absence of concern for testing in bilingual teacher education programs appear to result more from the historical belief by teacher educators that any teacher is able to select or prepare tests and testing techniques and to analyze the results effectively. This is simply not the case. Because of the special nature and special needs of bilingual students, competency in effective testing procedures and measurement devices calls for greater emphasis in this area in our programs for bilingual teachers.

Historical Contribution. Competency 10 (Figure 1) relating to the teaching of history deserves extended comment here for two reasons. First, it calls for a different emphasis in the presentation of history from that generally offered in the undergraduate curriculum. For the future bilingual teacher, initial courses in history should emphasize contributions made by various cultural groups to the growth and development of the United States. Later courses in history, then, may be infinitely more effective if taught with a wise proportioning of at least two languages. Teachers tend to teach as they have been taught, regardless of theories communicated. Example is more enduring than precept. While the other-than-English language may serve as a vehicle for appropriate content, the content also can and should serve as an effective vehicle for improving the level of usability of that language. Certainly those for whom English is the mother tongue have been taught in all subject areas in English. In the process, presumably, their understanding of English has been advanced. The communication content of language instruction has often tended toward a miscellany of unrelated sentences; often the vocabulary that is taught bears little or no relation to the subjects being studied outside the language class. Although the instructional program for second-language learners must proceed systematically from lesson to lesson with its own carefully planned curriculum, it can and should direct attention to carefully selected content from science, social studies, mathematics, and other subject-matter fields. Teacher education for bilingual classrooms should take this into account.

Cultural Awareness. It is almost trite to state that concern for and patience with people of other cultures, and an acceptance of their varied cultural values and patterns of behavior are central to successful bilingual teaching. In fact, bilingual education is an integral component of education designed to develop multicultural awareness or sensitivity. Cultural sensitivity is considered in competencies 6 and 7. Extreme care must be taken, when organizing the portion of the curriculum dealing with culture, that teachers do not force their own cultural values, standards, and mores on students from another culture. This statement does not preclude the obligation to gradually orient persons from other cultures to the new culture in which they are living. But this awareness can best be accomplished by a give-and-take process in which teachers indicate a willingness, even a desire, to learn to understand (and in some instances, to accept) the values and patterns of other cultures. Those preparing to be bilingual teachers, who have grown up totally in the culture of the United States, need ample opportunity to work and shop and find their recreation with children and adults of other cultures. This opportunity occurs best in informal situations, especially in those related to community-based and socially oriented activities. The teacher who learns from other cultures is respected. A respected teacher carries weight as exemplar to students from other cultures.

Community Involvement. Competency 8 (Figure 1) calls for bilingual teachers to become effective in community affairs. This requires the development of a variety of lower-level skills and competencies. For example, teachers first must learn to assess accurately the readability levels of printed instructional materials, especially materials that might be used with community groups. This accounts for delaying extensive involvement in community affairs until the inservice years, as indicated on the time line in Figure 1. Also, community-oriented activity should be delayed until the skills needed simply to survive as a beginning teacher have developed. Delay, however, does not mean denial. Care must be taken in developing a total bilingual curriculum not to ignore the development of this competency. For the truly successful bilingual teacher must eventually be able to perform comfortably in bilingual community settings.

Figure 2 provides a second approach to competency development through the bilingual teacher education curriculum. Figure 2 divides competencies into those related to scholarly command of the discipline to be taught and those related to pedagogy or professional preparation for bilingual situations. Figure 2 asks us to consider the increasing complexity of both aspects of excellence. At level 5 the teacher is presumed ready to be effective in the bilingual classroom. At level 7 command of the academic discipline is professionalized through appropriate pedagogy. It is only at this stage that the bilingual teacher becomes able to relate the discipline to the needs of students, and to motivate students to learn the content. The final level of competence is exemplified when the bilingual teacher becomes able to assess his or her own teaching of one or more disciplines and to select from alternate teaching strategies in order to increase teaching effectiveness.

One final concern related to curriculum calls for consideration here. It is often referred to as the "teacher-proof curriculum." Experience indicates that no teacher-proof curriculum exists. While the curriculum can be well planned and organized to include experiences and opportunities leading to the development of essential competencies, these can surface only under the guidance and supervision of teachers who themselves are knowledgeable in the whole field of bilingual education. Even this contact is not enough to assure success. There is greater

Figure 2

Subject Area and Pedagogical Competencies Developed through a Bilingual Teacher Education Curriculum

	Levels	Competencies Related to Subject Areas or Disciplines *	Competencies Related to Pedagogy or Teacher Training
	1	Learning vocabulary, topics, and principles of the discipline	Learning vocabulary of psychology and teaching
	2	Developing skills of the discipline	Developing skills related to the teaching act
Increasing complexity	3	Understanding structure of the discipline or process skills	Understanding the structure, nature, and teaching strategies for bilingual situations
	4	Ability to apply the discipline to other fields and other fields to major discipline	Ability to present the discipline to bilingual children or other bilingual populations
Levels needed to be truly effective as a teacher in bilingual settings	5	Ability to use the discipline to solve theoretical problems	Ability to determine those factors that influence the effectiveness of learning the discipline by the bilingual child
	6	Ability to use the discipline to solve practical problems	Ability to control those factors
	7	Ability to relate the discipline to the needs of bilingual students and to motivate bilingual students to learn the discipline	
	8	Ability to accurately evaluate one's own teaching of a discipline and to change teaching strategy to improve effectiveness	

*Disciplines include at least two languages, one of which is English.

probability of success when the master teachers themselves are still growing and learning. An effective curriculum fails without effective methodology.

Methodologies or Teaching Strategies

The importance of methodology in the education of bilingual teachers has been considered, but it needs amplification. As indicated earlier, successful teaching in a bilingual or in any setting can occur only if appropriate methodology is used in the teacher education program itself. Unfortunately, conventional methods of teaching in institutions of higher education do not reflect methods appropriate to teaching in elementary and secondary schools. There is some probability that college and university teachers who have taught at the lower school levels, and who have been prepared to teach there, will be more effective exemplars than those who have not had this mellowing experience. To date relatively few teachers who have met state certification requirements have had contact with master teachers teaching in bilingual situations. Finding ways to increase contact between developing bilingual teachers and master bilingual teachers becomes a high priority if quality education is to occur at the school level in the years to come.

At first glance it might appear that preservice and inservice education of teachers in effective methodology for bilingual settings should not be difficult, or at least not more difficult than the preparation of teachers for more conventional educational settings. On the other hand, this may not be the case, since teachers for traditional school settings need to develop expertise only in the discipline to be taught and the strategies for teaching. Those being prepared for bilingual teaching situations also must develop effective strategies for bilingual classrooms.

To understand the uniqueness of teaching in bilingual settings it will be helpful to consider ways of working with children in kindergarten through early elementary grades and then look at teaching strategies appropriate for older children in intermediate grades and secondary school.

Young children can learn a second language through imitation and through involvement in activities that most children enjoy. Anyone who has taught in or observed groups of youngsters in kindergarten through, let us say, fourth grade, knows the effectiveness of simple games, songs, and stories that involve much repetition and many actions that demonstrate the meanings of words. In the same vein, using pictures and repeating names of pictured objects, or naming storied persons or animals and acting out storied relationships are time-honored and effective procedures which bring surefire involvement in meaningful use of language.

Throughout relationships with young children the importance of the teacher's attitudes, communicated through behavior, can not be overemphasized. It may seem unnecessary to mention that one never laughs at a child's mistake and never permits a class to ridicule a youngster for some chance error in linguistic or social behavior. A word of advice may be in order, though, concerning responses to a child who seems not to understand something the teacher has said. Understanding will not be improved by the teacher's raising his or her voice, or shouting, as though speaking to a deaf person. Rephrasing in two or three different and simpler ways may be the best answer. If not, then the teacher should know that frequently children understand what they read better than what they hear. So the blackboard for group-wide use or a magic slate or writing pad in hand for individual encouragement may provide the assistance the child needs. In cases where writing is called for, the teacher will find that printing legibly will reinforce the oral image of spoken repetition with the steady image of the visualized word.

Cultural awareness plays a major role in language teaching, even for young learners. A child's name is important. He or she responds to its pronunciation *as he or she pronounces it.* Similarly, the matter of physical contact may be extremely important. Children from some cultures may cringe from a well-intentioned and friendly pat on the back or shoulder.

Older children and adults also can learn a second language through imitation and involvement in activities. But the structuring of the class should recognize the demands of increased maturity, in both content and placement of responsibility. It will be valuable for us now to look at the number of patterns of classroom management or teaching strategies that are available to the bilingual teacher. The relationships among these strategies are summarized in Figure 3.

Figure 3
Relationships Among Teaching Strategies

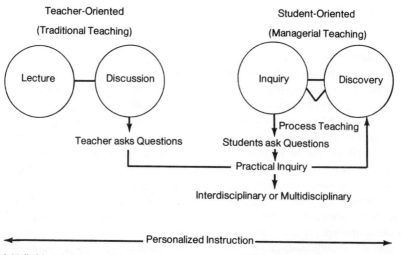

The Second Handbook of Research on Teaching (Travers, 1973) is one of many useful sources of information regarding teaching strategies. The *Handbook* reports that over a period of ten years emphasis in method of teaching at the school level has shifted from lecture strategy towards discussion strategy. During the early 1960s about 60 percent of classroom instruction followed a lecture format and about 40 percent a discussion format. The reverse percentages describe the situation existing by the early 1970s.

Lecture denotes a situation in which the teacher talks directly to students. It is essentially one-way communication. *Discussion* denotes oral interaction between teacher and student, and frequently among the students themselves. It involves at least two-way communication. In discussion, teachers pose questions, and the students attempt to answer or do answer the questions raised by teachers. The research literature indicates an increase in the use of discussion strategy with each advance in grade level. Educational research also indicates that not a few teachers, impatient with student hesitation or unaware that thoughtful answers take time, answer their own questions. When this situation occurs, discussion ceases. Little learning takes place and little motivation for further learning is engendered.

In the early 1940s teachers in the several academic fields were caught up in enthusiasm for teaching the structures of disciplines, following the lead of Jerome Bruner and Joseph Schwab. In more recent years this strategy has come to be called *process teaching*. Changes in terminological fashion have been so frequent, though, that process teaching and discovery teaching and inquiry teaching have become confused in many educators' minds. Since these three strategies are related and all three methodologies or classroom strategies do have contributions to make to the successful bilingual classroom, it will be helpful here to examine their similarities and differences. Inquiry teaching involves any technique or strategy which causes students to question or to inquire. Discovery teaching involves any technique that causes the students to seek answers to the questions posed either by themselves or by the teacher. The answers obtained through discovery can be obtained through a number of channels: from memory, through reasoning, through the use of appropriate laboratory or community investigations, or from library resources. Accepting these two definitions, it becomes possible to define process teaching. In process teaching inquiry and discovery complement each other.

It is important to keep in mind that process teaching as a classroom strategy is not the same as discussion. It differs in that the discussion strategy calls upon teachers to ask questions, while the process strategy generates situations in which students ask the questions. Classrooms or other teaching environments designed to elicit questions from students (inquiry) produce a greater probability of continued motivation to learn. Of course the other half of the process (discovery) also must occur to assure continued motivation and learning. Students need teacher guidance on how and where to find the answers to the questions they themselves have asked during the inquiry.

The definition of process teaching leads naturally to the currently emerging strategy of managerial teaching. The relation of managerial teaching to multicultural education stands out in the *Journal of Teacher Education* for May–June 1977, which is almost wholly devoted to multicultural education and the academic disciplines.

Managerial Teaching and Personalization of Instruction

Managerial teaching is a strategy which calls upon teachers to serve as managers of educational activity, or as organizers of learning experiences. The role of manager demands more of the teacher than to be a mere information source. This strategy calls for extensive planning by teachers, much of which must occur outside the formal classroom hours. This planning manifests itself in the form of student activity during normal classroom hours, and extended learning activities beyond these formal hours.

Managerial teaching lends itself comfortably to individualization, or as we now hear, personalization of instruction. As managers, teachers can plan specific or personalized learning activities for individual students or groups of students. For personalized instruction to occur, the teacher must empathize with each child in his or her desires or difficulties in learning. Managerial teaching with emphasis on personalization of instruction assumes optimum significance in classrooms where there are children speaking in two, three, or more different languages — a situation not at all uncommon in urban schools, and becoming more common in rural schools.

Effective classroom managers balance elements of the science of education and the art of teaching. They employ the science to determine appropriate placement for each student. They call upon the art of teaching to help each child find a meaningful pattern for the myriad diverse inputs of the school day. The use of managerial teaching strategy is essential to success in bilingual classrooms. It is worth repeating here that the probability is low that teachers will learn to use a managerial teaching strategy in bilingual settings if they experience only lecture and discussion in their college or university courses. Teacher education programs for bilingual teachers must not only exemplify managerial teaching strategy, but must also provide future bilingual teachers with opportunity, under supervision, to test out their competence to handle it themselves. Managerial strategy, when used in either teacher education or school classrooms, approximates the optimum relationship between teaching method and the method of the independent research worker in his or her own field.

There are important reasons why lecture and discussion strategies may be inappropriate in bilingual classrooms. First, both of these more

traditional strategies treat the entire classroom (usually from twenty to thirty-five students) as a single learning unit. Second, use of these strategies tends to place the teacher in a central and dominating position. Neither of these situations opens opportunity for students to try out their facility with language or otherwise become exploratorily involved in the learning process, which is so essential to the development of a positive self-image. In addition, neither lecture nor discussion generates much interaction among students—a denial in the first instance of this most significant avenue to language learning.

But now a word of caution. All of us tend to expect to learn in ways in which we have always been used to learning. And the number of schools that have provided non-English-speaking students with prior experience with managerial teaching is decidedly limited. Most English learners will have been inured to teacher-centered classrooms; they may well feel lost if suddenly put into small groups or showered with too much responsibility for self-direction. And their parents, when told about the new classroom, may well feel that their children are not getting good instruction. So testing out one's competence should carry every indication of gradualism and a constant alertness to the readiness of children to adapt to new procedures.

Multidisciplinary Scholarship and Teaching Strategy

Every minute of the day the teacher in a multicultural setting faces dramatic evidence of the physiological and psychological individuality of children, of the economic or political pressures behind the migration of their parents, of the subtle and sometimes sharp diversities of their customs and values, and, of course, of the woeful blockages to communicative interaction in their strange new situations. The teacher is aware of their desperate need in coping with these aspects of their lives.

But to cope with the children's problem the teacher is relatively powerless without a wide spectrum of professional information. The teacher's preparation for working in the bilingual classroom should, under optimum conditions, draw on pertinent phases of the psychology of early childhood and the psychology of adolescence, on sharply focused concepts of cultural anthropology and urban sociology, on the linguistic bases of English language and selected aspects of sociolinguistics dealing with the role of language in human development and formulation of personal and societal values and ways of looking at life.

This kind of broadly multidisciplinary curriculum underlies the ability to carry on a successful managerial teaching strategy. Later paragraphs will provide more detail on courses in such a curriculum. At this point, though, it will be instructive to look at the relationship of the multidisciplinary preparation and the use of managerial teaching strategy.

From the immediately preceding paragraphs special attention should be paid to such phrases as "pertinent phases," "sharply focused concepts," "selected aspects," and the like. In other words, conventional courses in a number of disciplines could demand of the prospective teacher a lifetime of study and, ultimately, the need to sort the wheat from the chaff in its application to the bilingual classroom. The key concern for designers of an appropriate curriculum must be the professionalization of the academic courses included in the curricular pattern, i.e., organizing and teaching them as models for adapting their content to bicultural bilingual teaching.

Managerial teaching requires that the teacher as manager set problems or stimulate his or her students to pose problems whose solutions require content from more than one discipline. The teacher guides students to sources of information from several disciplines and, where necessary, helps them to clarify the relationships that contribute to the solution of the problems. The one means to ensure that bilingual teachers will be able to channel the findings of many disciplines, all active in the out-of-school world, is to organize and teach courses in such a way that students have ample opportunity to deal with the resolution of realistic problems. The nature of each problem selected should be such that the prospective bilingual teacher will draw upon knowledge and information at the cutting edge of more than one discipline. In some instances teachers from several disciplines may well be invited to make up the team of experts which offers a problem-oriented, multidisciplinary course.

Two examples should help to clarify the nature of managerial teaching. In a beginning course related to the understanding of other cultures the question to be dealt with might be "How can we use a local restaurant to orient ourselves to an unfamiliar culture?" The first activity in dealing with this problem could be selecting the restaurant and securing its menu, which might appropriately be written in the language of the target culture. Translating and determining the meaning of the words in the language of the culture must first occur. Once the items of food on the menu are understood, reasons for differences in these foods from those found in restaurants catering to English-speaking clientele could be considered. Perhaps information from the fields of agriculture and geography are needed here. Comparing the current prices of ethnic dishes with conventional restaurant costs might require information from the field of economics. Literature on nutrition and health could serve as information source regarding the nutritional value of the foods on the menu. Sociology, communications, and psychology come into play in considering appropriate behavior in the restaurant. What are the verbal and nonverbal gestures that might be used to compliment the chef, the waitresses, and others? What about the nature and meaning of the music to be heard while eating? What is its history and significance in the target culture? Eventually, eating at the restaurant gives students opportunity to conclude this type of problem-oriented study with both pleasant and practical experience. This culminating field experience might be used to assess the significance of the problem and the effectiveness of the process—not excluding the feeling of accomplishment on the part of the students.

In a more advanced course, another kind of problem might be set. What are the similarities and differences in migration patterns of several minority groups that have entered the United States during the nineteenth and twentieth centuries? Consideration of this question calls for comparative demographic data; it calls upon language, politics, economics, history, and education. An extended period of time is required to consider this question in any depth. It might call for visits to areas where peoples from various cultures are residing or have resided. Or representatives from the cultural groups might be invited to the class to present information pertinent to the inquiry. Finally, the field of art could be called upon, first to reveal cultural values expressed in the arts, and then to display the findings graphically or pictorially to the rest of the student population.

Even from these two examples, it is clear that courses taught with a problem orientation are necessarily based on several disciplines. This is especially true if the problems are those of today's society. Joseph Schwab, one of the early proponents of inquiry teaching, refers today to the process of considering such problems as practical inquiry because consideration of one problem leads the student to ask further questions about the society of which he is a part or wishes to become a part. It is clear that practical-inquiry teaching is a strategy that is closely related to problem-oriented teaching. This strategy must take a significant place in the education of bilingual teachers if their teaching is to be meaningful in the world of the bilingual child.

References

Acosta, R., and Blanco, G. *Competencies for University Programs in Bilingual Education.* Office of Bilingual Education, U.S. Office of Education. Washington, D.C.: U.S. Government Printing Office, 1978.

Alatis, James, and Twaddel, Kristie, eds. *English as a Second Language in Bilingual Education.* TESOL. Washington, D.C.: Georgetown University Press, 1976.

American Association of Colleges for Teacher Education. *Directory: Multicultural Education Programs in Teacher Education Institutions in the United States: 1978.* Washington, D.C.: American Association of Colleges for Teacher Education, 28, 1978.

————— "Multicultural Education." *Journal of Teacher Education,* no. 3 (May–June 1977).

Bernabe, Luz Valentínez. "Teacher-Student Relations as a Factor in Bilingual Education." In *Proceedings of the First Inter-American Conference on Bilingual Education,* edited by Rudolph C. Troike and Nancy Modiano. Arlington, Va.: Center for Applied Linguistics, 1976.

Blanco, George M. "The Preparation of Bilingual Teachers." In *Proceedings of the First Inter-American Conference on Bilingual Education,* edited by Rudolph C. Troike and Nancy Modiano, Arlington, Va.: Center for Applied Linguistics, 1976.

Casso, Henry J. *Bilingual/Bicultural Education and Teacher Training.* Washington, D.C.: National Education Association and ERIC Clearinghouse on Teacher Education, 1976.

Center for the Study of Culture in Education. *Materials Prepared for the National Policy Conference on Bilingualism in Higher Education,* 20-22 February 1977. San Francisco: University of San Francisco Press, 1977.

Cordasco, Francesco. *Bilingual Schooling in the U.S.* New York: Webster Division, McGraw-Hill Book Company, 1976.

Croft, Kenneth. "Teachers of English to Speakers of Other Languages." TESOL, *A Composite Bibliography for ESOL Teacher-Training.* Washington D.C.: TESOL, 1977.

Dissemination and Assessment Center for Bilingual Education. *Teacher Training Bibliography.* Austin, Tex., 1975 (revised 1976).

ERIC Clearinghouse on Teacher Education and American Association of Colleges for Teacher Education. *Multicultural Education and Ethnic Studies in the U.S.* Washington, D.C.: February 1976.

ERIC Reports. *A Model In-Service Program for Training Mainstream Teachers of Spanish Speaking Pupils.* 1975.

Erickson, Frederick. *The Politics of Speaking: An Approach to Evaluating Bilingual-Bicultural Schools.* Bilingual Education Paper Series. Los Angeles: National Dissemination and Assessment Center at California State University, Los Angeles, 1978.

Fanselow, J. and Light, R., eds. *Bilingual, ESOL, and Foreign Language Teacher Preparation Models, Practices, Issues.* TESOL. Washington, D.C.: Georgetown University Press, 1978.

Goldstein, Wallace C. *Teaching English as a Second Language: An Annotated Bibliography.* New York, London: Garland Publishing Inc., 1975.

Gordon, Eliane C. *Manual for Teachers of Spanish Speaking Children.* New Brunswick, N.J.: IRES Institute, Rutgers University, 1975.

Haugen, Einor. "Bilingualism in the Americas: A Bibliography and Research Guide." *American Dialectic Society Publication* 26. University, Ala.: University of Alabama Press, 1956.

Hunter, William A. *Multicultural Education Through Competency-Based Teacher Education.* Washington, D.C.: American Association of Colleges for Teacher Education, 1974

Klassen, Frank H., and Gollnick, Donna M. *Pluralism and the American Teacher: Issues and Case Studies.* Washington, D.C.: Ethnic Heritage Center for Teacher Education, American Association of Colleges for Teacher Education, 1977.

Modiano, Nancy "Uso de Modelos Nativos de Instruction para el Entrenamiento Chiapas." In *Proceedings of the First Inter-American Conference on Bilingual Education,* edited by Rudolph C. Troike and

Nancy Modiano. Center for Applied Linguistics. Arlington, Va.: Center for Applied Linguistics, 1976.

Multicultural Program of the University of San Francisco (with) the Bay Area Bilingual Education League (co-sponsors). *Second National Policy Conference on Bilingualism in Higher Education,* at California State University at Los Angeles, 4-7 March 1978.

Natalicio, Diana S. "Linguistics and Teacher Education: Chicano Spanish." In *Swallow IV: Linguistics and Education,* edited by M. Reyes Mazon. San Francisco: Institute for Cultural Pluralism, School of Education, University of San Francisco (no date).

National Council for Accreditation of Teacher Education. *Standards for Accreditation of Teacher Education.* Washington, D.C., 1978.

National Dissemination and Assessment Center *Bilingual Education.* Paper Series, Dissertation and Data-Based Journal Articles on Bilingual Education. Los Angeles: National Dissemination and Assessment Center at California State University, Los Angeles, 1978.

National Indochinese Clearinghouse. *A Manual for Indochinese Refugee Education, 1976-1977.* Arlington, Va.,: Center for Applied Linguistics, 1976.

National Institute of Education. *The Desegregation Literature: A Critical Appraisal.* Washington, D.C.: July 1976.

National Institute of Education. *Multicultural/Bilingual Division: Fiscal Year 1977-1978, Program Plan.* Washington, D.C.: June 1977.

Northwest Regional Educational Laboratory. *Oral Language Tests for Bilingual Students: An Evaluation of Language Dominance and Proficiency Instruments.* Portland, Ore.: Northwest Regional Educational Laboratory, 1976.

Ogletree, Earl J., and García, David. "Part VIII: Reshaping Teacher Education for the Spanish-Speaking Child." *Education of the Spanish-Speaking Urban Child.* Springfield, Ill.: Charles C. Thomas, 1975.

Padayley, Jon, and Froman, Jo. "A Community Oriented Approach to Technical Training." In *Proceedings of the First Inter-American Conference on Bilingual Education,* edited by Rudolph C. Troike and Nancy Modiano. Arlington, Va.: Center for Applied Linguistics, 1976.

Pacheco, Manuel T. "Preparing Teachers for Non-English Home Language Learners." In *Designs for Foreign Language Teacher Education,* edited by Alan Garfinkel and Stanley Hamilton. Rowley, Mass.: Newbury House Publishers, Inc., 1976.

Palmer, Judith W. "Developing a Competency-Based Bilingual Teacher Training Program." ERIC ED 108 528, 1975.

Pérez, Carmen Ana. "Instructional Methods and Supervised Teaching." *National Conference of EPDA Bilingual Education Project Directors: Preparation and Certification of Teachers of Bilingual-Bicultural Education* 1976.

Pettigrew, L. Eudora. "Competency-Based Teacher Education: Teacher Training and Multicultural Education." ERIC ED 092 486, 1973. (Available through Computer Microfilm International Corporation, P.O. Box 190, Arlington, Va. 22210.)

Schneider, Susan G. *Revolution, Reaction or Reform: The 1974 Bilingual Education Act.* New York: Las Americas Publishing Co., 1976.

Travers, Robert M., ed. *Second Handbook of Research on Training.* Chicago: Rand McNally, 1973.

U.S., Department of Health, Education, and Welfare. "Bilingual Education Programs." *Federal Register* Part 3 (11 June 1976).

––––––. *A Study of State Programs in Bilingual Education.* Prepared for the Office of Education by Development Associates, Inc., March 1977. ED 142 056.

U.S., House of Representatives. *Hearings before the Subcommittee on Elementary, Secondary and Vocational Education of the Committee on Education and Labor.* Washington, D.C.: U.S. Government Printing Office, 1977.

Valencia, Atilano A. "Teacher Training in Bilingual-Bicultural Education." In *Bilingual-Bicultural Education for the Spanish-English Bilingual.* Berkeley, Calif.: Bilingual Media Productions, 1972.

Waggoner, Dorothy. *State Certification Requirements for Teachers for Bilingual Education Programs, June 1976.* Washington, D.C.: National Center for Education Statistics, 1976.

A Bilingual Homebound Tutorial Program for All Ages: Survival English with a Cultural Difference

Robert A. Gilman
College of Education
University of Nevada

Gayle de Frutos
Reno, Nevada

Karen A. Christensen
Reno, Nevada

The recent and unprecedented rate of growth in the hotel and casino service industry has attracted large numbers of low-income, minimally skilled people seeking employment in Reno, Nevada. Aggressive recruiting efforts undertaken in southern California and other areas of the Hispanic Southwest account, at least in part, for the fact that many of those who have come are monolingual speakers of Spanish.[1]*Most, but not all, of this group are of Mexican origin (see Figure 1). Because employment is available twenty-four hours a day, seven days a week, individuals may work two jobs to support themselves and their families. For most of them, lack of facility in the English language constitutes a critical barrier to community acceptance, better-paying jobs, and greater opportunity and personal self-fulfillment in general.

* See notes on page 128.

Figure 1

Breakdown on Students in the Centro de Información Latino Americano's Homebound Tutorial Program
October 1978

Total Enrollment		157	
Sex	Male	97	
	Female	60	
Country of Origin	Mexico	136	
	Cuba	3	
	El Salvador	4	
	Spain	3	
	Guatemala	1	
	Argentina	3	
	Panama	1	
	Venezuela	1	
	Peru	1	
	Colombia	4	
Job Orientation	Service Workers	107	
	Housewives	14	
	Students	12	
	Laborers	12	
	Unemployed	8	
	Handicapped	3	
	Farm Workers	1	
Age Groups	Under 18	31	20.0%
	19-25	48	31.0
	26-35	37	23.0
	36-55	39	25.0
	56-65	1	0.5
	over 65	1	0.5

In 1975, at about the time when this and related needs were beginning to be heavily felt in the Reno area, a coalition of local Hispanic clubs and societies founded the *Centro de Información Latino Americano* (CDILA—Latin American Information Center). Incorporated as a nonprofit, private charitable organization, the centro's original purpose was to serve as an information and referral clearinghouse that could link rapidly increasing numbers of Hispanic clients to general community, social, and economic assistance services, including English as a Second Language (ESL) classes. However, in the face of a general lack of awareness of the special needs of Hispanics, coupled with a widespread indifference to their welfare—long a characteristic of the extremely politically conservative Reno area—the centro soon discovered that its very name had become a misnomer.

While it is true that much progress has been achieved through persistent advocacy and media blasts to make other agencies (and politicians during the 1978 election campaigns) aware of the need for establishing and improving programs for Hispanics, the centro initially was forced to provide many key services itself: job placement, housing information; interpreting in courts; translation of examinations and legal, health, driving, and other vital information; direct financial assistance and emergency loans; assistance to those in need of returning to their homes outside the area; outreach work with the aged; and drug abuse counseling; as well as the originally envisioned information and referral services.

Perhaps the biggest surprise of all for the organizers of the centro was the almost total absence of appropriate or adequate classes for Hispanics, despite the existence of extensive community college and public school programs.[2] Responding to over one hundred requests for relevant ESL classes by Hispanic clients, in 1977 the centro conducted an indepth study of existing ESL classes. The study revealed that these classes were ineffective for the vast majority of the monolingual, Spanish-speaking community for the following reasons:

1. Reno has a limited system of public transportation, making it virtually impossible for those without private transportation to travel to ESL classes.

2. Because of their work schedules in a twenty-four hour community, many Hispanics cannot attend ESL classes at the hours they are given.

3. The ESL teachers, with few exceptions, are monolingual and therefore unable to communicate and establish rapport with Spanish-speaking students in their own language.

4. Many ESL classes cannot use a bilingual bicultural mode because they are composed of students from different areas of the world.

5. Many of the people who might profit most from ESL instruction are discouraged from seeking it because of physical disabilities, cultural alienation (including difficulty in communicating with Anglo Americans, especially in a structured classroom environment), illiteracy, isolation, advanced age, and numerous other factors.

In the face of such obvious and pressing needs, and confronted with the lack of adequate existing programs, the director of the centro, José Esteban Valle, in November 1977 submitted a proposal to the Administration of the Comprehensive Employment and Training Act (CETA) for a one-year research and demonstration project designed to employ a staff of bilingual and bicultural language instructors who would travel to the houses of Hispanics who had requested this service. There they would offer, on a regularly scheduled basis, ESL classes specifically tailored to individual needs. Fortunately, the proposal was quickly funded for one year, and the program began operation in January 1978.

From its inception, in contrast to traditional ESL programs, the centro has emphasized a culturally sensitive program which respects the Spanish speaker's language and background. All tutors and staff are bilingual and are immersed in the cultural milieu of their clients and students. Two additional advantages should also be noted:

1. Because the program is federally funded, it does not rely on volunteers.

2. Because it is not associated with a local school district, community college, or university, it is not restricted by the regulations or local biases of these institutions.

Student Characteristics

As Figure 1 indicates, the vast majority of the students in the ESL classes have identified Mexico as their country of origin. It is also important to note that in terms of job orientation, service workers predominate; and that in regard to age and sex characteristics, 74 percent of the students are under the age of thirty-six (the majority of those twenty-five or younger are single males).

Unfortunately, it proved difficult to collect reliable data about previous educational backgrounds because of the students' reticence about admitting weak or minimal education backgrounds. It is hoped that this very useful data, as well as other relevant data, can be collected in the near future.

Staffing and Organizational Aspects

The staff of the Homebound Tutorial Program consists of five full-time, paid bilingual tutors and one secretarial aide. One of the tutors serves as the head tutor and is responsible for the total administration of the program. She schedules and coordinates classes, maintains records of student progress reports, familiarizes staff with ESL teaching methods and techniques, screens and keeps a waiting list of prospective students, and prepares instructional materials for the tutors. She also periodically observes and monitors tutorial sessions, holds monthly teacher meetings and workshops, conducts weekly individual meetings with the tutors, and reports progress monthly to the executive director and board of directors at the centro. Also, she tutors a half-time teaching load. The duties and responsibilities of the tutors are to attend an orientation session with the head tutor, tutor Hispanics in English in their homes, provide transportation for students to and from classes when necessary, prepare daily individualized lesson plans, and maintain student files and progress reports. In addition, the tutors must attend monthly teacher meetings and workshops and attend weekly individual meetings with the head tutor.

The homebound tutorial classes are established with a minimum of one to a maximum of six students per class and meet from three to six hours weekly. Tutors must instruct a minimum of twenty students and must teach for a minimum of twenty-five hours per week. Two hours per day are allotted for preparation of lesson plans, and additional time is granted for maintenance of student files and progress reports.

Before students can be scheduled for homebound classes, they must be screened by the head tutor. In this initial interview, the tutor explains the goals and objectives of the program, establishes a time and place for the classes, and determines the approximate instructional level of the students (either beginning, intermediate, or advanced). The student is then fitted into the schedule of a tutor. If a student cannot be fitted into the schedule of one of the tutors, his or her name is put on the waiting list until accommodation is possible.

The homebound tutorial school year is divided into two six-month semesters. Generally, a full year of instruction is necessary for students to reach a satisfactory level of competence in English.

As noted earlier, emphasis within the classes is on individualized instruction to meet the varied needs of each particular student; tutors devise and prepare materials to meet these needs. A pragmatic rather than an academic approach to learning is employed. The tutors teach by doing—field trips and practical learning situations are included in class plans to help the students more comfortably assimilate into the community. These and other qualities of an ideal tutor for our program are summarized in Figure 2.

Figure 2
Ten Attributes of an Ideal, Homebound Tutor

An ideal bilingual tutor in our program should:

1. Speak, write, and read Spanish and English and be well versed in the grammar of both languages.

2. Have experience or training in language teaching and be familiar with basic techniques (e.g., drilling, pronunciation correction, grammatical explanations).

3. Be open to instructional suggestions from students, coworkers and professionals and constantly attempt to improve teaching methods through study and awareness of theories and changes in the educational field.

4. Plan lessons to meet the immediate needs or specific interests of students and use varied review procedures to ensure retention of the target language.

5. Use the student's language to establish rapport and empathy in the student-tutor relationship, for complicated structural explanations, and to reinforce the student's culture. The tutor should strive to communicate in the target language as much as possible and to use the student's native language decreasingly as he or she progresses.

6. Be aware of the student's educational background and not judge his intelligence by his ability to learn English.

7. Be punctual for class sessions and demonstrate warmth, friendliness, and courtesy while, at the same time, not "smothering" the student with his own help and advice. The tutor should be prepared to refer the student to professional agencies that can more effectively deal with problems that are unrelated to learning difficulties.

8. Have had extensive contact with both his own and the student's culture and should be sympathetic to both.

9. Demonstrate cultural sensitivity by being aware and noncritical of the customs, taboos, and mores of the student's home culture, while helping the student to understand and feel comfortable in the unfamiliar culture.

10. Teach by *doing* rather than *telling* and include field trips and practical learning situations in class plans in order to help the students more comfortably assimilate into the community.

The tutors are guided by specific recommendations which take into account the students' cultural context. These suggestions are outlined in Figure 3.

Figure 3
Cultural Recommendations and Suggestions for the Homebound Tutor

1. Use "Usted" with students, even teenagers, to maintain teacher–student respect. The instructor should be friendly and warm, but this touch of formality encourages the student to see his studies as a serious matter.

2. Latin cultures promote respect for the teacher. Take advantage of this factor, particularly if you are teaching in an informal, home-oriented situation, to maintain the students' motivation. Indicate that you are there to help, but that your time is valuable and someone else could benefit from your services if a student is not willing to make every effort to learn. Letting the student know that you are serious will help him or her to be a better student.

3. Acting Anglo American, or giving students tips on how to act in order to deal effectively with Anglo Americans, will help them realize that their goal in language learning must be communication—understanding of both language and culture. Point out that most Anglo Americans:

    a. Say "thank you" and "please" more often than may seem necessary
    b. Look people in the eye when speaking to them, and expect the same
    c. Don't make fun of people's defects, especially physical ones.

4. Avoid making value judgments in comparing one culture with another. Do point out differences, but don't reveal personal preference or imply superiority of one culture over another. A positive attitude toward both cultures is, of course, ideal in a bilingual instructor.

5. Help students acquire the basic communication skills necessary to take advantage of various services in the community—the county health department, hospitals, the state employment security department, and the department of motor vehicles, for example. In class, role-play possible encounters between the students and various agency personnel; then, if possible, take them on field trips to these places to reinforce or act out what they have learned. Realize that the students cannot take advantage of services with which they are not familiar, so familiarize them in advance of the actual need. In addition, help students to:

    a. Be aware of the difference between assertiveness and rudeness
    b. Realize that sometimes they must admit they have not understood and must request further explanations. Point out that most people will try to help if they request help. Teach them to appeal to the teacher in all of us when requesting explanations.
    c. Be persistent; if they are not adequately served, they can request a referral to someone who *can* help them.

6. If you are teaching in a home situation, you may have some problems or reservations about asserting authority while a guest in your students' homes. To avoid or overcome these difficulties you can:

    a. Always be thoroughly prepared for the teaching session and let the students know what is expected of them in the way of learning objectives
    b. Take roll, visibly, and refer to your prepared lesson plan

c. Carry with you materials and aids (a small blackboard, portable tape player, flash cards, etc.). In addition to enhancing your teaching, these aids will let the students know that your attitude is serious and that you are in control of the direction of the class.

7. When subtlety or suggestion fail, assert your authority as teacher rather than allowing valuable time to be wasted or the class to be disrupted. Ask that radios, televisions, or stereos be turned off; that interruptive phone calls be cut short; that students be prepared for class upon your arrival. Most students will appreciate your serious interest in their learning. Be ready, however, to take advantage of a spontaneously arising learning situation: a door-to-door salesman, a promotional phone call, a TV commercial or program. Remember that practical learning experiences are often the best kind.

8. According to students' ages, modality, and interests, take them on field trips to offer them practical learning situations. The grocery store, a nearby park, a discount department store, or the local library are good places to begin. Then take them to a basketball game, a coffee shop, a fair or local event. Offer language preparation beforehand and followup discussion afterwards.

9. Anticipate the reversal of some of your own stereotypes. Consider each student as a unique individual and not as a nationality. Everyone will differ in personality, interests, learning ability, and approaches to learning. Explore with each student the best way for him or her to learn. Encourage the best use of the tools each one has at hand. Concentrate not on what the student does not know, but on how much he or she does know and is learning. Particularly if the student's contact with school has been very limited, or if the student has failed in school, you must make him or her feel that it is possible to learn. Help the student set reasonable goals and then offer praise as he or she progresses toward them.

Capsule or Content Areas — Capsules may be made up by the tutor to meet the immediate and long-range needs of the student. They may serve as primary materials, or to complement a textbook. Depending on the age, interests, and orientation of the student, certain capsules may be omitted or others added.

The following are sample content areas:

a. Self-identification (personal and family information)

b. Basic greetings

c. States of being (tired, sick, etc.)

d. Time-telling and weather (hours, days of the week, seasons, etc.)

e. Telephone communication (emergency phone calls, calling in sick to work, etc.)

f. Housing and home furnishings

g. Health

h. Consumer and business skills

i. Food — restaurant and grocery store

j. Stores — purchasing clothing and neccessary items

k. Jobs — employment and job applications and interviews

l. Making appointments

m. Asking and giving directions

n. Job awareness

o. Citizenship preparation and testing

    In making up or supplementing capsules, the tutor may make use of employment application forms (acquired from local stores or businesses), the telephone book, recorded telephone messages (time, weather, etc.), menus from local restaurants, local maps, newspaper ads, and numerous other materials that may be encountered. He or she should be careful to include for each capsule vocabulary lists, dialogues, drills, and activities. The capsules can be reinforced by field trips and other practical learning experiences. They should be reviewed often to ensure retention of vocabulary and to help the student gain facility in speaking.

    Texts — In choosing a text the tutor should, above all, consider the age, educational background, and interests of the student. In a homebound program for adults (many of whom may have had little or no formal education), a book with minimal grammatical explanations, many pictures, and simple drills is best. At the same time, the teaching and reinforcement of structural patterns should be evident in the text. The student needs to be able to understand and produce questions and sentences, not to recite lists of vocabulary.

    Above all, it is necessary to select a text which will allow for maximal practice of oral English, while at the same time introducing the student to written English.

Proven Results—Some "Success Stories" in the CDILA's Homebound Tutorial Program (HTP)

By and large, the HTP has been warmly received by the people it has sought to aid. Most have taken great advantage of this opportunity to acquire or improve English language skill. In many cases, their efforts have translated into better jobs, higher salaries, and greater personal satisfaction and confidence. The following are some examples of our students' improvement:

1. Julio L. was promoted from casino dealer to floorman, where he is required to file written reports.

2. Rey S. was promoted from waiter to captain, and is now speaking on the phone and filing written reports.

3. Miguel G. progressed from dishwasher to busboy.

4. Dolores R. progressed from factory worker to busgirl to waitress.

5. Paul C. received a raise after five months, whereas his fellow employees had worked for a year without salary increases.

6. Carmen E. was promoted from hotel maid to maid supervisor.

7. Rafael T. was able to pass the Nevada driver's test and get a driver's license.

8. María B. became a U.S. citizen.

9. In addition, four students who were illiterate in Spanish became literate and began to learn English.

These are but a few illustrations of how students have benefited from the Homebound Tutorial Program. Still others have become more active in the community, have begun to attend monolingual ESL classes, or have improved their personal situations, achieving much greater self-confidence in general.

Finally, it should be noted that the HTP has only begun to scratch the surface in terms of satisfying a previously unmet and rapidly growing need. By November 1978, there were over 100 persons waiting to enter the program who, because of limited staff and resources, could not be served. Further, the centro was seeing some 550 clients per month, many in urgent need of tutorial, culturally sensitive ESL classes.

Suggestions for the Profession

Despite the newness of the program, we have now reached the point where we can offer the following tentative suggestions, often based on what we learned the hard way, to those who might be interested in starting a similar homebound ESL tutoring program:

1. Counseling and teaching should be carefully coordinated. Many of our students needed job and psychological counseling as well as language lessons.

2. Follow-up studies should be conducted; one reason is that success stories will motivate future students.

3. Adequate evaluation tools should be designed before starting the program. We made up our own pretest and posttest, which proved inadequate to evaluate a highly individualized program.

4. Students must be motivated to see the great personal and, especially, economic value of free ESL lessons as early in the instructional process as possible. Those who enroll without a serious purpose are wasting scarce resources.

5. Screening and orientation must be carefully designed not only for students, but also for tutors who may join the program after it is already in progress. Frequent inservice sessions should also be offered for all tutors.

6. There is a need to compare our experience with those who have attempted similar programs.

In conclusion, despite the problems encountered, we believe that we have made a promising start in establishing the value of a bilingual, culturally aware program to teach adult Hispanics of all ages English in their homes.

Notes

1. According to informal estimates, 4,500 people, or 30 percent of the approximately 15,000 Hispanics living in the Reno area in late 1978, may be in this category. Because many are undocumented residents, more exact figures are impossible to obtain.

2. Hispanic dropout rates from traditional programs approached 100 percent and many clients expressed a strong aversion to enrolling in any existing ESL class.

Developing Bilingual-Vocational and Vocational English as a Second Language at the College Level: System Approach Techniques

Arturo A. Kotesky
Elgin Community College
Elgin, Illinois

with the collaboration of
Linda G. Mrowicki
Arlington Heights, Illinois

The Bilingual Access Program (BAP) at Elgin Community College (ECC), Elgin, Illinois, is a federally funded, five-year project being developed under an Advanced Institutional Development Program (AIDP) grant. Each fiscal year, during the five-year grant period, the Bilingual Access Program will implement different vocational programs in a bilingual mode. A total of ten programs will be completed, including twenty-eight vocational and paravocational courses, and they are to be offered continuously. The Bilingual Access Program has been established to supplement regular vocational programs as a means to provide training to limited-English-speaking adults so that the exiting participants can possess skills related to employment opportunities existing in the Fox River Valley and Chicago metropolitan area. The bilingual access model is a unique

129

approach for implementing regular college vocational programs in a bilingual mode to specifically serve a large, Spanish-speaking population within and around the college's educational district.

This paper describes in detail the bilingual access instructional delivery system, a general system approach to bilingual access and Vocational English as a Second Language (VESL) materials, the instructional design for developing bilingual access support materials, the instructional design for developing ESL/VESL components, teaching the vocational class in an ESL context, sequence of milestones within the bilingual access instructional design process, the paper's conclusions, and a series of appendixes showing sample output products.

Bilingual Access Instructional Delivery System

Figure 1 represents the instructional components within the bilingual access model, also identified as bilingual access instructional delivery system. The system was conceptualized as a means to provide technical training and English skills to limited-English-speaking (LES) adults, supplementing human and nonhuman resources already available at Elgin Community College (ECC). The delivery system deals with the actual implementation of instruction within the classroom and laboratory learning environments and includes the following components within each vocational program: an English as a Second Language (ESL) pretraining course, vocational and paravocational instruction in an ESL context, a series of Spanish bilingual instructional support materials and bilingual student assessment instruments, and a Vocational English as a Second Language (VESL) course unique to each vocational program. Each one of these components is analyzed in detail throughout this paper, considering the pertinent development and implementation phases. Figure 1 also gives a perspective on the supportive relationship of the various components within the bilingual model delivery system. The college schedule features two semesters, and LES students are expected to come into the Bilingual Access Program three weeks prior to the regular instructional period. Students' ESL competencies are assessed to determine their entry point in the bilingual program. The ESL pretraining course as well as other ESL courses are available within the college so that LES students can meet the English language entry level skills requirements. ESL/VESL curriculum development and implementation are carried out by the college's Adult Basic Education program at the Community Outreach Placement and Assessment Center (COPA). The ESL/VESL curriculum development process is described extensively in other sections of this paper.

Vocational and paravocational instruction constitute the second component within the delivery system. Vocational and paravocational faculty members, under various college divisions, conduct the classroom and laboratory training tasks. These instructional activities are implemented according to an ESL context concept. An operational

Figure 1
Bilingual Access Instructional Delivery System

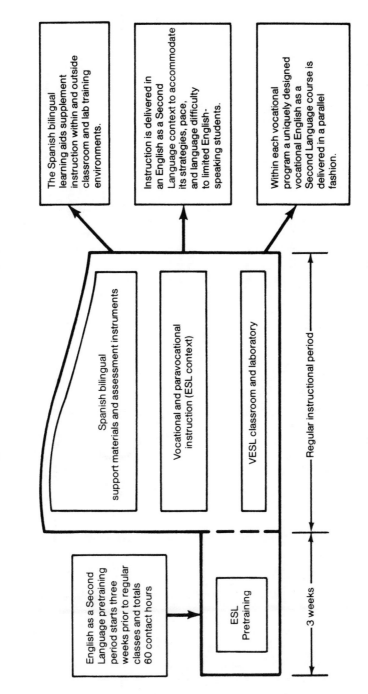

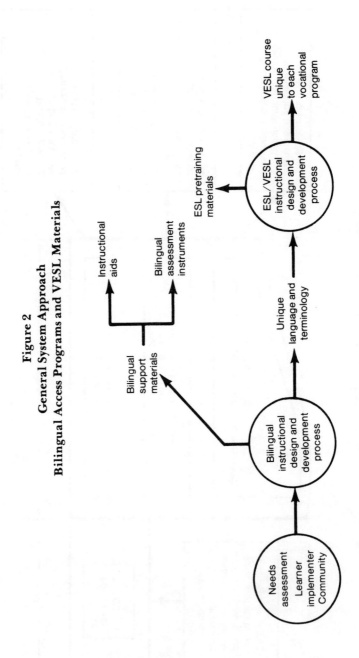

Figure 2
General System Approach
Bilingual Access Programs and VESL Materials

definition of the ESL context concept as related to vocational programs is proposed later within this paper.

The bilingual or Spanish instructional aids constitute the third element within the bilingual delivery system, and are designed to supplement vocational and paravocational instruction in a contingent manner, and to support LES students' individual activities on a self-paced basis. As shown in Figure 1, Spanish bilingual learning aids decrease in number as the student progresses through the semester. Within each course, bilingual student assessment instruments are also provided as part of the bilingual support materials.

The VESL course is the fourth component and it is uniquely designed to meet the language requirements specific to each vocational program. VESL instruction is delivered in a parallel fashion during the regular semester instructional period. Instructional coordination activities are carried on throughout the semester to ensure a one-to-one correspondence between vocational instruction and VESL instruction.

A General System Approach to Bilingual Access Programs and VESL Materials

Figure 2 shows the major subsystems within the BAP including the project's design and conceptualization and the project's curriculum design and development process. The first subsystem is a needs assessment study that was implemented to set up a valid and solid foundation for the bilingual project. Learner and community needs, as well as institutional goals, are the project's guiding points. Kaufman (1976) defined needs assessment as the determination of the gaps between current outcomes and required or desired outcomes based on referent of external survival and contribution, reconciliation of differences among the educational partners, and placement of needs (outcome gaps) in priority for intended actions. The Bilingual Access Program proposal, which is available upon request, funded by AIDP, is a thirty-page document that provides the rationale upon which is founded the bilingual access model, identifies programs and courses to be developed and implemented in a bilingual mode, and delineates the milestones to be completed during the five-year period — from 1978 to 1982. Identified vocational programs and dates of implementation are included in Appendix A.

The second subsystem is the bilingual instructional design and development process. Several tasks are accomplished within this process, although they revolve mostly around the content analysis of the identified programs and subject matters. Subject matter content and task analyses are conducted by the subject-matter specialist (SMS) and the bilingual instructional designer/coordinator of the project, based upon the "Instructional Design Model for Bilingual Access Support Materials" (Kotesky, 1978, 1979). Major results of this subsystem are bilingual support materials, including bilingual instructional aids and student assessment instruments, and the unique language and terminology pertaining to each vocational program. The last element constitutes a crucial part of the information for the development of VESL components within each vocational program.

The third subsystem is identified as ESL/VESL instructional design and development process, in which the college's ESL specialists are involved. A framework referent for the accomplishment of this developmental task is provided by the "Instructional Design Model for Developing ESL/VESL Components" (Kotesky, 1978, 1979). Major output results of this subsystem are the ESL pretraining course and a unique VESL course for each vocational program.

Instructional Design for Developing Bilingual Access Support Materials

Several professionals contribute within the bilingual instructional design and development process, namely subject matter specialists, English/Spanish translators, audiovisual production specialists, clerical staff, bilingual instructional designers and project coordinators, and any other professional whose expertise may be required at different stages of development.

The instructional design for developing bilingual access support materials is shown in Figure 3 and specifically encompasses the following sequential components:

0.0 Conduct needs assessment
1.0 Identify vocational programs and paravocational courses
2.0 Specify instructional goals
3.0 Identify target population
4.0 Conduct instructional analysis
5.0 Develop bilingual student assessment instruments
6.0 Identify and develop Spanish/bilingual support materials
7.0 Conduct formative evaluation

A feedback mechanism or revision process is also included. Components or steps 0.0, 1.0, and 3.0 are considered a given framework since they are an integral part of the BAP/AIDP proposal. *Specify instructional goals,* component 2.0, includes statements of participants' achievement at course completion. These statements should not necessarily be expressed in measurable behavioral terms (Mager, 1972). Following is an example of an instructional goal specified within Food Production I course, Culinary Arts Program: "The participant will acquire experience in the preparation of entrees, soups, salads, sandwiches, as well as experience in sanitation procedures." Component 4.0, *conduct instructional analysis,* is central to this design model. The following are subactivities carried out within this component:

Figure 3

Instructional Design Model for Developing Bilingual Access Support Materials

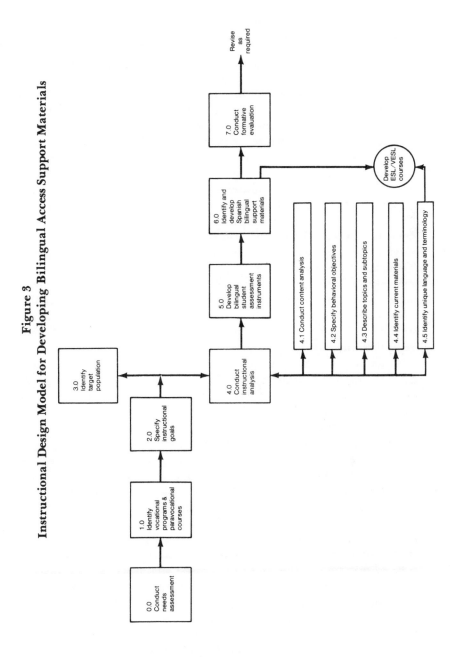

4.1 Conduct content analysis
4.2 Specify behavioral objectives
4.3 Describe topics and subtopics
4.4 Identify current materials
4.5 Identify unique language and terminology

For each course, a completely revised and updated course outline is developed. This is essential since in most cases it has been found that course outlines constitute a delineation of broad instructional tasks. The content analysis process, therefore, helps identify many activities and subactivities that are expressed in written form, thus generating a hierarchical course structure containing a series of subordinate and superordinate skills. The instructional analysis, component 4.0, encompasses content analysis and task analysis activities. Subcomponents 4.1 through 4.5 are accomplished using the instructional analysis forms shown in Appendix B. During the development process, a continuous interaction is required between the SMS and the bilingual instructional designer. Depending on each course's semester-credit-hours, a range varying from forty to one hundred or more hours of interaction is required. Terminal behaviors are specified within each topic, and topics and subtopics are described in terms of classroom or laboratory training activities (Mager, 1968; Gagne and Briggs, 1974). Current support materials used by the English-speaking instructor within each topic and subtopic are also identified along with the related subtechnical and general terminology. All terminal behavioral objectives are later fed back into the content analysis process to complete the course outline. Subtechnical and general terminology constitute an input element for the design and development of instructional situations within the VESL component in relation to technical information and concepts delivered by the vocational instructor.

Component 5.0, *develop bilingual student assessment instruments,* constitutes another unique consideration within this bilingual project. At least four assessment instruments per course are required by the project and the evaluation items are developed in one-to-one correspondence with the stated objectives and training activities.

Identify and develop Spanish/bilingual support materials, which constitutes component 6.0, is more or less a continuous task after the instructional analysis is completed for one course. This particular activity is based primarily on the information sheets and may include a survey of available resources appropriate to topics and/or subtopics; adaptation of available resources under copyright permission; translation of available materials under copyright permission; internally produced support materials; or a combination of the above alternatives. The column entitled "Tentative Support Materials for Bilingual Vocational Program" is filled in on the instructional analysis forms (Appendix B) as component 6.0 is completed. Monitoring of usage of the learning aids is accomplished through a document entitled, "List of Spanish Instructional Aids," shown in Appendix C, which provides information to the student, to the instructor, and to learning resource center personnel.

Component 7.0, *conduct formative evaluation,* is accomplished during the project implementation phase and falls beyond the scope of this paper.

Instructional Design for Developing ESL/VESL Components

The third major subsystem within the general system approach is the ESL/VESL instructional design and development process (Figure 4). Based on the model's component, specify VESL instructional goals, two major parallel activities are prescribed which are supportive of each other: develop ESL components and develop VESL components. Essential input information to this sequential model comes from component 4.0 within the instructional design model for developing bilingual access support materials, previously described (Figure 4).

Develop ESL Components. The ESL pretraining course is an integral part of the bilingual access instructional delivery system. English entry level skills have been defined for students enrolling in the Bilingual Access Program. According to the ESL assessment, LES students may or may not be required to sign up for ESL pretraining courses. Other options are also offered at Elgin Community College through the COPA Center to those students whose English skills fall below entry level requirements. The pretraining course has a technical focus and the instructional activities are based on grammatical structures and patterns predetermined under component E, *identify basic English language requirements.* Component G, *develop ESL pretraining course,* includes the following instructional segments: grammar, listening and comprehension, mathematics, and reading (Mrowicki, 1978a). Moreover, it can be said that this sixty-contract-hours, three-week-long course has been designed to meet the English language instructional requirements within most vocational fields to help LES students prior to pursuing regular instruction within their selected areas of training.

Develop VESL Components. As pointed out earlier in this paper, a unique VESL course, having direct correspondence with the language requirements specific to each vocational program, is developed and delivered in a parallel fashion throughout the semester. Major sources of information for VESL development are the unique subtechnical and general language and terminology within each vocational program, the SMS, and sometimes the vocational textbook. Vocational English as a Second Language (VESL) can be defined as the teaching of special-purpose English to LES persons, utilizing the vocabulary, situations, and lexicon specific to a vocational field or job (López-Valdez, 1978). In that line, it can be stated that the ESL specialist's experience in vocational

Figure 4
Instructional Design Model for Developing ESL/VESL Components

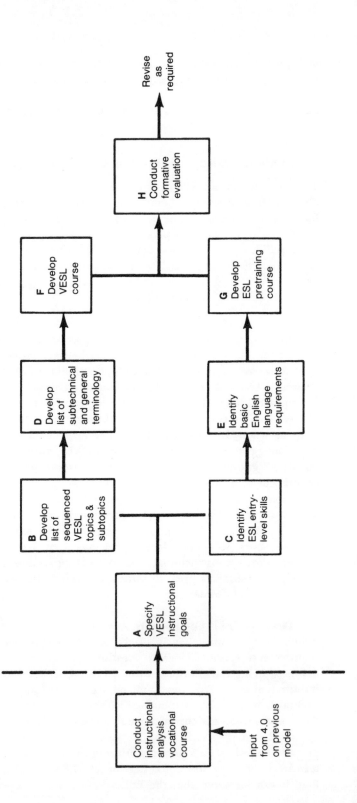

instruction and curriculum development is essential for creating VESL instructional classroom situations. Therefore, the input information is only a part of a very complex and cumbersome curriculum development process. It is essential that LES students learn the necessary language skills, grammar, and vocabulary to perform successfully both in the vocational classroom or laboratory and on the job.

Developing a list of sequenced VESL topics and subtopics, component B, takes into consideration the vocational course structural hierarchy already available through the reviewed and updated course outline. This is done to avoid job duplication and to achieve the expected one-to-one correspondence between vocational instruction and VESL instruction. Under component D, *develop list of subtechnical and general terminology* all terms are classified and listed according to the preidentified vocational topics and subtopics. In addition, the ESL specialist, with the assistance of the SMS, analyzes the vocational course in terms of priority of language skills in listening, speaking, reading, and writing. An example of the language skills assessment for the Machine Tool Operations programs is displayed in Appendix D. *Develop VESL course,* which is component F, constitutes the last component to be described. According to pertinent experience at ECC, Mrowicki (1978 b) considered the following segments within a VESL component: course overview, terminal behavior objectives or instructional goals, methodology, and VESL topics. The last segment also includes vocabulary study, grammar study, and reading.

In summary, VESL components are conceived to provide support to the LES student, equipping him or her with the required English skills to allow a transfer of language knowledge to the technical activities carried out by the vocational instructor.

Teaching the Vocational Class in an ESL Context

The bilingual access instructional delivery model calls for vocational instruction using an ESL context concept. This ESL context is described below in relation to actual vocational instruction as well as instructional events that should take place in the classroom to produce effective learning. Instructional events are activities that make up instruction for any single behavioral objective to be achieved by the learner within a lesson. Gagne and Briggs (1974) stated the following instructional events as a means to activate and support the internal processes of learning:

1. Gaining attention
2. Informing the learner of the objective
3. Stimulating recall of prerequisite learnings
4. Presenting stimulus material
5. Providing learning guidance
6. Eliciting performance

7. Providing feedback about performance correctness

8. Assessing performance

9. Enhancing retention and transfer

Not all instructional events are used and some are made to occur by the teacher, some by the learner, and some by the instructional materials. Gagne and Briggs (1974) suggested a set of ideal external and internal conditions to the learner within the delivery of instruction in a typical classroom situation. Such an arrangement would mean that subject-matter content is presented considering the appropriate instructional events, thus helping create the student's positive attitude toward learning; it would also mean that adequate hard learning materials exist. Delivery of instruction to LES students goes beyond all previous considerations, and it is due to this new condition — the presence of LES students in the classroom or lab environment — that the ESL context concept comes about. In fact, because of the intrinsic characteristics of the LES students, the vocational/paravocational instructor is asked to generate an ESL context to produce effective learning in those students. The following suggestions could be taken into consideration to produce an ESL context framework:

1. Simplify your English whenever possible.
   a. Keep the vocabulary as simple as possible. For example, use the word *turn* instead of *rotate.*
   b. Keep the grammatical structures as simple as possible. For example, use the active instead of the passive: Instead of saying, "The lathe is started by pushing the button," say "You start the lathe by pushing the button."
   c. Break long sentences into short simple ones. For example, instead of saying "You remove the tools which are mounted in the back by turning the headwheel counterclockwise," say "Look at the tools mounted in the back. You remove these tools by turning the headwheel counterclockwise."
   d. Speak at a normal pace, or a little slower than normal. But do not speak too slowly. Sometimes slow speech is as difficult to understand as fast speech.
   e. Try to speak with a neutral accent. Avoid a regional accent if your students might have difficulty understanding it.

2. Introduce concepts in a number of ways. Do not always rely on a lecture to get a point across. Try, for example, demonstrating or using diagrams, charts, or audiovisual aids to explain a concept.

3. Check concept comprehension in ways to which even the most limited-English speaker can respond. For example, instead of demanding long verbal responses, have the student demonstrate the task. Or when asking questions, ask *yes/no* questions first, then *or* questions, and finally *why* questions. *(What* and *where* questions are the most difficult to answer because they involve the most English of the

student.) Another alternative would be to accept all answers which contain the correct information. Do not point out grammatical mistakes. If you correct mistakes, your students might become too self-conscious to respond.

4. Remember, in your vocational class, communication is the primary goal.

Sequence of Milestones within the Bilingual Access Program

For each fiscal year during the five-year period, a series of milestones have been identified as shown in Figure 5. The identification of vocational programs leads to the identification of vocational and paravocational faculty members that will be collaborating with the bilingual project during any given fiscal year. With the support of the deans, the COPA director, and the AIDP faculty development coordinator, in service activities are conducted for participating ECC faculty including ESL/VESL staff members. This one-day workshop deals with the development procedures of the Bilingual Access Program for that particular fiscal year. Considerations are given to the project's overall philosophy and orientation, bilingual and ESL/VESL curriculum development, tasks and deadlines to be met, and delineation of responsibilities among parties involved within the various activities. Bilingual and ESL/VESL curriculum development are accomplished

Figure 5
Sequence of Milestones
Bilingual Access Program

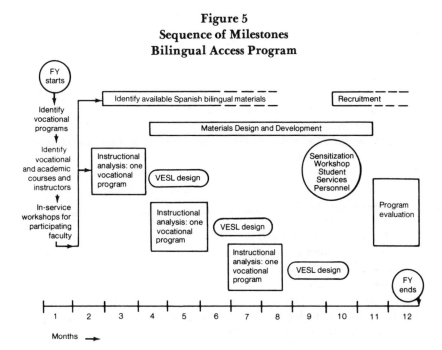

according to the preplanned sequence and deadlines. At the beginning of the period, a national and international survey is initiated in order to identify available bilingual Spanish resources that could be applicable to the selected vocational programs. Materials design and development is a continuous process which takes into consideration internal and external constraints in terms of final product development. Bilingual vocational programs are offered during the fall semester, and the outreach and recruitment process for the following year is initiated around the ninth month of the fiscal period. Sensitization workshop activities are also conducted around that time to help create within the institution a receptive climate toward LES students. A program evaluation report is completed at the end of the fiscal year according to federal guidelines.

Conclusions

The Bilingual Access Program at Elgin Community College is a unique approach to bilingual vocational education and can be considered a model program in the United States.

The output products developed under the BAP are self-contained instructional materials, and they can be used at any time by the institution with its available human and nonhuman resources; thus it is more cost effective than other bilingual vocational models.

Spanish bilingual supplemental learning aids and ESL/VESL components open college-level training opportunities to LES students, placing them in a successful, competing position with Anglo students.

The bilingual access model can be used in the United States not only for Spanish speakers, but for other limited-English-speaking groups, as well.

References

Gagne, R.M., and Briggs, L.J. *Principles of Instructional Design.* New York: Holt, Rinehart and Winston, 1974.

Kaufman, R.A. *Needs Assessment: Internal and External.* Unpublished manuscript. Tallahassee, Fla.: Instructional Systems Development Center, Florida State University, 1976.

Kotesky, A.A. "Instructional Design Process Toward the Implementation of Bilingual-Vocational Products." Elgin, Ill.: Bilingual Access Program, Elgin Community College, 1978.

———. "Implementing College Regular Vocational Programs into a Bilingual Mode: Two Instructional Design Models in Operation." Paper presented at the National Convention of the Association for Educational Communication and Technology, New Orleans, Louisiana, March 1979.

López-Valdez, E.J. "Needs Survey: Serving the Limited-English-Speaking." Arlington Heights, Ill.: Bilingual Vocational Project, Bilingual Education Service Center, 1978.

Mager, R.F. *Preparing Instructional Objectives.* Belmont, Calif.: Fearon-Pitman Publishers, 1968.

_____ . *Goal Analysis.* Belmont, Calif.: Fearon-Pitman Publishers, 1972.

Morwicki, L.G. *English as a Second Language Pre-training Materials.* Course description and activities, Elgin, Ill.: Community Outreach Placement and Assessment Center, Elgin Community College, 1978a.

_____ . *Vocational English as a Second Language Course for Machine Tool Program.* Unpublished workbook, Elgin, Ill.: Community Outreach Placement and Assessment Center, Elgin Community College, 1978b.

Appendix A

ECC Regular Vocational Programs	Date of Implementation
Machine tool operations	Fall 1978
Welding	Fall 1979
Culinary arts	Fall 1979
Restaurant management	Fall 1979
Plastics processing and manufacturing	Fall 1979
Secretarial science	Fall 1979
Group child care	Fall 1980
Automotive service technology	Fall 1980
Emergency medical technology	Fall 1981
Dental assisting	Fall 1981
All bilingual programs will be continuously in operation	Fall 1982

Appendix B
Instructional Analysis Sheet
AIDP/Bilingual Vocational Program
Elgin Community College

Course: Machine Tool Processes I (MTO-105)

Date of Analysis: June, 1978

Instructional Analysis Conducted by: Maurice Munch (Voc. Instructor)
Arturo Kotesky (B-V Coordinator)

Topic #	Name of Topic or Subtopics	Activities Description	Type CR	Type LAB	Time hours	Current Support Materials	Tentative Support Materials for B-V Program	Unique Language and Terminology
2 A)	Measuring Tools; types, uses, accuracy	Study of different kinds of linear type measuring tools				Text-Chapter 2 Hands-on Experience	Varios Instrumentos de Medicion	different similar kind type linear type measurement tool scale measurement scale
Instructional objective		SWBAT identify and manipulate linear type measuring tools and their specific scales	.5		.5			
1.	2A-1							
SUB → TOPICS	Semi-Precision Measuring Tools: Steel Rule and its Counterparts	Study and perform measurement of linear dimensions using rough measuring tools	.5		.5	Text-Chapter 2 Hands-on	Measurement Skills (Filmstrip/Sound materials in a Bilingual Mode with technical terms in English)	linear non-linear rough-fine rule steel rule inch subdivisions part of an inch smaller equal larger

S.T. #	SUB TOPICS					
2A-2 Semi-Precision Measuring Tools: Combination Set	Study and manipulate a variety of accessories of steel rules	.5	.5	Text-Chapter 2 Variety of Instruments		linear square angle protractor center trace layout precision
2A-3 Semi-Precision Measuring Tools: Depth Gages	Study and manipulate more precise linear measuring instruments	.5	.5	Text-Chapter 2 Demonstrations Hands-on	Depth Gages (Film-Strip/Sound Bilingual materials with technical terms in English)	accessory base base accessory slide precise precision

Appendix C
Lista de Materiales de
Ayuda/Curso: MTO-105
List of Spanish Instructional
Aids/Curso: MTO-105

AIDP/Bilingual Access Program
Elgin Community College

Prepared by: Arturo A. Kotesky (B-V Coord.)
Date: July 31, 1979

RLRC PERSONNEL INFORMATION INFORMACION DEL ESTUDIANTE PARA SOLICITAR EL MATERIAL			INSTRUCTOR'S INFORMATION
Material # Aid #	Titulo Del Material De Ayuda Title of Instructional Aids	Type of Material	Topics Covered in Outline
1	Lista de Materias MTO-105	Print	Course Outline
2	Conocimientos Básicos de Talleres	Print	1A 1B
3	Organización y Funcionamiento de Talleres	Print	1C
4	Varios Instrumentos de Medición	Print	2A 2B
5	Measurement Skills	Tutorial Kit English/Spanish	2A-1 2B-1
6	Depth Gages	Filmstrip/ Spanish sound and script	2A-3
7	Micrómetro y Vernier	Print	2B-4 2B-5
8	The Outside Micrometer	Filmstrip/ Spanish sound	2B-4
9	The Inside Micrometer	Filmstrip/ Spanish sound and script	2B-4

Can and Should the Laredo Experiment Be Duplicated Elsewhere? The Applicability of the Concurrent Approach in other Communities

Rodolfo Jacobson, Ph.D.
University of Texas of San Antonio

The United Independent School District (formerly the Consolidated Independent School District) of the City of Laredo, Texas, was one of the first school systems, prior to the passage of federal bilingual education legislation in 1968, to implement bilingual programs in as many as three local elementary schools: the two public schools Nye and Clark and one Catholic school, Mary, Help of Christians. From the very beginning, the program was a maintenance design utilizing a teaching technique known as the "concurrent approach." The concurrent approach seeks to incorporate some behavioral norms of bilingual communities and to bring them and the bilingual teacher's language choices into closer agreement with the students' cultural and linguistic heritage, as well as with their expected roles as members of United States society.

In the early days of the program, not much was known about the nature of this approach except for the fact that both languages were used concurrently and teachers as well as students were expected to alternate between them in a random "flip-flop" fashion. When I joined the district as a consultant and outside evaluator of the program in 1975, the extent to which both languages were actually maintained appeared questionable, as Spanish was limited to the social studies class only twenty minutes each

. Even within the bilingual social studies class the observed pattern was
∟t the teacher would ask questions in Spanish and the children respond
ın English. To actually implement a maintenance program and make the
concurrent approach work, the schools had to increase the amount of
Spanish used in the program, to improve attitudes toward Spanish among
teachers and students, and to explore in detail the nature of the concurrent
approach. Dolores Earles, the former project director, and Guadalupe
Puente, the present director, have both been most receptive to my
recommendations and we have succeeded, over the years, in developing a
bilingual program that is unique, at least in Texas, and that I like to refer
to as the "Laredo Experiment." It is as remarkable as, but somewhat
different from, other bilingual experiments such as the St. Lambert
Experiment (Lambert and Tucker, 1975), the Culver City Project (Cohen,
1974: 55-68), and the Redwood City Project (Cohen, 1975).

After four years of observations, evaluations, and inservice workshops,
the Laredo program has become a true maintenance program for children
from kindergarten through grade 3 because English and Spanish are now
used at an approximate fifty-fifty ratio. In addition, teachers have
acquired a clear understanding of what the concurrent approach actually
is, that is, (1) how to define it, (2) what its theoretical foundations are, (3)
what its rationale is, and (4) how to implement it in the classroom.

Definition

The concurrent approach is a strategy by which the bilingual teacher
presents the school curriculum (except language arts) in both languages
concurrently. The teacher switches from one language to the other and
back to the first, but only as far as this switching is pedagogically and
linguistically justifiable in light of four criteria:

1. A balanced language distribution
2. The continued teaching of content
3. A conscious alternation between the two languages
4. A means of accomplishing specific objectives.

Theoretical Foundations

This approach is supported by the theories that (1) the bilingual individual
stores and retrieves information in either one of two languages, so that
we can never be certain which language allows him or her to perform a
task more successfully at a given moment; and (2) the interactional norms
governing the verbal behavior of many communities where two languages
are in contact allow their members to switch from one to the other code, in
particular when engaged in informal intraethnic communication. Because
of the first theory, the teacher does well to use the two languages
concurrently, since the students will be reached regardless of the language

that is the medium of learning the subject. The second theory, on the other hand, allows the teacher to use, in the classroom, strategies that are familiar to the child, thus bringing together community behavior and school practices. Whereas *intrasentential codeswitching* may conflict with the child's language development, *intersentential codeswitching* will not, and the adapted codeswitching strategy achieves a most desirable rapprochement between community and school.

Rationale

On the basis of these theories, we may specify the following factors as essential in formalizing the rationale for the concurrent approach:

1. Any fairly educated bilingual adult can separate the two languages when he or she so desires; as a corollary, the concurrent use of the bilingual's two languages does not lead to a confusion between the two codes, as some of its objectors have tried to make us believe.

2. From a sociolinguistic viewpoint, the teacher and the class are participants in the same social situation and we may expect the former to analyze the situation meaningfully and to identify a series of cues to which teacher and students should react appropriately.

3. Switching from code to code while teaching content is a relevant strategy for anyone who finds codeswitching to be a normal practice in his or her own community.

4. The bilingual individual usually distributes the two languages, allowing equal time to both. Where bilingual imbalance exists, it may be due to attitudinal factors in that the speakers grant higher prestige to one language compared with the other.

Implementation

In order to implement the approach, the teacher must focus on the two main ingredients of a language alternation technique, viz. the language attitudinal perspective and the series of responses to cues identified in the classroom situation. Accordingly, the concurrent approach is designed to plan teaching in such a way that equality between the bilingual's two languages is achieved. The prestige granted to each code is the affective element that enables the teacher and students to strive for a linguistic balance. The system of cues, on the other hand, is the inventory of potential factors that tell the teacher when code alternation is appropriate. These cues have been drawn from four general areas: (1) classroom strategies, (2) curriculum, (3) language development, and (4) interpersonal communication. The specific cues associated with each one of these areas may serve as guidelines for teachers to balance out both linguistic codes.

Teachers are trained in many aspects of education, but not usually in monitoring their use of language, and even less in monitoring their distribution of the two languages in a bilingual program. Therefore, a training session should include theory, class observations, coding sessions, advanced planning, videotaped performances, and peer critiques. By fully understanding the approach's rationale and its actual implementation during token lessons, teachers become convinced of its feasibility. Workshops of this nature have been conducted in Laredo and elsewhere and have been organized with the following segments in mind:

1. The rationale of the concurrent approach and its conceptual framework: the prestige of codes and the system of cues

2. Cue-response analysis: recorded and videotaped minilessons are studied, transcribed, and coded

3. Advanced planning of language distribution: lesson plans in two languages with switch rationalization

4. Lesson drafts for approval

5. Videotaped minilessons

6. Peer critiques: lesson replay and instant evaluation

7. Special topics, such as "Spanish terminology" and "Role of the monolingual teacher in a team approach."

A one-week workshop has been satisfactory in motivating teachers to use this technique and to ensure their competency in controlled switching. Reactions to this practice-oriented workshop have been positive, and later class observations have shown that teachers were more effective in integrating the switching technique in their classes.

The concurrent approach is one strategy that lends itself most effectively to a maintenance program, but to use this technique the teacher must become psycholinguistically and, above all, sociolinguistically sophisticated by detaching himself or herself from teaching tasks, and must make those language distribution choices that are most conducive to bilingual learning. Workshops of the kind outlined above are needed to accomplish the teachers' detachment and develop in them the language analytical attitude without which no advanced planning can be agreed on. The teachers in the Laredo program have acquired this psycho-sociolinguistic sophistication and are succeeding in rendering both groups, Anglo American and Mexican American children, bilingual and bicultural. These children have developed the necessary feeling of appropriateness, so that they can choose the language they wish to use at a given moment.

Is there anything special about Laredo, or about any other bilingual bordertown for that matter, or could this experiment be duplicated in other areas of the United States where two languages and cultures come in close contact? A border situation encourages or needs the coexistence of two codes, especially if the speakers of either code are respected. In a materialistic society respect is contingent upon higher socioeconomic status. In this sense, Laredo is special, since a high percentage of middle-class Mexican Americans live there and their economic situation has in no way been dependent upon their acculturation to Anglo American society. In other words, linguistic or cultural loyalty and socioeconomic mobility are not contradictory terms in Laredo. This is not necessarily true for other bilingual cities where most Mexican Americans are members of the lower socioeconomic class and cannot climb the ladder of social and economic success unless they strip themselves of their ethnic features, whether cultural or linguistic. Therefore, for the Laredo program to be duplicated elsewhere, we must first be able to identify within the community an attitudinal climate similar to the one in Laredo: both languages must have prestige, both cultures must be respected, and biculturalism-bilingualism must not be viewed as standing in the way of good U.S. citizenship.

As we examine this situation from a more pedagogically relevant perspective, we would address ourselves to three basic questions:

1. How can children with diverse language proficiencies be taught in two languages?

2. To what extent will children still satisfy the demands of a basically English-speaking society?

3. What does bicultural bilingual learning mean in terms of the child's future role in our society?

Schools in communities with a lesser degree of bilingualism compared with Laredo exhibit great diversity in language proficiency. Most "bilingual" children find themselves at the two extremes of the bilingual spectrum and only a few of them qualify as reasonably balanced bilinguals. How can we then teach school subjects alternating between two languages, if most of the children fully comprehend instructions in just one of them? Obviously, the concurrent approach cannot work under such conditions, unless the weaker language is first strengthened. The alternation approach must wait until the children, through the ESL or SSL component of the bilingual program, have acquired a certain bilingual balance. Thus, the concurrent approach becomes a long-term objective but can gradually be introduced as the children gain proficiency in the second language (L_2).

Conclusions

Few educational programs are as misunderstood as bilingual education programs. From the uneducated parent of a minority child up to the politician, it is the common belief that bilingual education means teaching the child in the vernacular language alone. Even those who know better argue that Spanish-speaking children in a bilingual program do not become proficient enough in English because of exposure to Spanish during their education. Our experience with bilingual children as well as recent research has shown otherwise. Children motivated to learn a second language do so quickly and to the dismay of their parents, whose teachers they often become after interacting with other-language-speaking peers for only a short time. Are we motivating non-English-speaking children when we place them in a monolingual English language school? Or, are we not rather alienating them from English and Anglo American values as we force the children away from their language and culture? Non-English speaking children can become as proficient in English as their monolingual peers, if they are allowed to be loyal to their heritage and at the same time are motivated to function successfully in the mainstream of United States society.

Bilcultural bilingual learning, then, carves out for the bilingual children their future roles in our society. As adults they will be able to relate to family and friends and at the same time function adequately in the broader society. Whether they interact as bilinguals now and as monolinguals at some other time will depend entirely upon their sensitivity, that is, their feeling for appropriateness, thus becoming truly coordinate bilinguals.

The concurrent approach is felt to be instrumental in achieving these goals for our children: (1) they will internalize content in their two languages; (2) their English will not be any worse off as a result of their exposure to Spanish, as long as the attitudinal perspective is attended to; and (3) through bicultural bilingual learning they will understand their role as members of our pluralistic society, remaining loyal to their heritage and at the same time becoming fully integrated in the broader United States society.

The concurrent approach holds great potential for children whose parents, as well as communities, believe that being bilingual is an asset, not a liability, and that bilingualism should be pursued as a goal in all those areas of our country where speakers of different languages and members of diversified cultures are in contact.

References

Cohen, Andrew. "The Culver City Spanish Immersion Program." *Language Learning* 24 (1974): 1.

―――― . *A Sociolinguistic Approach to Bilingual Education*. Rowley, Mass.: Newbury House, 1975.

Jacobson, Rodolfo. "How to Trigger Codeswitching in a Bilingual Classroom." In *Southwest Area Linguistics Now and Then*. Edited by B. Hoffer and B.L. Dubois. San Antonio: Trinity University, 1977.

―――― . "Anticipatory Embedding and Imaginary Content: Two Newly Identified Codeswitching Variables." In *Bilingual and Biliterate Perspectives*. Edited by A.G. Lozano. Boulder: University of Colorado, 1978a.

_____ . "The Social Implications of Intra-sentential Codeswitching." In *New Directions in Chicano Scholarship*. Edited by R. Romo and R. Paredes. San Diego: University of California, 1978b.

_____ . "Codeswitching in South Texas: Sociolinguistic Considerations and Pedagogical Applications." *Journal of the Linguistic Association of the Southwest* 3, nos. 1 and 2 (1978c).

Lambert, Wallace E., and Tucker, G.R. *Bilingual Education of Children: The St. Lambert Experiment*. Rowley, Mass.: Newbury House, 1975.

College-Level Bilingual Education: Curriculum Planning and the Relationship of English and Home Language Development

Ricardo Otheguy
City College
City University of New York

Ruth Otto
Newark College of Arts and Sciences
Rutgers University

Laura Siffeti
Essex County College
Rutgers University

No question in bilingual higher education in the Hispanic areas of the United States needs greater clarification than whether to use Spanish as the language of instruction in subject-matter courses in college, and support this instruction with developmental Spanish classes. As often happens with educational questions, and as happened with this one when it was being asked at the elementary and secondary levels, answers are given and positions are taken on the basis of strongly held assumptions rather than research evidence or experience.

We have learned in conversations with professors and administrators in the New York-New Jersey area that opposition to instruction in Spanish is based on intellectual assumptions and not—as many in the field of bilingual education tend to think—on social or affective grounds (Otto and Otheguy, 1979). That is, this opposition often rests on highly developed ideas about language and language learning and not on simple-minded beliefs about assimilation and social cohesion, or on prejudice toward linguistic minorities. In this paper we will discuss the three assumptions that we have found to underlie objections to Spanish-medium instruction in the colleges, and argue that while they appear plausible, there is in fact little to support them and much to suggest that they may not be valid. These assumptions are the following:

1. Learning a second language is a difficult and time-consuming task that occupies all of the student's attention, and classes in Spanish take up time needed to develop English.

2. Development of Spanish competes with development of English, and the college student who needs English as a Second Language (ESL) instruction should put his mind to only one language at a time.

3. College-age students already know their language and nothing is to be gained by further developing Spanish in students from Hispanic backgrounds.

The supposition that language skills and content courses taught in Spanish take up time that could be better spent on English assumes, first, that the only student who could profit from such courses is the one in need of ESL classes who cannot afford to be distracted from the difficult task of acquiring college-level English. But many U.S. Hispanics are fluent speakers of English with no need for ESL, who could yet profit from exposure to and practice in one of the educated, standard varieties of their home language. We have had direct experience with many Hispanic students who welcome the chance to take college-level courses in Spanish, even when they may be more comfortable in English. In so doing, these students are lending support to the old idea that an educated person is one who is literate in more than one language, a notion that was uncontroversial until recently even in the United States.

Second, the position that content courses taught in Spanish take up time that is needed to develop English assumes that for those Hispanics who do need ESL, every hour spent on Spanish could be better spent on English, on the principle that there is no limit to the amount of time that college students can profitably be exposed to a second language. But there is no evidence at all for this position, which is reminiscent of some of the early objections to home-language instruction at the elementary level. It is probably a good idea to reinforce ESL with subject-matter instruction in English, provided the student has enough English to follow the class. And it may very well be that if a student takes all his content courses in Spanish his English development will be slowed. But this does not mean that the same will be true if the right mix of the two languages is found. The notion that instruction in Spanish robs the college ESL student of precious hours needed to develop English assumes that English proficiency will increase with every hour of additional exposure or instruction. (For a recent statement of this belief in a direct link between amount of instruction and proficiency in a second language, see Epstein, 1977, p. 25.) But this view lacks empirical support and flies in the face of even the little we know about the acquisition of a second language. In this task, factors such as attitude toward the language and experience with it outside the school setting have more influence on outcomes than simple accumulation of time (Gardner and Lambert, 1972; Krashen, Seliger, and Hartnett, 1974; and Naiman et al., 1975).

The second factor underlying objections to Spanish-medium courses is the unexamined assumption that development of fluency and literacy in college students in one language *competes* with their development in another. But there is no reason to prefer this view over its opposite, namely the often-expressed although equally unexamined assumption that development of literacy and fluency in one language *contributes* to their development in another (Gaarder et al., 1972, p. 622; and Kobrick, 1972, p. 58). We have no direct evidence that developing the home language of college ESL students helps their acquisition of English. However, there is plenty of indirect evidence that native-language development in general contributes to rather than competes with development of a second language, and that developing the Spanish of U.S. Hispanics in college will have beneficial effects on the development of their English.

The first piece of indirect evidence is found in the tradition of contrastive studies going back to Weinreich (1953). These studies can be interpreted as supporting the conclusion that transfer of learning is a constant feature of human linguistic behavior — that the skills acquired in learning one's first language can be applied in handling one's second. This suggests that development of skills in Spanish will pay off in the development of English. But these studies also show that this transfer is successful only sometimes, that sometimes it is imperfect and inaccurate, and that highly developed skills in the first language interfere with the second. This would suggest that the colleges had better leave the students' Spanish alone lest it interfere with English development.

If we look at immersion programs (Lambert and Tucker, 1972; and Tucker, 1977) we also find contradictory or limited answers. The success of these programs suggests that under certain circumstances development of one language does not compete with development of another. And with respect to reading ability in particular, there is strong evidence of positive transfer of skills from one language to another (Tucker, 1977, p. 12ff). But in immersion programs it is the second language that is being developed and thus they are only of limited interest for our question. Furthermore, and even allowing that these programs aim to develop a second, not a first, language, they could be interpreted as demonstrating the opposite of our point, for they show that improvement of one language is not dependent on concurrent development of another.

But two factors further limit the evidence from both contrastive studies and immersion programs. Most immersion programs reported in the research literature involve children from dominant middle-class families in Canada, whereas students in college bilingual programs in the United States tend to be of low socioeconomic status from less integrated populations. Moreover, research in both immersion programs and contrastive studies is usually carried out in groups where there is a sharp line between first and second language, whereas we are talking about cases where often the line between first and second language isn't clear.

Studies that apply more directly to the bilingual situation in the United States suggest that the competing-languages rationale against Spanish-medium courses is invalid. In interviews with college ESL students, Helen Aron found a number of striking differences between the first language experience of students who had been promoted to the next level of college ESL and that of those who had not made the grade (Otheguy and Aron, 1979). First, according to the students' self-report, those who did well in ESL were much more likely to have completed secondary school in their home country than students who didn't do well. Second, the students who passed their ESL courses tended to do more reading in their first language than those who failed. Third, those who passed ESL felt that their command of their first language was greater than the average in their home communities, whereas the students who failed ESL reported that their ability in their first language was average or below average. These findings are similar to the widely reported studies on semilingualism in Scandinavia, where children of Finnish background in Swedish schools have been found to do better in Swedish the better they know their first language, leading Paulston (1977, p. 93ff) to conclude that "the evidence is perfectly clear that mother-tongue development facilitates the learning of the second language, and there are serious implications that without such development neither language may be learned well."

The relevance of these studies to the question of whether to have Spanish-medium and Spanish-development courses in college lies in suggesting that ESL students with a strong foundation in their first language are likely to do better in English than those with less-developed abilities in their first language. These studies, of course, do not address directly the issue of whether to develop the first language of those that do not start out with this strong foundation. But they suggest that the ESL skills of college Hispanics will be considerably improved if home-language skills are improved, both through developmental Spanish classes and through subject-matter courses taught in Spanish. This is a line of thinking that is consistent with the claim by Cummins (1976, 1977) that a certain minimum threshhold of first-language competence must be reached before a student can benefit from bilingual education.

In short, there is no clear support for the idea that subject-matter and developmental college courses in Spanish will compete or interfere with development of English, and a great deal of indirect evidence that investing time and effort in the students' Spanish will pay off in concomitant improvement of their English.

The third assumption underlying opposition to subject-matter and developmental courses in Spanish at the college level is the belief that the colleges should not need to develop Spanish because the students already know it from home. This outlandish yet widespread assumption draws on several sources.

For instance, there is the belief that Hispanic students in the United States are native speakers of Spanish comparable to the way Anglophone students are native speakers of English. Here is another manifestation of the age-old equation of ethnicity with language, and of the conviction that every human being has a clearly defined native language that he fully masters, both of which ideas have been shown to be false (Boas, 1911, p. 3ff; and Hymes, 1974, p. 71ff). Whether students who are not classifiable as native speakers of Spanish can be classified as native speakers of English begs the question of the appropriateness of the "native" versus "second" categorization, which though useful to describe some bilinguals may not in fact be useful to describe others. For our purpose, the question is beside the point. It is enough to recognize that in the United States context "Hispanic" is not necessarily synonymous with fluent, let alone literate, in Spanish, and that therefore there is no support for the claim that no development of Spanish is needed by Hispanic students.

Another factor contributing to the belief that since college Hispanics already know their language no further development is needed involves the indirect influence of research into theoretical questions on educational practice. A factor that has dominated the intellectual climate in which linguistic problems are discussed by ESL and bilingual educators, particularly during their period of graduate and certification training, is the theory of transformational grammar. This approach to linguistic analysis and theory has had a profound effect on all language-related fields, despite the fact that nonpractitioners understand it poorly or not at all and that practitioners have repeatedly denied its relevance to pedagogical, curricular, or policy problems relating to language (Chomsky, 1966). As a result of superficial familiarity with the work of transformationalists, the idea has been popularized that the mechanism of language acquisition is not only innate but independent of the mechanism by which other skills are acquired (Chomsky, 1968). Transformationalists have also developed a highly abstract conception of language competence that bears only the faintest and most indirect connection to language use, and which they acknowledge themselves is so far removed from human language performance that it provides no insights into the system that makes linguistic communication possible (Chomsky, 1971).

As filtered down through the fields of applied linguistics and language pedagogy, these ideas have promoted, first, a belief that development of linguistic competence is no longer taking place in college students. Thus, they may profit from exposure to reading and writing techniques, but their linguistic competence itself bears no further development, since it is fully in place by early childhood (Dale, 1976, p. 128). Second, these ideas have promoted a mindless linguistic egalitarianism, under which all native speakers are assumed to have equal knowledge of their language, which is thus somewhat magically exempted from the usual human variation that pervades all other skills, and as a consequence is also exempted from the need of development through education. Imperfect learning may exist among second-language speakers, and the language of different groups may of course receive different degrees of social approval. But if cultural value judgments are set aside and only native speakers are considered, variation between individuals exists only at the level of mere performance. Knowledge of the linguistic system, that is, knowledge of the language, is assumed to be the same for all.

But note that these beliefs have not resulted from the findings of transformational grammar as filtered down to educators; that is, they are not the result of what linguists of this school have empirically learned through language analysis and then shared with us. Rather, they result from preanalytical, philosophical assumptions. But the transformational assumption that language is a knowledge, highly determined by innate structures and held equally by all speakers, provides us with no framework within which to discuss this or any other education question.

We might better conceive of language as do many nontransformationalist linguists (e.g., Diver, 1975), as an instrument or a tool. Then competence becomes competence to use the tool, to apply it to whatever purpose the tool is designed for, and to acquire mastery over its use through a gradual, life-long process. Skill in speaking, reading, and writing is thus not something apart from and overlaid on linguistic competence, it is competence itself. These skills can be reasonably expected to increase with time and practice, according to factors that affect the development of all other skills, such as need, aptitude, motivation, and, most important for our purpose, training, encouragement, correction, and support—in short, what we usually call education. Similarly, we can reasonably expect skill in the use of this tool to vary from one individual to the next, and within the same individual, according to a variety of factors, one of which must be exposure to education.

Opposition to Spanish development at the college level cannot find support in a view of linguistic competence that considers language development to be complete by early childhood and essentially the same among individuals. In addition to the testimony of our daily experience, there is plenty of evidence for the opposite view. Such works as Labov's "The Logic of Nonstandard English" (1970) are correctly interpreted as warnings against equating competence in a socially favored dialect with greater skill in the use of language. But they should also be interpreted as evidence that this skill does vary among individuals, a fact that has been empirically supported by other studies, as well (cf. Stolz, 1967). The evidence provided by Gleitman and Gleitman (1970) not only supports the existence of individual differences in the mastery of one's native language but also demonstrates that the degree of mastery tends to increase with education. In a carefully controlled set of experiments on paraphrase, they showed that the level of success in linguistic tasks that are socially neutral varies among individuals and tends to increase with level of education (1970, p. 137ff). This is probably due to the fact that education in any field tends to increase demands on the user of language and to produce greater language proficiency. Gleitman and Gleitman conclude that there is no support for what they call the linguistic egalitarianism that follows from transformational assumptions. Research by Loban (1976) has also demonstrated that all first-language skills continue to develop well into adolescence and at different rates for different people.

The facts thus suggest that linguistic competence should be seen as the skill to manipulate language, one that varies among individuals and that increases with practice and education. For our case, they suggest that a central mission of a college bilingual program should be to develop skills in Spanish with as much diligence as in English.

This is the way that native languages have been treated in all cases where the teaching of mainstream, majority students is guided by common sense and tradition rather than by the questions, doubts, and demands of research evidence that attend the education of minorities. No institution of higher learning behaves as if language development did not take place among college students and were therefore outside its purview. For any majority group, the need to develop native language skills in college is considered obvious and uncontroversial. Thus the third and final assumption underlying opposition to Spanish-medium instruction in the colleges turns out under examination to be as invalid as the other two.

Given that Hispanic students need to develop first-language skills as much as and often more than other students in college, and given that far from competing with improvement of English this development is probably an indispensable precondition for it, we find that Spanish-medium courses and courses to develop skills in speaking, reading, and writing Spanish appear as natural components of a college bilingual program.

The success of this approach depends on how seriously these courses are seen as an integral part of the students' educational program, treated with the same attention — and subject to the same level of demands — as the English part of the curriculum. In this respect it is imperative that proficiency in writing some standard variety become a demand made for Spanish as much as for English, that testing and assessment be carried out in both with the same care, and that efforts toward developing language skills be made equally for both languages, so that bilingual programs will result in the creation of truly educated bilinguals and in full integration of Spanish into the life of the college or university.

References

Boas, R. *Handbook of American Indian languages*. Bureau of American Ethnology. Washington, D.C.: U.S. Government Printing Office, 1911.

Chomsky, N. "Linguistic Theory." In *Language Teaching: Broader Contexts,* edited by Robert G. Mead, Jr. Middleburg, Vt.: Northeast Conference on the Teaching of Foreign Languages, 1966.

―――. *Language and the Mind.* New York: Harcourt Brace Jovanovich, Inc., 1968.

―――. *Problems of Knowledge and Freedom.* New York: Vintage Press, 1971.

Cummins, J. "The Influence of Bilingualism on Cognitive Growth: A Synthesis of Research Findings and Explanatory Hypotheses." In *Working Papers on Bilingualism* No. 9 (1976): 1-48.

―――. "The Cognitive Development of Bilingual Children: A Review of Recent Research." ERIC ED 147 727, 1977.

Dale, P. *Language Development: Structure and Function.* New York: Holt, Rinehart and Winston, 1976.

Diver, W. *Introduction to the Columbia University Working Papers in Linguistics,* vol. 2. New York: Dept. of Linguistics, Columbia University, 1975.

Epstein, N. *Language, Ethnicity, and the Schools: Policy Alternatives for Bilingual-Bicultural Education.* Washington, D.C.: Institute for Educational Leadership, 1977.

Gaarder, B., et al. "Teaching Spanish to Native Speakers of Spanish." *Hispania* 55 (1972): 619-631.

Gardner, R.C., and Lambert, W.E. *Attitudes and Motivation in Second Language Learning.* Rowley, Mass.: Newbury House, 1972.

Gleitman, L., and Gleitman, H. *Phrase and Paraphrase: Some Innovative Uses of Language.* New York: W.W. Norton, 1970.

Hymes, D. *Foundations in Sociolinguistics.* Philadelphia: University of Philadelphia Press, 1974.

Kobrick, J. "The Compelling Case for Bilingual Education." *Saturday Review* (29 April 1972).

Krashen, S., and Hartnett, D. "Two Studies in Adult Second Language Learning." *Kritikon Litterarum* 2 (1974): 220-228.

Labov, W. "The Logic of Nonstandard English." In *Monograph Series on Language and Linguistics* vol. 22, edited by J. Alatis. Washington, D.C.: Georgetown University Press, 1970.

Lambert, W., and Tucker, R. *The Bilingual Education of Children.* Rowley, Mass.: Newbury House, 1972.

Loban, W. *Language Development: Kindergarten through Grade 12.* Urbana, Ill.: National Council of Teachers of English, 1976.

Naiman, N., et al. *The Good Language Learner.* Toronto: Ontario Institute for Studies in Education, 1975.

Otheguy, R., and Aron, H. "Level of First-Language Skills and their Effect on Second-Language Learning." Unpublished manuscript, 1979.

Otto, R. and Otheguy, R. "Bilingual Education Goes to College: A Look at Program Objectives." *TESOL Quarterly* 12 (1979).

Paulston, C. "Research." In *Bilingual Education: Current Perspectives,* Volume 2 (Linguistics). Arlington, Va.: Center for Applied Linguistics, 1977.

Stolz, W. "A Study of the Ability to Decode Grammatically Novel Sentences." *Journal of Verbal Learning and Verbal Behavior* 6 (1967): 867-873.

Tucker, R. "The Linguistic Perspective." In *Bilingual Education: Current Perspectives,* Volume 2 (Linguistics). Arlington, Va.: Center for Applied Linguistics, 1977.

Weinreich, U. *Languages in Contact.* New York: Linguistic Circle of New York, 1953.

Pedagogy

The Misplaced Child:
Does Linguistically Different Mean
Learning Disabled?

Katherine Archuleta
California State Department of Education
Sacramento, California

Hermes T. Cervantes
Denver Public Schools
Denver, Colorado

The assessment and subsequent placement of linguistically, culturally, and ethnically different students into classes for the learning disabled has come under considerable criticism from minority group members as well as from other members of the academic community (Bernal, 1975; DeAvila and Havassy, 1975; Jackson, 1975; Kamin, 1974; Mercer, 1974; Mercer and Brown, 1973; Samuda, 1975; and Williams, 1975).

Indeed, the concern stems not only from the ambiguities, contradictions, and confusion within the field of learning disabilities (Coles, 1978) but also from the inappropriate assessment and placement procedures typically used in assigning bilingual bicultural children to special education classrooms (Mercer, 1973). It is the ability to diagnose the presence of learning disabilities in children (whether linguistically, culturally, or ethnically different or not) and prescribe effective remediation that is being questioned.

The eight most frequently recommended academic tests for a learning disabilities battery are the Illinois Test of Psycholinguistic Abilities, the

Bender Visual-Motor Gestalt Test, the Frostig Developmental Test of Visual Perception, the Wepman Auditory Discrimination Test, the Lincoln-Oscretsky Motor Development Scale, the Graham-Kendall Memory for Designs Test, the Purdue Perceptual-Motor Survey, and the Wechsler Intelligence Scale for Children. All have been found to have suspect predictive or diagnostic validity (Newcomer and Hammill, 1975; Robinson and Schwartz, 1973; Henderson, Butler, and Gaffney, 1969; Black, 1976; Gamsky and Lloyd, 1971; Flynn and Byrne, 1970; Larsen, Rogers, and Sowell, 1976; Pyfer and Carlson, 1972; Wikler, Dixon, and Parker, 1970; Meier, 1971; Fisher, 1971; Black, 1973; Rudel and Denckla, 1976; and Farr, 1969).

Other investigators have revealed that Hispanic and Black children have been disproportionately identified as having serious learning disabilities in California (Mercer, 1973) and other states of the Southwest (Baca, 1974). For example, Mercer noted that 100 percent more Blacks, about 300 percent more Mexican Americans, and about 50 percent fewer Anglo Americans were labeled "mentally retarded" than would be expected from their proportions in the populations.

Fortunately, efforts are currently being extended to develop more valid assessment techniques and to ensure educational placements in the best interest of children. These efforts are, to a large extent, the result of a series of landmark legal cases such as *Hobson* v. *Hanson,* 1967; *Arreola* v. *Santa Ana Board of Education,* 1968; *Diana* v. *California Board of Education,* 1969; *Spangler* v. *Pasadena Board of Education,* 1970; *Steward* v. *Philips,* 1970; *Larry P.* v. *Riles,* 1971; *Ruíz* v. *California State Board of Education,* 1971; and *Lau* v. *Nichols,* 1974 (Oakland and Laosa, 1976). Such litigation eventually led to Public Law 94-142, The Education for All Handicapped Children's Act of 1975.

P.L. 94-142 set guidelines for the evaluation procedures to be utilized in the assessment of students for special classes. The law requires that all testing and evaluation procedures for special education services (1) be selected and administered so as not to be racially or culturally discriminatory, (2) be given in the native language of the student, and (3) include a sample of the individual's adaptive behavior. A discussion of each of these mandates follows.

Nondiscriminatory Assessment

Culture-free tests, culture-fair tests, adaptations of present tests for cross-cultural applications, and culture-specific tests are efforts that have been used in the assessment of linguistically, culturally, ethnically, and socioeconomically different students. Most efforts have been sharply criticized (Samuda, 1975) though promising approaches have been reported (DeAvila, 1975, Bernal, 1975). These investigators have hypothesized that the developmental stages described by Piaget can provide a cross-cultural framework for assessment.

With respect to culture-specific tests, Mercer and her colleagues (1977) have developed a system of multicultural pluralistic assessment that uses socioeconomic status, family size, family structure, and urban acculturation when interpreting Wechsler Intelligence Scale for Children, Revised Scores. This procedure has been examined by Baca and Cervantes (1978, 1979) and found to be promising.

Native Language Assessment

Bilingual educators continue to express concern over the need for adequate assessment instruments for evaluating language dominance and language proficiency. Silverman, Noa, and Russell (1976) report that most of the currently available language tests have technical limitations with respect to criterion-related validity as well as reliability considerations. However, there are numerous promising tools, such as the Language Assessment Scale and the Language Assessment Battery which not only describe the individual skills but also prescribe remedial activities for those deficits observed.

Assessment of Adaptive Behavior

Adaptive behavior, or "the effectiveness with which an individual copes with the natural and social demands of his environment" (Grossman, 1973), is a required aspect of P.L. 94-142. This recommendation was based upon research findings which revealed that the social role performance of students labeled significantly learning disabled tended to be undistinguished from that of the adults in the community (Mercer, 1973).

Of the two typically used scales, Baca and Cervantes (1978, 1979) suggest that the Adaptive Behavior Inventory for Children included in the Mercer and Lewis Scale is significantly more applicable for culturally, ethnically, or linguistically different individuals.

Recommendations

The assessment of culturally and linguistically diverse students, as well as the debate over the appropriateness of traditionally used achievement and intelligence tests, continues to be of concern to teachers and administrators. Bilingual educators should be aware of current research and discussions that may affect or, even more seriously, mislabel their students. With this in mind, the following are recommended:

1. That the specific purpose for assessment be determined prior to any testing

2. That all tests be examined with respect to their technical features such as reliability and validity as well as their appropriateness for use with culturally and linguistically diverse groups

3. That guidelines specified in P.L. 94-142 be followed by local school districts

4. That technical assistance be requested in the areas of nondiscriminatory assessment from regional training and resource centers

5. That assessment of language be in the primary language of the child

6. That adaptive behavior scales be used for all special education placements

7. That staff inservice training be provided to enhance the skills of district staff members in the appropriate and nondiscriminatory assessment of linguistically and culturally different students.

References

Baca, L. "A Survey of the Testing, Labeling and Placement Procedures Utilized to Assign Mexican American Students into Classes for the Educable Mentally Retarded." Unpublished doctoral dissertation, Greeley, Colorado, University of Northern Colorado, 1974.

Baca, L., and Cervantes, H.T. "The Assessment of Minority Students: Are Adaptive Behavior Scales the Answer?" *Psychology in the Schools* 15, no. 3 (1978): 366-370.

Bernal, E.M. "A Response to 'Educational Uses of Tests with Disadvantaged Students.' " *American Psychologists* 30, no. 1 (1975): 93-95.

Black, F.W. "Neurological Dysfunction and Reading Disorders." *Journal of Learning Disabilities* 6 (1973): 313-316.

Black, F.W. "Cognitive, Academic and Behavioral Findings in Children with Suspected and Documented Neurological Dysfunction." *Journal of Learning Disabilities* 9, (1976): 182-187.

Cervantes, H.T., and Baca, L. "Assessing Minority Students: The Role of Adaptive Behavior Scales." *Journal of Non-White Concerns* 7, no. 3 (April 1979): 122-127.

Coles, G. "The Learning Disabilities Test Battery: Empirical and Social Issues." *Harvard Educational Review* 48, no. 3 (August 1978): 313-340.

DeAvila, E.A., and Havassy, B.E. "Piagetian Alternative to I.Q.: Mexican American Study." In *Issues in the Classification of Children*, vol. 2. Edited by N. Hobbs. San Francisco: Jossey-Bass, 1975.

Farr, R. "Reading: What Can Be Measured?" Newark, Del.: International Reading Association, 1969.

Fisher, K.L. "Effects of Perceptual-Motor Training of the Educable Mentally Retarded." *Exceptional Children* 38 (1971): 264-266.

Flynn, P.T., and Byrne, M.C. "Relationship Between Reading and Selected Auditory Abilities of Third Grade Children." *Journal of Speech and Hearing Research,* 1970, vol. 13, pp. 725-730.

Gamsky, N.R., and Lloyd, F.W. "A Longitudinal Study of Visual Perceptual Training and Reading Achievement." *Journal of Educational Research* 64 (1971): 451-454.

Grossman, H.J. *Manual on Terminology and Classification in Mental Retardation.* Washington, D.C.: American Association on Mental Deficiency, 1973.

Henderson, N.B.; Butler, B.; and Gaffney, B. "Effectiveness of the WISC and Bender Gestalt Test in Predicting Arithmetic and Reading Achievement for White and Non-White Children." *Journal of Clinical Psychology* 29 (1969): 206-212.

Jackson, G.D. "On the Report of the Ad Hoc Committee on Educational View from the Association of Black Psychologists." *American Psychologists* 30, no. 1 (1975): 88-93.

Kamin, L.J. *The Science and Politics of I.Q.* New York: John Wiley and Sons, 1974.

Larsen, S.C.; Rogers, D.; and Sowell, V. "The Use of Selected Perceptual Tests in Differentiating Between Normal and Learning Disabled Children." *Journal of Learning Disabilities* 9 (1976): 32-37.

Meier, J.H. "Prevalence and Characteristics of Learning Disabilities Found in Second Grade Children." *Journal of Learning Disabilities* 4 (1971). 1-16.

Mercer, J.R. "A Policy Statement on Assessment Procedures and the Rights of Children." *Harvard Educational Review* 44, no. 1 (1974): 125-141.

———. *Labeling the Mentally Retarded.* Berkeley: University of California Press, 1973.

Mercer, J.R., and Brown, W.C. "Racial Differences in I.Q.: Fact or Antifact? In *The Fallacy of I.Q.* Edited by C. Senna. New York: The Third Press, 1973.

Mercer, J.R., and Lewis, J.F. *System of Multicultural Pluralistic Assessment.* New York: The Psychological Corporation, 1977.

Newcomer, P.L., and Hammill, D.D. "I.T.P.A. and Academic Achievement. A Survey." *Reading Teacher* 28 (1975): 731-741.

Oakland, T., and Laosa, L.M. "Professional, Legislative and Judicial Influences on Psychoeducational Assessment Practices in Schools." In *With Bias Toward None: Non-Biased Assessment of Minority Group Children.* Lexington, Ky.: Coordinating Office for Regional Resource Centers, 1976.

Pyfer, J.L., and Carlson, B.R. "Characteristic Motor Development of Children with Learning Disabilities." *Perceptual and Motor Skills* 35 (1972): 291-296.

Robinson, M.E., and Schwartz, L.B. "Visuo-Motor Skills and Reading Ability: A Longitudinal Study." *Developmental Medicine and Child Neurology* 15 (1973): 281-286.

Rudel, R.G., and Denckla, M.B. "Relationship of I.Q. and Reading Scores to Visual, Spatial and Temporal Matching Tasks." *Journal of Learning Disabilities* 9 (1976): 169-178.

Samuda, R. *Psychological Testing of American Minorities.* New York: Harper and Row, 1975.

Silverman, Robert J.; Noa, Joslyn; and Russell, Randall H. *Oral Language Tests for Bilingual Students.* Northwest Regional Educational Laboratory, 1976.

Wickler, A.; Dixon, J.F.; and Parker, J.B. "Brain Function in Problem Children and Controls: Psychometric, Neurological, and Electroencephalographic Comparisons." *American Journal of Psychiatry* 125 (1970): 94-105.

Williams, R. "Moderator Variables as Bias in Testing Black Children. *Journal of Afro-American Issues* 8, no. 1 (1975): 70-90.

Assisting Nonlearners in Bilingual Programs

Sister Patricia Ann Preston
Mount Mary College
Milwaukee, Wisconsin

The principal purpose of bilingual education is to teach bilingual, or potentially bilingual, children — to teach them in such a way that they can learn, no matter what the subject matter is. A considerable amount of time has elapsed since the renewed interest in bilingual bicultural education in our country gave rise to many varieties and levels of programs. Evaluations using many criteria and tests have been reported, and much success has been recorded. However, for the classroom teacher and for the parent and child, only one thing is really important: has the child learned? Even the best teacher in the best-planned and most successful program looks back at a number of children who, while apparently not suffering from any of the known learning disabilities, have not learned despite the special efforts of teachers.

Teachers, like other professional practitioners, have limited time, space, and focus within which to work. Yet the child in the teacher's classroom is subject to innumerable variables which are not within the teacher's province: home environment, dominant and subdominant cultures, physical disorders, social contexts outside of school, parenting methods, nutrition, etc. Recognizing the influence of such factors on the problems of nonlearners, teachers can refer these children to other professionals who focus on these particular domains; they can also act as citizens to support the rights of their students. However, in school the teacher has to teach the child. Evidence of successful teaching is the fact that the child has learned. Therefore, if the child does not learn, no matter what variables outside the teacher's domain contribute to the child's learning difficulty, the fact remains that the teacher has not taught. And that is a point of deep frustration for many teachers today.

Identification of Nonlearners

In order to teach the nonlearning child, it is necessary to discover what is obstructing the learning process. The rapid growth of diagnosis and special teachers for children with identifiable learning disabilities has helped ameliorate the problems of many children. However, in most bilingual and many monolingual classrooms there are still a number of children with no demonstrable learning disabilities other than the fact that they do not learn, neither in the regular, the bilingual, nor the remedial classroom. Who are these nonlearners and how can they be recognized? Organized research is very much needed here. From personal observations made while working with many children and teenagers experiencing school problems, I offer a few signs:

- The child able to copy accurately numbers or letters with pencil and paper, but unable to follow a motor or linguistic or geometric pattern

- The child able to count, but not able to use the numbers in a meaningful way or to reverse a procedure (count backwards, reverse an addition fact)

- The older child with very simplistic classification systems (i.e., "What is an animal?" — "Something that goes on the ground." — "A car moves on the ground. Is the car an animal?" — "Must be")

- The child unable to follow simple two- or three-step directions, regardless of language or languages used

- The child able to decode in reading, but unable to recode the same words on cards into a meaningful sentence

- The teenager who knows the function of an object (i.e., a broom) but not its name in either language

- The older child unable to select the key sentence in a paragraph or put a meaningful title to a story.

Evidence from Research

Often the nonlearning child in a bilingual classroom appears to be a balanced bilingual or English dominant although from a home in which the parents speak another language. It would appear that these children should be able to learn more quickly than the non-English-dominant child, but in fact this does not happen. Research with Finnish emigrant children in Swedish schools has raised a debate about the existence of a phenomenon which the Scandinavian researchers call "double semilingualism" (Paulston, 1976)—that of a person, placed in a bilingual setting, who appears to forget his or her first language more rapidly than he or she acquires the second one, resulting in knowledge of some of each language, but not enough of either to function adequately in school. These studies are "particularly significant in that both countries are highly developed, industrialized, modern societies with [high] school achievement norms both for children in Sweden and Finland. In addition, they are societies where problems of health-care, diet, and unemployment are not intervening variables. Such variables are often cited as contributory factors in the lack of school achievement by minority children; (Paulston, 1977, p. 159). Skutnabb-Kangas (1975, p. 4) points out that the studies which showed evidence of what these researchers call semilingualism all involve bilingual children from working-class homes belonging to a minority group, who are being instructed in the majority middle-class language, their own first language carrying low prestige in both the school which they must attend and the society in which they live.

Results of those studies uphold the hypothesis that those students who have best preserved their first language are also best in acquiring the second language. An examination of siblings showed that those who moved to Sweden at an average age of ten preserved their Finnish language skills at an almost normal level after four or five years of Swedish schooling and also approached the normal level of Swedish language skills for Swedish pupils their age. Those who moved at age twelve also achieved Swedish language skills well, although at a slower rate than the ten-year-olds. However, children under the age of six at the time of emigration and those born in Sweden often did not develop Swedish language skills beyond the twelve-year-old level, no matter how much schooling they had. Children who moved at age seven or eight, the age for beginning formal schooling in Sweden, underwent the most serious educational disturbance.

As Paulston (1977, p. 143) points out, the cognitive development of children in bilingual programs is poorly explored in empirical studies, probably because of the political danger of confronting some of the real educational issues of a child's total development. Such fears are based on those studies which gave rise to the belief that bilingualism is detrimental to the cognitive growth of a child. Ample evidence indicates that bilingualism in itself is not necessarily detrimental to the school achievement of most children, but rather is often highly beneficial. I trust that those of us who believe in the value of bilingual bicultural education are now sure enough of the ordinarily beneficial effects of bilingualism that we can confront some of the very realistic educational problems, apart from any political overtones, that those trying to teach bilingual children have to face. I also believe that by exploring some of these problem areas we will disarm much of the opposition which has been raised against bilingual education.

Assumptions Prevalent in Today's Schools

In order to understand better the reason for the nonlearner's inability to respond to regular teaching or remedial assistance, it is helpful to look at some present practices and assumptions in our schools. In many places, it is assumed that the child is ready for school at a certain chronological age (innate cognitive development happens just as innate bone and muscle development happens). If it is recognized that the child is not ready for school, then the parents are advised to delay entrance for another year, or the school system attempts to provide opportunities for the child to become ready (preschool programs such as Head Start, for example). What is done in such compensatory programs? The child's experience is expanded by group field trips, stories, art projects, etc. The child's vocabulary is expanded by learning to label and classify common objects, animals, workers, etc. And great emphasis is placed upon socialization, assisting the child to become more independent, and raising self-esteem through interaction with other children, usually in a nonstructured, completely child-centered situation. Repeated evaluations of such programs have shown that the children do expand their experience and vocabulary and do learn to share, work, and play with other children, but there is little evidence that the potential "nonlearners" in these programs actually become ready for school and therefore learn well in subsequent grades. The exception to this is mainly found in preschool programs which integrate a definite cognitive and linguistic developmental program with the young child's other social, emotional, and physical needs (Chazan and Cox, 1976, p. 197).

Two other assumptions very evident in many schools are that schools and teachers do not have a responsibility for especially assisting the "nonready" child, and that remedial or compensatory education is merely a matter of repeating endlessly the regular kindergarten through grade 3 reading and math curricula.

However, I strongly believe that every child has a right to learn, which means a right to be taught at a level and in a way that the child can learn. I also believe that every child, adult, and senior citizen can learn, if teaching begins at the level where previous learning has stopped and is conducted in a way that permits the individual to decompose and recompose previously acquired knowledge so that new knowledge can be integrated within the individual's cognitive and linguistic structure. I believe, therefore, that educators have a responsibility to teach in such a way that students can learn.

How can this be done for the nonlearner described above? A good start has been made in areas where educators go into the homes to help teach parents of young children how to use their ordinary times with the child in such a way that the child's cognitive and language development will be coordinated with his or her physical, emotional, and social development. Also, it is hoped that programs of parent and community education will help to lessen the numbers of nonready children in the future. However, with today's highly mobile society and the trend toward the employment of mothers of young children outside the home, it is likely that there will continue to be significant numbers of nonlearners attending our schools.

Probable Causes of Limited
Academic Competency in Some Children

What could be a probable cause of the limited language and academic competency of some children placed in a bilingual setting, and how might they be helped to attain their potential educational level? It is important to note that not all bilingual children from working-class minority groups have this limited competency. It is my hypothesis that the phenomenon is brought about by a combination of factors which includes linguistic, social, cognitive, emotional, physical, and environmental conditions.

From my experience and a review of current theories of language and cognitive development, bilingualism, and sociolinguistics, I propose that there is an integral and reciprocal relationship between cognitive and language development, and that both of these are affected by the quality and quantity of social interaction and environmental stimulation available to the child from birth on. If the regular acquisition of language skills is impeded by physical, social, environmental, or affective conditions, there will be a concurrent impediment in the development of cognitive skills, and vice versa. If the limitation or delay in the cognitive or linguistic developmental processes of the child lasts over a significant period of time—particularly during those years of extraordinary, fundamental development, ages birth to nine years—then it is likely that the child will display the type of school performance shown in the studies of the Finnish children and experienced daily in many U.S. classrooms.

A brief review of some of the major theories of language and cognitive development and some of the factors which affect development may help clarify the matter. Piaget's work on cognitive development remains the most influential and extensive. It basically describes stages through which every child passes in an invariant sequence, which is assumed to be a fixed feature of the interaction between the child and his or her environment. Thus these stages are both inherent in the child and dependent on experience (Wallace, 1976, p. 15). Operations of thought are internalized actions, and each child is an open, active, self-regulatory system which tends toward order through equilibration. As he or she matures, the child in interaction with the environment undergoes a change of perception, for example, and this can be seen as a disturbance of the child's previous cognitive equilibrium. The child then makes use of self-regulatory processes which restore equilibrium by producing new rules and concepts through decomposing and recombining those which he or she already possesses, thereby bringing the child to a new level of operational thought, a new structure of thinking. Thus, if the child's environment lacks stimulation, or is so cluttered that he or she cannot distinguish any specific experience long enough for it to make an impression, the child's innate processes of decomposition and recombination will not be fully used.

In contrast, Vygotsky, although maintaining an independent developmental course for language and thought, shows that at about the age of two the developmental curves of thought and language come together in the phenomenon of naming (1962, p. 119). In Vygotsky's concept, the function of language is first social, then egocentric, at which point it begins to serve as a means of regulating one's behavior and clarifying one's cognitive operations; later, egocentric speech turns into inner speech. This is the exact reverse of Piaget's sequence which proceeds from nonverbal autistic thought through egocentric thought and speech to socialized speech and logical thinking. According to Vygotsky (1962, p. 53), the use of language to serve as a means of regulating one's behavior and clarifying one's cognitive operations serves a facilitating role in the development of thought.

Vygotsky, and other psycholinguists who follow him, points to the fact that a child understands and responds to a word in a broad, general sense long before the specific symbolic concept of the word is grasped. Likewise, the toddler uttering that first important word pronounces only one word, but that word represents a whole sentence, or in reality a number of possible sentences (Vygotsky, 1962, p. 126), whose meaning usually becomes easily understood by the mother. The process of refining both the understanding and the communicative act through language takes place through the child's interplay with the environment, as the cognitive development helps to refine the symbolic language development and vice versa.

Following Vygotsky's work, Uznadze (Cummins and Gulutsan, 1975, p. 91) perceives the cognitive/linguistic development in terms of a set, similar to Piaget's concept of "assimilative schema," which disposes the individual to respond in a particular direction in any interaction with the environment. Thus, the child's set acts as a "filter to determine which stimuli the individual attends to and how he organizes them in order to make a response. Uznadze distinguishes two levels of mental activity—the level of sets or 'acts of everyday behavior' and the level of objectification which is the basis of conscious thought processes" (Cummins and Gulutsan, 1975, p. 91). The ability to objectify situations arises in the context of social interaction and is closely linked with language, through which the individual can halt a set by means of the process of objectification and then program a new set to organize the activity. Most children receive sufficient social interaction to reach the level of sets or acts of everyday behavior, and so our nonlearner is able to function satisfactorily in normal, everyday situations. However, the child must receive feedback from the social environment to internalize those functions on the higher level of objectification, so that these functions can later be used for the decomposition and recomposition process necessary to program new sets that will lead to the child's full intellectual development. Bruner (1973) notes that for school tasks, a child must be freed from the concrete, perceptual, context-bound uses of language, the sets of everyday behavior, for the more abstract functions. Bernstein (1971), Deutsch, (1965), and others have demonstrated the greater likelihood of a child raised by persons from lower socioeconomic levels to be less proficient in the elaborated code conducive to selective formal operations such as abstraction, integration, deduction, organization, etc.

Slobin, concerning himself with the child's strategies for organizing language, takes as a premise that in order for a child to construct a grammar "(1) he must be able to cognize the physical and social events which are encoded in language, and (2) he must be able to process, organize, and store linguistic information. That is, the cognitive prerequisites for the development of grammar relate to both the *meanings* and the *forms* of utterances" (Slobin, 1973, p. 176). Yet Chomsky (1968), McNeill (1970), and others postulate that the development of the child's mastery of the structures of language are largely determined innately. However, although the child may be able to master the fundamental structure of a language through innate processes, the function of the language seems to be more dependent upon social interaction. If the young child's home environment does not offer cognitively rich dialogue with adults so that the child can move to the cognitive level essential to a frame of reference for a meaningful language structure, or if the child's use of language in its function as part of the self-regulatory, clarifying device for the stabilization of a cognitive discovery does not receive appropriate response from another speaker, then the entire process of development can proceed only within a framework that is dangerously weakened by gaps in functions which form the rudiments of successive development in language and thought.

Hypothesis of Gaps in the Cognitive/Linguistic Developmental Network

I propose that these gaps in the cognitive and linguistic foundation of the child are the major cause of the nonlearner's inability to respond to instruction. These gaps can easily be disguised by the child's well-known ability to learn by rote. Thus, a child, through memorizing the correct, expected response to a given task or verbal interaction, can appear to have mastered a cognitive skill or a competency in language function which is not really there. Unfortunately, the empty spaces left in the construction of the various networks of thought and meaning, covered over by often meaningless use of words expressing very fuzzy notions, seldom cause the child major difficulty until he or she reaches the school system and is presumed to have a fully developed cognitive/linguistic competency at the kindergarten or first grade level. Even there, through rote the child may be able to progress through the first stages of the educational system making minimal progress, until the cognitive relationships which underlie subtle syntactic forms of coordination, subordination, causality, and reversibility become much more dominant in the instructional mode, usually by the third or fourth grade.

Although the child's apparently innate abilities to structure language and equilibrate may be functioning, insufficient environmental reinforcement inhibits the full development of that competency. If, in addition, the child is confronted with two language systems to be ordered and internalized, then the complexity of the task to be performed with limited external assistance is likely to result in even greater cognitive and linguistic confusion. John noted that "the use of language for purposes of problem solving unfolds at an accelerated pace between the ages of four and seven, the very time when [many] non-English-speaking children are exposed to a second language. Caught between two languages, the young child needs special assistance in organizing his world" (John, 1971, p. 63). Without that help, the child in a normal, psychologically healthy way responds to the complexity of the task by either ignoring the task or turning it into one he or she can handle, often with results that are totally meaningless.

An Initial Framework for
Possible Solutions to the Problem

Therefore, the challenge is to discover the means of filling up the gaps in the cognitive and language systems which somehow were left open during those critical years from birth to age seven, so that the child has a solid foundation upon which to build further cognitive and linguistic structure. This means that we must take the second grade child who cannot add two more to the three apples in the basket and end up with five apples, if there is not a means of memorizing the correct answer available, and move back one step to see if the child understands the concept of counting up to three by stopping at three. If the child cannot do that, then the process of teaching that basic cognitive area of seriation, including "beginning" and "end," must include not simply language, nor simply motor activity, but also an integrated motor, symbolic, and verbal recomposition of the previously learned concept of numbers to include the new concept of "counting up to" or "stopping at," and then the next new concept of "going farther" or "adding." If either the motor interaction with the child's environment (taking three steps, catching three balls, putting three objects in a box) or the linguistic expression of that interaction (symbolizing the action by means of words) are lacking, then the child will still not have an integrated, solid structure upon which to internalize further mathematical concepts or syntactic and semantic structures.

Instead of continuing our current approach to assisting nonlearners by extending language production (heavily using rote) or providing remediation several levels above that at which the child has his or her first big gaps in cognitive and language functioning, the diagnostic teacher should be ready and knowledgeable enough to return to the most fundamental stages of operational, enactive thought, and progress with the child through the various stages of cognitive development. The teacher should constantly use language as a clarifying, self-regulatory, refining, and integrating process. In this way the child has both the operational experience and the most abstract, verbal representation available to break down new complexes into manageable units which can then be reconstructed into new, meaningful structures at a higher level of thought and language.

Any child exhibiting signs of semilingualism should be instructed intensively in his or her dominant language exclusively, if at all possible, until the child has a sufficiently firm grasp of language and thought to be able to cope successfully with the added complexity of a second language system. It may also be that successful teaching of nonlearners in the bilingual classroom may influence the teaching processes in all classrooms, where undoubtedly monolingual children suffer from the same lack of a firm, integrated cognitive and linguistic foundation.

References

Bernstein, Basil. *Class, Codes and Control.* London: Routledge and Kegan Paul, 1971.

Bruner, Jerome. *Beyond the Information Given.* New York: W.W. Norton and Company, 1973.

Chazan, Maurice, and Cox, Theo. "Language Programmes for Disadvantaged Children," *Piaget, Psychology and Education.* Edited by V.P. Varma and P. Williams. London: Hodder and Stoughton, 1976.

Chomsky, Noel. *Language and Mind.* New York: Harcourt Brace Jovanovich, Inc., 1968.

Cummins, James, and Gulutsan, Metro. "Set, Objectification and Second Language Learning." *International Journal of Psychology* 10 (1975): 91-100.

Deutsch, Martin. "The Role of Social Class in Language Development and Cognition." *American Journal of Orthopsychiatry* 35 (1965): 78-88.

John, Vera. "Cognitive Development in the Bilingual Child." In *Monograph Series on Languages and Linguistics,* Vol. 23. Edited by James E. Alatis. Washington, D.C.: Georgetown University Press, 1971.

McNeill, D. *The Acquisition of Language: The Study of Developmental Psycholinguistics.* New York: Harper and Row, 1970.

Paulston, Christina Bratt. "Linguistic Aspects of Emigrant Children." Unpublished manuscript, 1976.

_____ . "Theoretical Perspectives on Bilingual Education Programs." *Working Papers on Bilingualism,* No. 13 (1977): 130-180.

Skutnabb-Kangas, Tove. "Bilingualism, Semilingualism and School Achievement." Paper presented at the Fourth International Congress of Applied Linguistics, Stuttgart, August 1975.

Slobin, D.I. "Cognitive Prerequisites for the Development of Grammar." In *Studies of Child Language Development*. Edited by C.A. Ferguson and D.I. Slobin. *Studies of Child Language Development*. New York: Holt, Rinehart and Winston, 1973.

Vygotsky, Lev. *Thought and Language*. Cambridge, Mass.: M.I.T. Press, 1962.

Wallace, J.G. "The Course of Cognitive Growth." In *Piaget, Psychology and Education*. Edited by V.P. Parma and P. Stoughton. London: Hodder and Stoughton, 1976.

Materials Development for Individualized Instruction in the Bilingual Classroom

Myriam Met
Cincinnati Public Schools
Cincinnati, Ohio

Vuong G. Thuy
Temple University
Philadelphia, Pennsylvania

Materials, particularly testing materials, dealing with cultures other than Anglo American are often found to be biased. In addition, commercial materials are generally written for certain groups of students. Therefore, commercial materials often do not meet individual student's needs.

Frequently, then, the teacher has to do something about the materials available in order to meet the instructional objectives and the needs of individual students. This problem is particularly acute in bilingual classrooms.

In the presentation or adaptation of materials, there are three principal variables: the teacher, the student, and the existing materials. The adaptation process itself involves a series of steps in order to render materials useful for individualized instruction.

Identification of the Student's Needs

Research, as well as common sense, tells us that instruction is improved when individual needs and differences are taken into account. By using various techniques including contrastive analysis, not only will the student's needs be determined, but also the differences affecting his or her learning and academic performance will be identified. The student's cultural, educational, linguistic, and socioeconomic background should also be taken into consideration. The knowledge of this background, including the learning and teaching styles with which the teacher is familiar, often leads to effective or affective teaching. Attention should be given to how physical and emotional needs influence the student's learning and performance.

Survey of Existing Materials

It is usually not feasible in terms of time and patience for the teacher to go through jungles of books and materials, or to search for appropriate but rare materials such as those needed in bilingual classrooms. Fortunately, there are always excellent sources which can help solve this problem, such as selected or annotated bibliographies, book reviews, educational and professional journals, and publishers' catalogs. As for bilingual educational needs, a national network for forty-two Title VII Bilingual Education Centers (twenty for resource and training; nineteen for materials development; and three for dissemination and assessment) can be good sources. These centers, funded by the Office of Bilingual Education, are located throughout the United States and serve various languages. Since they have close and cooperative relationships not only among themselves but also with various institutions in the country, their well-trained personnel can help in locating the needed materials. A large number of these centers have bilingual resource libraries.

Another source for help is teachers themselves. Through the years, many teachers have made their own materials because of the lack of appropriate materials to meet the instructional objectives and the needs of individual students. However, one should be careful with teacher-made materials because they have often been developed to meet the specific needs of a particular teacher or student.

Evaluation of the Student's Needs and Available Materials

After the student's needs and available materials have been identified, it is necessary to evaluate them to determine what should be done with the materials. The following are some suggested criteria:

1. *Student's Needs.* The student's needs can be evaluated by trying to find the answers to the questions below:
   a. *Immediate Needs*
      • What seems to *prevent* him from making steady learning

progress (cultural, educational, linguistic, socioeconomic, emotional factors, etc.)?
- What does he need in order to achieve steady learning progress?
- Can some of these needs be met by appropriate materials?

b. *Future Needs*
- What will he need to *maintain* steady learning progress?
- Can his future needs be met by the use of appropriate materials?

2. *Materials*. The following questions can help determine the appropriateness and quality of materials, depending on the instructional objectives and the student's identified needs:

a. Are the objectives of the material clearly manifested by the rationale of the author?

b. How consistent is the content of the materials with the objectives?

c. Are the teaching-learning methods used in the material sound?

d. Does the material have continuity of learning sequence?

e. Does the material show how it can be used by the teacher or student?

f. Is the material *technically* accurate (e.g., culturally and linguistically, as in the case of language materials)? Is it culturally biased?

g. Does the material provide the teacher or student with the tools to achieve whatever goal has been set?

h. Does the material provide sound devices to reinforce learning?

i. Does the material provide sufficient diagnostic and test instruments?

j. Does the material meet the identified needs, interests, and abilities of the student?

k. Does the material coordinate well with regular school curriculum?

l. Is the material easily adaptable to meet the identified needs of the student?

Adaptation

The adaptation or preparation of materials involves manipulating certain material items such as omitting, replacing, rearranging, and adding items to meet the student's specific needs and instructional objectives.

Testing of Teacher-made Materials

After materials have been adapted or prepared, they must be tested. Often they require modifications or changes. If that is the case, the above procedures must be repeated in the revision phase of materials adaptation or preparation.

Individualized Instruction

Individualized instruction allows for remediation, reinforcement, and enrichment of pupils' skills. Individually tailored materials may be designed to accommodate cultural and linguistic differences in pupils' learning styles and patterns. Or, materials can be adapted as explained above so that students may work individually, in small groups or teams. The most current means of individualizing instruction is the learning center.

In the learning center, learning is student managed. Students acquire, maintain, and extend their skills by working alone or with a limited number of other students without the direct supervision of the teacher. Materials are designed so that the presence of the teacher is not required: Students are presented with instructional objectives and directed to perform given activities to meet the stated objectives.

Often the student may choose from several activities, each of which allows him or her to meet the instructional objective in a different way. Since most materials are self-correcting (the student can tell immediately if he or she is right or wrong), the pupil receives immediate reinforcement. This instant feedback feature of learning center materials allows instructional recycling to occur much sooner, for the student and teacher know exactly what skills must yet be mastered.

The learning center provides a variety of approaches to mastering and practicing the instructional objectives and can be used to introduce new material or simply to reinforce large group instruction. It affords multiple opportunities to use a variety of sensory modalities with children. For example, those who learn best by listening use recordings for receiving instruction. Those who prefer tactile materials manipulate concrete objects. Those who need to "see it in writing," work with print media.

Teacher-made Materials and Individualized Instruction

In preparing instructional activities, the teacher must bear in mind some basic criteria. The teacher must have a clear idea of the instructional objectives and the student's needs with regard to those objectives. This implies a diagnostic/prescriptive approach in which instructional recycling is an integral component. Other criteria, as stated earlier, include an awareness of the student's cultural background, individual learning styles, and sensory mode preferences, all of which contribute to the design of effective individualized materials.

1. **Learning Center Materials: Tasks**

    Students involved in learning center activities may be required to perform a variety of tasks to develop comprehensive skills. They may listen and respond to audio-recorded materials. Students may view video-recorded materials (e.g., filmstrips) and perform follow-up activities as instructed. To develop sequencing skills, they may place picture or word cards in their correct order. Sorting activities develop classification skills and may be used to reinforce such concepts as the basic food groups; animals (mammals, reptiles, and other species); modes of transportation (land, sea, and air); and historical events (e.g., eighteenth, nineteenth, and twentieth centuries).

Probably the most common of all tasks is matching. Matching activities may be at the simple recognition level or may require higher-level skills. The following are some matching tasks which lend themselves well to individualized instructional materials:

a. two identical items (concentration) — important for prereading skills
b. lower-case with upper-case letters of the alphabet
c. roman with cardinal numbers
d. pictures with the initial consonant
e. spelling words with their pictures
f. synonyms, antonyms, homonyms, and homophones
g. go-togethers (comb-brush, chair-table)
h. singular/plural forms of words (wife/wives, libro/libros)
i. contractions (can/can't)
j. a picture with the sentence which describes it
k. grammatical transformations
   - past/present (have/had, voy/fui)
   - passive/active (John threw the ball/The ball was thrown by John)
   - pronominalization (Mario dió el libro a Juan/Se lo dió)
l. a historical event with the date
m. a historical event: cause/effect
n. a scientific cause/effect relationship
0. a mathematical operation and its result: ($15 \times 14/29$; areas of a circle: $2 \pi r_2$)

2. **Practical How-to's of Learning Center Materials: Formats**
   Activities for learning stations generally are developed for specific tasks and may take a variety of formats. Some formats, of course, lend themselves more easily to certain tasks than others. Below is a description of some very basic patterns for learning center activities:

   a. *Open-ended Game Boards*
      These activities are basically paths to be completed. Students begin at the start and advance along the path according to the rules established by the teacher (or students). The first one to reach the finish line wins. In the simplest version of this activity students roll the dice and advance the corresponding number of spaces if they answer a question correctly. The variations on this idea are infinite.

   b. *Open-ended Pictures*
      Pictures are pasted or drawn on paper or cardboard. Record a

series of questions on a cassette. The student listens to the cassette while looking at each picture. The student then responds to the questions (which may range from true/false to complete sentences). Instead of using a tape, you may write a series of questions on ditto sheets or cards; the student responds in writing. Students may also be asked to use the pictures as the basis of an original written exercise, ranging from one to two sentences to a composition.

c. *Classifying*

On a large sheet of paper, draw from four to five columns and from three to four horizontal lines. At the top of each column is a category designation. Make cards which correspond to the size of each box on the paper, and on each put the name or picture of an item which belongs to one of the categories. Students place cards in their corresponding category. Another approach is to use a bulletin board to which envelopes are attached; students sort the cards by placing them in the envelope for each category.

d. *Concentration*

Make two sets of cards, each set one half of a pair. Words or pictures may be used. Place all cards face down. Students try to match up the pairs. The student with the most pairs wins. Students may simply name matching items or find items that go together (shoe/sock). In an ESL classroom, negatives may be reviewed (e.g., card 1 — This is a ball; card 2 — This is *not* a ball).

e. *Bingo/Lotto Games*

Each student has a game card on which from six to twenty items are written or pictured. As the caller draws items at random, the student marks or covers the corresponding item on his card.

f. *Spinner Games*

Divide 9" circle (a pizza board is excellent) into eight to twelve wedges. Use a paper fastener to attach a spinner in the center. Students then turn the spinner and perform a task such as naming the picture the spinner points to. For example, fruits are pictured on the perimeter of the circle. As the spinner points, the student must name the fruit (or spell it) to place the fruit in his basket. The first student to collect one of each fruit wins.

h. *Clothespin Match-ups*

Divide a 9" circle into eight to ten wedges. In each wedge write, draw, or otherwise indicate one-half of a pair of items to be matched, and place the other half of the pair on a plastic clothespin. The student must place each clothespin on the corresponding wedge.

i. *Yarn Match-ups*

Divide a board (about 8½" by 11") into two columns and then

into five horizontal sections. In the column on the left, place five halves of matching pairs. In the column on the right, place the five other halves in random order. In the left column tie a length of yarn. Punch holes on the right hand column. Students match each pair of items by pulling the yarn from the left column through the hole on the right.

Variation

On the perimeter of a circle place a number of items. Punch a hole next to each. In the center draw or write one item. Tie the same number of strings in the center as there are items on the perimeter. Students are to connect the string to *only* those items on the perimeter that match the central item on some characteristic (e.g., they begin with the same letter, or the number in the center equals the number illustrated on the perimeter).

j. *Puzzle Halves*
On a card (about the size of a keypunch card) place a pair of items which match, one at each end of a card. Then, using a zig-zag motion, cut the card in halves (no two cards will ever be cut the same way). Students join the appropriate halves.

k. *Puzzle Match*
Remove the pieces from a framed hardboard puzzle of about twelve to thirty pieces. With a felt-tipped marker outline the spot where each piece belongs. Cut out pictures of matching pairs; in the outlined space place one half of a pair. Place the other half on the back of the corresponding puzzle piece. Students match up pairs by placing the puzzle pieces in the appropriate spots.

l. *Fishing*
Using a dowel from which a magnet is hung on a string, students "catch" fish from a basket. Fish may be cut from oak tag, with a paperclip or a few staples passed through each fish's mouth. Students keep each fish which they "earn" by identifying the picture, spelling a word, performing a mathematical operation correctly, etc.

m. *Popular Games*
Children's games, such as *Candyland* (for teaching colors) and *Chutes and Ladders* (for teaching numbers) are relatively inexpensive learning station activities. Others, such as *Silly Sandwich* and *Mother's Helper* may be adapted for developing language skills in the ESL classroom.

3. **Providing Feedback**
Many of the tasks and formats discussed above lend themselves well to pupil self-evaluation. If materials are properly designed, students may work independently of the teacher, and yet get immediate feedback on

the correctness of their response. In classifying activities, materials may be made so that only the correct number of items in a category will fit in the space provided (e.g., four spaces correspond to the four items which should be placed in that category). Some matching activities often have a built-in correcting device since there is only one correct match for a given item. Additional feedback may be provided using color coding: On the back of clothespin match-up wheels or yarn match-ups a different color dot is placed for each item. When colored clothespins are used, the student can check the color of the clothespin with that on the circle. If wooden clothespins are used, the colored dot is placed on the back of the clothespin. In yarn match-ups, the color of the dot is placed on the back of the right half. Puzzle matches are self-correcting in that only the pieces that fit together will form a match.

What Should the Teacher Make?

It should be clear from the previous discussion that making or adapting materials for the classroom involves choices and decisions. Decisions can be facilitated if the teacher has first done a thorough needs assessment. The teacher must also have an explicit philosophy of how pupils best learn, for it is this philosophy that determines how instructional materials are to be presented to the students. Further, the teacher must decide how the material is to be used. Will it precede, replace, or reinforce direct instruction from the teacher? Will the materials be used by students individually, in small groups, or in larger groups? Are the materials suitable for children with limited skills? Other considerations include providing ways for students to check, correct, and prescribe their own work. Since making or adapting learning materials takes time, teachers may wish to design them so that they may be used by children at varying achievement levels. A good example of this is open-ended pictures which can be used by children with limited or extended skills alike. By including different instructions for each ability level, the teacher can expand the scope of the materials.

Some Handy Tips

Discarded texts and workbooks are excellent sources of pictures, word and math problems, etc. The opaque projector is useful for tracing or enlarging pictures for those who lack drawing skills. Garage sales and bazaars are excellent sources for dice, game boards, old puzzles, etc.

Organizing for Independent Work

The effectiveness of independent learning activities is enhanced by proper management techniques. The teacher must not only design materials on the basis of student's needs, but also ensure that students have adequate opportunity to use them. Teachers must schedule time for pupils at learning stations, and perhaps assign work with specific materials. Good management techniques also include clear instructions on the purpose and use of materials. Pupils should know where to be, when they are to be there, what to do when they get there, and where to store materials when done. Directions should be both oral and posted in writing. Provision should be made for evaluation of pupil progress.

Time and Money

It is a truism of our technological society that many of our time-saving devices cost us dollars. This is certainly true in the kitchen where convenience foods save time but are more costly than cooking from scratch. There are many who believe that convenient foods can't match the quality of a homecooked meal. The kitchen is analogous to the classroom. Teacher-made materials *do* take time to make, but cost less. However, the real benefit is to the children — for teacher-developed materials are especially tailored to individual students' needs, interests, and abilities.

References

Forte, Emogene, and Mackencie, Joy. *Nooks, Crannies and Corners.* Nashville, Tenn.: Incentive Publications, 1973.

_____ et. al. *Center Stuff for Nooks, Crannies and Corners.* Nashville, Tenn.: Incentive Publications, 1973.

Helstrom, Carole. *Learning Centers and Teacher Made Materials K-6.* Englewood, Colo.: Educational Consultant Associates (n.d.).

Herr, Selma E. *Learning Activities for Reading.* Dubuque, Iowa: William C. Brown, 1961.

Iorton, Mary B. *Activity-Centered Learning for Early Childhood.* Reading, Mass.: Addison Wesley, 1972.

Kaplan, S.N. et. al. *Change for Children.* Santa Monica, Calif.: Goodyear Publishing Company, 1973.

Sancho, Anthony R. *Creating for Bilingual-Bicultural Learning Centers.* Newport Beach, California: Chess and Associates, 1975.

Voight, Ralph Claude. *Invitation to Learning: The Learning Center Handbook, Vol. I.* Washington, D.C.: Acropolis Books, Ltd., 1974.

_____ . *Invitation to Learning: Center Teaching with Instructional Depth, Vol. II.* Washington, D.C.: Acropolis Books, Ltd., 1974.

Language Experience for the Bilingual Child

Nancy Hansen-Krening
University of Washington
Seattle, Washington

Teachers of bilingual children frequently ask, "How do we take our students from a spoken second language to using that language in reading and writing?" "Language experience" has been one answer to that question.

Language experience is a commonsense approach to using oral language for teaching skills in listening, speaking, reading, and writing. Language experience uses the existing language and experiences of the bilingual bicultural child to create self-written reading material for that child.

In this approach, the communication cycle begins with the bilingual bicultural child's out-of-school experiences. The language is the language of the child and the experiences are the experiences of the child. Slowly this cycle turns and expands as the teacher introduces the language to be learned and presents new experiences for the child to participate in, think about, and discuss. The child is actively involved in a continuous process of listening, speaking, writing, and reading. For example, the child first writes stories about his or her family, friends, or any important out-of-school experience. Whether this is a story dictated to the teacher or a story written by the child, the language is the conversational language of the child and the experiences are experiences that the child wants to record in print; neither language nor experience is shaped by the teacher. After the story is completed, the child uses that story for reading material. Gradually *teacher*-planned activities are introduced as a stimulus for reading and writing. Then the student's stories reflect individual responses to those teacher-planned activities. As the students become involved in these new experiences, the teacher supplies labels for developing concepts and introduces new language to label those experiences. As the children become involved in the learning process, they expand their listening, speaking, reading, and writing vocabularies. As their vocabularies grow, children understand more of what they hear and speak; their reading and writing vocabularies grow even more as their comprehension at all levels is increased.

Basic Skills

Within the integrated, cyclical process of learning communication skills, bilingual bicultural children are also learning, through language experiences, basic decoding and comprehension skills. This is done in a natural, uncontrived manner because language experience establishes an immediate purpose for learning those skills. For instance, rather than learning sound-symbol relationships (phonics) in isolation, children literally see that letters represent spoken sounds, spoken words. They first watch as the teacher forms letters and words to represent the student's spoken words. As their writing skills develop, the students themselves begin to make sound-symbol relationships and use those relationships to symbolize the sounds of their new language. They see the purpose for learning printed symbols and the sounds those symbols represent. Conceptualizing the sound-symbol relationship is a crucial first step in becoming independent, successful readers and writers.

As they are learning these sound-symbol relationships, children are also, in context, learning the purpose of a standardized spelling of the symbols for spoken words. They learn that a standard form of spelling enables other people over a variety of geographical areas to read and understand their writing. Students also see the practical need for legible printing or handwriting. By using their own stories for reading material, students quickly realize that illegible printing or handwriting interferes with reading.

Language experience also ensures an immediate relationship between the bilingual child's listening and speaking vocabulary and his or her reading and writing vocabularies. Developmentally, listening and speaking vocabularies form the basis for reading and writing vocabularies. These four vocabularies, in combination, are often called "meaning" vocabularies because they represent words for which children have meaning. In any reading program, what a child understands and can use in print is determined by what he or she already understands in oral language. Teachers who use language experience use the child's oral language to prepare reading materials for that same child. This guarantees a match of listening and speaking vocabularies with reading and writing vocabularies. Using the child's oral language is not a limiting process, because the teacher is responsible for planning new experiences which will expand the child's meaning vocabularies. It is a continuous process of growth.

The Child

The bilingual child is the primary resource for the teacher of reading and language arts. It is the child who creates learning material — not a book, not a workbook, not a dittoed worksheet, but the child. Because this is demonstrated overtly every day, language experience constantly validates the child as a valuable, worthwhile entity. It esteems the student's out-of-school life. It uses rather than abuses the child's home language and culture. It says, "You are important. You have something to say that I want to hear." Individuals are respected. Differences are respected. Language is respected. As this respect is established, the children also gain mastery of new experiences and a new language.

All of these factors combine to create a sense of power, a sense of control in children. The individual child feels in control of what is being learned and what is being done. This feeling of control, of power, gives students a sense of self-direction and self-confidence, and a belief in their problem-solving abilities. These feelings are critical elements in effective learning.

Practical Application

There is a definite sequence in using language experience:

Step 1. At the first level or step in language experience, the teacher uses the experiences and the oral language of the child to initiate learning. For example, the teacher may simply have the student paint a picture of a favorite animal, anything that would stimulate the child's language and experience. Once the picture is finished, the teacher might say, "Let's talk about your picture, Anna." Anna might point to her picture and say, "Puppy." The teacher would then write the word "puppy" by Anna's picture. The teacher always accepts what the child says and records it verbatim. One-word stories, for instance, are not unusual with some children. One-word responses or expressions are an initial step in the developmental acquisition of more complex syntax.

Once she or he has recorded the child's word or words, the teacher reads what was written to the child. The child then reads the story to the teacher. This is an initial step in the bilingual child's transition from oral language to reading and writing. It also marks the initial acquisition of a sign vocabulary.

Step 2. At this step, the child is expected to dictate complete sentences. The teacher may still be totally responsible for taking dictation for the child. The teacher continues to read the sentences to the child, and the child then reads the sentences back to the teacher. After reading to the teacher, a student should be encouraged to read to his or her classmates.

Older students may now begin to shape their stories into simple paragraphs. Illustrations may become more detailed and as they do so, they may be used to stimulate a greater production of language. Art is more abstract than the actual object, but it is less abstract than words; because of this, it may act as a point of reference in stimulating writing. Another advantage of using illustrations is that a specific picture usually focuses on a particular topic; by identifying the main idea of a picture, children become familiar with the concept of topics and main ideas. In writing about those topics in their stories, they learn about the use of topic sentences in writing and reading.

Step 3. At this step the teacher encourages children to write one or two words on their own. Because of steps 1 and 2, the students have begun to develop a sight vocabulary and they use this vocabulary in their writing. If the teacher knows that the children can read a particular word, the teacher leaves a space for them to write the word in. Teachers will note that there is a close match between high-frequency sight words (as in the Dolch word list) and the words used in student stories. Because sight word vocabularies are growing, students can now open trade books and recognize words in print.

It is also at this step that specific work on phonics begins. Again, the adult draws upon the child's developing sight vocabulary. Using this vocabulary, the teacher identifies a series of words that represent the same initial sound or a particular phonics generalization and asks what the words have in common. For instance, Ben might have the words *book, baby,* and *bounce* in his sight vocabulary. The teacher would have him pronounce these words as she or he points to them. The purpose is for Ben to learn that the letter B represents a particular spoken sound. The teacher would then ask Ben, "What do you see about these words?" or, "What is the first letter of each word?" Later, when Ben is dictating another story, the teacher would consistently point out or ask Ben to point out other words that begin with the same sound. Ben would, at this time, be encouraged to write the first sounds he heard in words. This type of activity can be done with either one student or an entire class.

Step 4. At this stage bilingual students are ready to assume the major responsibility for their own writing. It is now that the students demonstrate their understanding of sound-symbol relationships in composing words. They must be encouraged to spell whole words entirely on their own. This does mean that there will be idiosyncratic spelling of words, but it also means that children become more self-directed, independent, and, most importantly, they experiment with the language which forms the basis for public school language.

As children now begin to branch out into reading commercially printed books, as they begin to share their writing with broader audiences, they become aware, both directly and indirectly, that there are standard forms for communication. These are not arbitrarily imposed standards, but rather are required for sharing written expressions with the broadest possible audience. Students learn that there is a practical, reasonable *purpose* for learning and using specific forms in transmitting messages to others.

Step 5. This is a demanding stage. Students are now actually required to correct misspelled words, work with standard usage, and conform to the requirements of capitalization and punctuation. At this step, they are moving from teacher-initiated corrections to proofreading and correcting their own work. Once they have demonstrated basic oral competency in the spontaneous use of their newly acquired language, they are ready to assume the responsibility for self-correction. As an aid to independent proofreading, students should read their writing aloud either to themselves or to another student. This technique helps them to hear where punctuation marks belong and where there is awkward, confusing, or incorrect syntax. This process also underlines the relationship between oral language and language that is written. Once the students have corrected the story and have rewritten it, they may go over the writing with the teacher. At this point, the teacher is able to evaluate pupil progress in reading and writing skill development; the teacher is also able to prescribe further work according to the individual's needs.

A Caution

There will be a broad range of abilities at every level. For some students, the first words that they write are words that must be spelled perfectly and written perfectly. For example, students may be able to produce only a few words in the second language, yet if they write these words themselves, they insist that the teacher tell them the correct spelling. These students are not satisfied with approximations in spelling or idiosyncratic spellings (as in stage 3). There are children at all of the beginning stages who may insist upon correction of misspelled words and standard usage, as well as correct capitalization and punctuation.

Some students will move quickly through all five of the stages, while other students will move very slowly. The stages are not absolutes, they are general and flexible.

Providing Variety in Language Experience

Language experience uses a variety of expressive forms. It cannot (and should not) always depend upon children's having a planned experience, drawing a picture about that experience, writing about the experience, and finally, reading what they have written. In any time of sustained learning environment, variety is necessary in order to sustain the interest in learning.

Fortunately, all forms of the arts lend themselves to use in language experience. The following are some ideas that can be used as both the planned experience for the child and as the form used for responses to that planned experience; with each set of activities, important reading and writing skills have been noted:

1. Music. Children are often less inhibited in music than they are in reading and writing. Because of this, children who are reluctant to express themselves in any other activity will become engrossed in writing lyrics for melodies. As they are composing and recording these lyrics, they are working with auditory discrimination, auditory memory, sequencing, and recalling details.

2. Art. Art encompasses many activities other than painting, drawing, and coloring; it also includes weaving, making banners and cloth pictures, stitchery, clay objects, and draft constructions (such as kites). Since art is a mediating symbol system, representing actual objects, it is more concrete than the printed word, yet less concrete than the actual object. Art objects may be used to stimulate and develop descriptive language which may be used in writing captions, titles, labels, and brief paragraphs or short stories.

3. Creative Movement. Movement exploration and creative movement help children develop such important concepts as space, time, weight, and force (large/small, slow/fast, heavy/light, push/pull). Children have direct experience with learning both variations of a particular movement and with words that describe that variation. Concepts grow and expand, which in turn expand the child's listening, speaking, reading, and writing meaning vocabularies.

4. Creative Dramatics. Reading comprehension is often difficult to teach bilingual children. There are many cultural and experiential nuances operating in comprehension of written and spoken languages. Because of differences among languages, and because it is difficult to assess the quality or depth of another person's level of comprehension — we frequently understand more than we can express with words — it may be necessary to employ alternative modes of expression. Creative dramatics allows children to express what they understand both with and without words. Either verbally or nonverbally, creative dramatics requires that children maintain a sequence of events, identify main ideas, remember details of the action and plot, interpret characters, and distinguish fact from fantasy. It teaches comprehension skills while allowing the teacher to assess each student's level of comprehension.

A Sample Lesson

The following is a suggested language experience lesson plan for a small group. Although the lesson focuses on describing textures, it could also include names of objects and colors. The uses would be determined by the needs and abilities of the students.

Objectives:	To provide learning experiences for bilingual bicultural children. To develop oral language of bilingual children.
For:	Children who possess almost no skills in reading and writing and whose verbal skills are just being developed.

First Day

Materials:	Have available various rough and smooth articles — bark, stones, plastic transparency, glass, satin, sand paper, scouring pad, cleaning brush, aluminum foil, objects around the classroom.

Lesson:

1. Introduce the concept of rough and smooth by holding up a piece of sand paper and a piece of plastic transparency. Identify each one separately and call them rough and smooth. Discuss with the children how the objects feel as they are passed around and try to think of other words that describe rough and smooth (bumpy, scratchy, etc.). Continue with other items listed and elicit from children how the articles feel.
2. Play a game requiring the students to take turns finding objects in the classroom that are rough or smooth.

Learning Center: Place the classroom objects on a table. Have the children sort them into groups of rough and smooth. They may label the objects in both their first and second languages.

Second Day

Materials:	Have corn meal, rice, fingerpaint, and water in flat containers such as a 9" x 13" cake pan; also a blindfold and a pan with soapy water. Have six bags and worksheets color coded. Worksheets should have six circles, one above each color. Inside the bags place rough and smooth textures (one in each). Have available sandblocks, tambourine, sticks, triangle.

Lesson:

1. Using the above textures, discuss how the children think the materials (rice, cornmeal, etc.) would feel if they could touch them. Blindfolded, they

> feel textures, trying to guess what they are and describing each texture.
>
> 2. Discuss the musical instruments, pass them around to see how they feel, then listen to the sounds of each one and discuss how the sounds differ. Try to elicit the concept that the sandblocks sound rough or scratchy, sticks rubbing together do not sound scratchy. Repeat activity with tambourine and triangle.

Learning Center: Have bags and color-coded worksheets available. The child reaches into bag without looking and feels the texture inside. If he or she likes to feel it, the child draws a happy face in the color-coded circle that matches the bag. If not, he or she draws a sad face.

Third Day

Materials: Provide a container to collect textured objects, large chart paper, construction paper, textured materials, paste, and crayons at learning center.

Lesson:
1. Take a walk with children to collect textured materials.
2. List rough and smooth objects and, if possible, put up a picture of each object beside the word.

Learning Center: Have materials available to make a texture collage — those collected during walk can be used.

Fourth Day

Materials: Have available tape and the filmstrip *Bumpy Lumpy* (Scholastic Beginning Concept, CSC Number VPM 74-25 FSS), filmstrip projector, screen, and tape recorder. Mark twenty texture blocks — 2" x 2" squares of wood or heavy tag. Fasten to the tops of two of each square materials of ten different texture. Use toweling, tacks, shells, wire, nails, macaroni, carpet, foam rubber, sand, or aluminum foil. A blindfold is needed.

Lesson: Show filmstrip and tape above. Show again, omitting the tape and allow the children to describe the textures they see.

Learning Center: Use texture blocks here. The blindfolded child picks up a block and must feel to find the identical block.

After matching all ten textures, he or she removes the blindfold and checks to see if he or she was right.

Fifth Day

Materials: Bring fresh pineapple, banana, coconut (shredded), and carrot. Have envelopes, scissors, and magazines at the learning center.

Lesson: Using the above food, feel the outside and describe, then compare it with the texture on the inside—are they the same or different, does the texture change as you chew it? Taste and discuss the food.

Learning Center: Have magazines available. Children may cut out and put in an envelope pictures of things they like to feel. This will be used later in the day for the children to share with the group.

Sixth Day

Materials: Collect pictures of rough and smooth objects. Put rough and smooth textures, pencils, paper divided by a line down the center, and a sample of finished project at learning center.

Lesson:
1. Discuss body parts and how they feel—edges of teeth and fingernails feel rough, skin feels smooth, etc.
2. Using pictures, sort according to rough and smooth. "If you could touch it, how would it feel?"
3. Ask children to bring something from home they like to feel.

Learning Center: The children, with your help, may write "rough" and "smooth," one on each side of the middle line of the paper. The children will choose an example of each and paste it under the descriptive word.

Seventh Day

Materials: Texture blocks, burlap or loose netting for weaving, yarn, plastic strips, grasses, and large teacher-made plastic needles.

Lesson:
1. Each child shares with the class textures brought from home and add to chart started on the third day.
2. Weave textures into netting.

Learning Center: Use texture blocks again.

Evaluation: The children will be able to:
1. Classify rough and smooth objects
2. Classify pictures that look rough or smooth
3. Use the descriptive words in other relevant situations
4. Begin to recognize and read the words in print.

Summary

It is an enormous challenge for teachers to work with students who are just beginning to make the transition from oral language to language in print. These children have a limited repertoire of public school language, yet they face great demands upon that language. They are required to develop mastery of a new set of symbols while almost simultaneously using those symbols expressively and receptively.

Language experience may or may not be a panacea for teachers and children, but it has demonstrated its value for bilingual children. It is a common-sense approach for helping bilingual children make the transition from oral language to language in print. It is more than simply a stopgap measure until something better comes along.

Social Factors in Second-Language Acquisition: Peer-Tutoring Intervention

Donna M. Johnson
RMC Research Corporation
Mountain View, California

Diane August
Stanford, California

This paper describes two studies that are currently being conducted through Stanford University. Both studies (Johnson, August) examine the effects of a peer-tutoring treatment designed to promote second-language acquisition through social interaction.

At a time when there are increasing numbers of limited-English-speaking students in the schools, and educators are required by law to meet their educational needs and to teach them English, there is still a serious lack of information concerning just how children acquire a second language (L_2) and how classrooms can be structured to promote second-language learning.

Quite often limited-English-speaking children are segregated from their native English-speaking peers for much of the school day. This common practice, accompanied by formal English instruction based upon techniques originally designed for adults, may not provide the best possible opportunity for rapid second-language acquisition.

We know from the literature on first-language and second-language acquisition and from experience that adequate exposure to language in use is essential for learning a language. It follows that the more language input the learner is exposed to, the faster the language should be acquired. However, one problem is that in school settings teachers have only so much time that can be devoted to interacting with each child. So, to learn a second language, children must make use of the language input they can get from their peers.

Two recent studies have demonstrated that learners vary in their ability and motivation to gain access to and make use of second-language input. Seliger (1977) studied a group of adults in an English as a Second Language (ESL) class over a period of one semester. He identified two types of students which he termed high-input generators and low-input generators. High-input generators were those students who initiated a large number of verbal interactions with their fellow students in the target language and thus got both the necessary input and the opportunity for involvement and practice. He found that these students made the greatest gain on final tests, particularly on measures of functional ability. The more they created practice situations for themselves, the more they learned.

Wong Fillmore (1976) conducted a longitudinal study of five children who were learning English as a second language, observing each one for an hour weekly as he or she played in a playroom with an English-speaking friend. She found that the children varied greatly in the way they approached the task of learning English and, as a result, achieved widely different levels of proficiency after one school year. The children who learned the least English were those who shied away from social interaction with English speakers, while the successful learners were those who were able to establish and maintain social contact with peers and adults who could give them the kind of input they needed for learning.

The most successful learners used what Wong Fillmore called social strategies, such as the following:

1. Joining a group and acting as though they understood what was going on even if they didn't

2. Giving the impression that they could speak the language by using a few well-chosen words

3. Counting on their friends for lots of help.

She noticed that the children's friends helped in several ways:

1. They believed that their friends could learn and acted on this belief by including them in their activities.

2. They made a real effort to understand what the learners were saying.

3. They provided the learners with linguistic input that could be understood.

The speech of their friends had certain characteristics that made it easy to understand. It was simplified yet entirely natural speech. It was repetitive. It was contextualized; that is, it was closely related to the activities the children were involved in at the moment. In addition, it was accompanied by gestures that helped to make meanings clearer.

So, if children can provide this kind of language input for one another, and if adequate exposure to such input is necessary for learning, then we need to find ways to help children get more access to this kind of input and to make good use of it. This is the purpose of the studies described herein.

In order to promote friendships and verbal interaction between second-language learners and fluent speakers of the second language, a peer-tutoring treatment was developed. There is a body of literature on peer tutoring (Allen, 1976), but the peer-tutoring treatment in the present studies is different from most peer-tutoring situations in that the goal of the tutoring sessions is to increase language practice during the rest of the day. In most of the peer-tutoring literature, the tutor is academically superior to the tutee and the outcomes investigated are generally achievement in the subject matter and attitudes toward the subject matter and school. Social outcomes are generally not examined. The more relevant literature comes from the sociology of education. Some scholars have demonstrated that working cooperatively in ethnically mixed small groups on a common task can promote cross-cultural friendships (Johnson and Johnson, 1979). In one such study by Hollifield (1978), conducted with ten-year-olds, students worked cooperatively in groups to study one part of a lesson and then to teach that part to other group members. As a result, they viewed their classmates as learning resources and increased their liking of group members. This is the kind of finding expected in the current studies. It is hoped that increased liking for the tutoring partner will lead to more communication in the second language and thus to more second-language learning.

Johnson Study

The first study was conducted in the summer of 1978 and the data are currently being analyzed. The hypotheses being investigated are the following:

1. Limited-English-speaking Mexican American children who undergo a peer tutoring treatment will interact verbally with fluent English speakers to a greater extent than will limited-English-speaking Mexican American children in a control group.

2. Limited-English-speaking Mexican American children who interact verbally to a greater extent with fluent English speakers will make more growth in English language proficiency than will limited-English-speaking Mexican American children who interact to a lesser degree with fluent English speakers.

Subjects. The primary subjects were sixteen Mexican American children from a school district in Mountain View, California. They were all fluent speakers of Spanish and all spoke some English, although their proficiency in English was limited. This group of students will be referred to as LES children. The study focused on their acquisition of English as a second language. The other participants in the study were eighteen fluent English speakers (FESs) from the Palo Alto-Stanford area. They were mostly Anglo Americans and knew no Spanish. No data were collected on these children, although they participated in the study by interacting with the LES children. The children ranged between five and nine years of age.

Setting. All thirty-four children were attending a seven-week bilingual summer program at Stanford's experimental school. It was a daycamp program with an open-classroom atmosphere and a wide range of activities for the children to choose from, both indoors and outdoors. The program was bilingual only in the sense that both English and Spanish were used by students and teachers, and a limited number of ESL and SSL vocabulary lessons were provided. There were some large group and small group activities directed by teachers, but for the most part, children were free to choose their own activities and their own playmates. The LES children attended three days a week for a total of twenty-one days. There were five teachers, three full time and two half time. Two were monolingual English speakers, two were fluent Spanish speakers, and one had a fair degree of proficiency in Spanish.

Overview of design. A matched pairs experimental design was employed. During the first week of the program all LES children were pretested on three measures of English language proficiency: the Peabody Picture Vocabulary Test (Dunn, 1965), the Language Assessment Scales (DeAvila and Duncan, 1977), and the Child-Child Communication Test developed by the researcher (Johnson, 1978). Also, during the first week, all LES children were observed to determine the degree to which they interacted in English with fluent English speakers (FESs). The Language Use and Interaction System (LUIS) was developed by the researcher for this purpose. Children were then matched on the basis of two variables: (1) overall English language proficiency as measured by the three tests, and (2) frequency of interaction in English with FESs as measured by the LUIS. Then members of the matched pairs were randomly assigned to a treatment and a control group.

The treatment was then carried out for a five-week period. It consisted of structured peer tutoring sessions in which LES children were paired with FES children. Control children worked on the same tasks, but under the direction of a teacher. All LES children were observed weekly during their free time to record their language use and interaction patterns. During the last week of the program, after the treatment had terminated, the LES children were posttested on the same three proficiency measures and were observed again for verbal interactions.

Observations. To measure the quantity and type of verbal interactions in which the students engaged, the Language Use and Interaction System was employed. The basic idea came from a coding and tabulation system used by Seliger in his study (1977), but the format is based on Stalling's Five Minute Observation System (1977). Observers focussed on one child at a time and the basic unit they coded was the utterance. The instrument allows for recording information concerning (1) the type of utterance (whether an initiation or a noninitiation); (2) characteristics of the person the child is addressing, such as language classification (LES or FES), whether a student or a teacher, whether an individual or a group; and (3) the language of the utterance (Spanish, English or codeswitching). In addition, information about the setting is recorded, including location, group size, teacher presence and role, activity, and who selected the activity.

Subjects were observed outside the treatment situation at times when they were free to interact with children of their own choice and to use the language of their choice. Observers attempted to be as unobtrusive as possible and when children asked what they were doing they said they were counting things; that response seemed to satisfy the children's curiosity. Each LES child was observed for forty minutes before and after the five-week treatment. In addition, during the five-week treatment period, each child was observed for twenty minutes each week. All observations were conducted in four equal time segments throughout a day.

Language proficiency testing. The three measures of English language proficiency were administered during the first and last weeks of the program, before and after the treatment. Forty items of the Peabody Picture Vocabulary Test, which measures comprehension of vocabulary, were administered. In this test, a vocabulary word is read to the student and he or she chooses the correct picture from a plate of four pictures. The Language Assessment Scales is an overall proficiency test with sections on comprehension and production of phonology, vocabulary production, syntax comprehension, and a story retelling task. It was administered and scored according to the publisher's instructions. The Child-Child Communication Test was developed in order to measure the kind of language children would be likely to learn by interacting with one another in an open-classroom setting. It involves a comprehension-imitation-production task and contains seven items. Each item is a picture of two children engaged in dialogue in a school situation. The tester explains each situation briefly in Spanish, then supplies the dialogue in English, and the child has to recreate the conversation. The child's speech is recorded and later rated against four criteria: quantity, grammaticality, comprehensibility, and appropriateness. The rating scale used is an adaptation of one developed by Overall (1978).

Treatment. The treatment consisted of structured peer-tutoring sessions. This was not the usual kind of peer tutoring in which the tutor helps out an underachieving tutee. The peer teaching in this study had a different purpose: to provide a structured setting for meaningful conversation through an exchange of information between a Spanish-dominant student and an English-speaking student. The outcome of interest was a social one. How would these sessions affect the students' behavior during the rest of the day? Would they choose to interact with their tutoring partners and children of the other language group?

The entire treatment session lasted about one hour, with the first thirty minutes devoted to training the tutors and the last thirty minutes devoted to peer tutoring. During the first thirty minutes, half of the treatment group children were taken aside and trained. This group included four LES and four FES children. Training consisted of teaching them an activity such as a cooking, science, or art project using primarily English. They were also taught the English vocabulary necessary to discuss each step of the activity. These eight children were designated as tutors for the day. Meanwhile the rest of the treatment group and all of the control group children were outside together engaged in free play.

During the second half-hour, the actual peer tutoring took place. Each of the eight trained tutors was paired with a tutee with whom he or she was compatible. The pairs were spread out around the room as much as possible and the tutors instructed their tutees. Two teachers supervised, but they let the children do the instructing. Language use for tutoring was English, since the FES children could not speak or understand Spanish. Meanwhile the control group was outside engaged in the same activity, but directed by a teacher. A control for curriculum was imposed by providing both groups with the same activities. Teacher effects were controlled by having teachers alternate weekly between the treatment and the control group for the one-hour session. The roles of the children as tutors or tutees alternated daily so that each child spent as many sessions in the tutee role as in the tutor role.

Expected findings. The data analysis is currently in progress but the expected findings are that (1) as a result of the peer tutoring experience, the children in the treatment group will interact in English with FESs during their free time more than children in the control group, and (2) those children who practice speaking English the most will achieve the most growth in English language proficiency.

August Study

A second study is currently being conducted which investigates the same hypotheses as the Johnson study. However, some of the procedures have been modified, and the study consists of two experiments. The first (referred to as the ESL experiment) investigates English language acquisition, and data collection was completed in April 1979. The second (referred to as the Spanish language experiment) examines Spanish language acquisition and is now in progress.

Setting. The setting for the August study is a public elementary school in Mountain View, California. The school population is largely lower social class, and is ethnically mixed. There are Anglo, Black, Filipino, and Mexican American children. Some of the Mexican American children are Spanish dominant, some are balanced bilinguals, and some speak only English.

Procedures for ESL experiment. In the ESL experiment the group under study was composed of fourteen limited-English-speaking (LES) Mexican American children. As in the Johnson study, to assess English language proficiency among these children, the Language Assessment Scales (LAS) and the Peabody Picture Vocabulary Test (PPVT) were administered. These language tests may not be sensitive to the kind of language gained as a result of verbal interactions. In order to make the LAS more sensitive to gains in communicative proficiency, the story recall task was scored differently. In the story recall task the child listens to a tape-recorded story and then must retell the story in his or her own words. To score the story, the rating scale was changed from a five-point scale to a ten-point scale in order to allow for the measurement of more variability in proficiency. In addition, the language sample obtained from the story retelling task was scored according to total words produced, mean length of utterance, and errors per 100 morphemes. In addition to the language proficiency tests, language samples of all the children were obtained. Each child was tape-recorded while teaching an activity to another child in English. Each child was taped once before the treatment began and once immediately after the treatment took place, each time with the same partner. These language samples provided more detailed information on the child's communicative proficiency.

In order to measure the amount of verbal interaction in English, the Language Use and Interaction System was adapted so it would be appropriate to this situation. Since the Mexican American children in this study were either dominant in Spanish, balanced bilinguals, or non-Spanish speaking, the categories of addressee were changed to reflect this. In addition, in order to simplify the instrument, only utterances and not initiations were coded.

The treatment itself was quite similar to that in the Johnson study. There were several differences, however. In the Johnson study, tutees were assigned to compatible tutors by the research assistant. In this study the LES children were given the opportunity to practice initiating interactions with the children who were dominant in the language they were learning. First, they were trained as tutors during their regular ESL class time. Then, during lunch recess each LES child chose an FES child to invite back to an activity center. The LES child was always the tutor and taught the activity to the FES friend. The LES tutor didn't redo the project, but only instructed his or her partner in the task. The children in the control group continued to receive their customary ESL instruction in the Distar Oral Language Program. During lunch recess they were in free play as usual. In addition, it was felt that the length of the treatment in the Johnson study was too short, so it was increased from fourteen one-hour sessions to thirty one-hour sessions.

After the treatment the children in the experimental group were observed in two different situations. First, as in the preobservation period, each child was observed during six five-minute segments while engaged in free play. Since language interactions during free play may not necessarily be representative of what a child is capable of producing in a more structured situation, each child was also observed in a more structured situation. The child was given the opportunity to interact with both fluent English-speaking and fluent Spanish-speaking (FSS) children. Two FES and two FSS children were randomly sampled from the school population. The child under study was placed in this group. These five children were given ten minutes to work together to build a block structure. The interactions between the child under study and the rest of the group were coded.

Procedures for Spanish language experiment. The maintenance of Spanish is an important component of Spanish-English bilingual education. For this reason the Spanish language experiment was carried out. It focuses on the acquisition of Spanish. All children participating in this study were Mexican American. Limited-Spanish-speaking children took part as tutors. It was expected that they would acquire more Spanish as a result of tutoring, since they chose fluent Spanish-speaking children as their partners. In this experiment, the same procedures were followed as in the ESL experiment with the following exceptions: (1) the children were tested for Spanish language proficiency, (2) they were observed for amount of interaction in Spanish, and (3) the peer-tutoring treatment took place in Spanish.

The data have not yet been analyzed. In both experiments it is expected that children in the treatment groups will increase their amount of interaction with other-language children significantly more than children in the control group. They will have been given the opportunity to initiate interactions and will have been provided with a structured situation in which they could interact successfully. Since it is expected that these interactions will be in the second language, their proficiency in the language they are acquiring should also improve.

Conclusion

In summary, a major part of second-language acquisition in children occurs as a result of talking to peers. For this reason, the focus of these studies was on social factors in second-language acquisition. These factors are important for both researchers and teachers to take into consideration when studying second-language acquisition or when designing programs intended to help children learn a second language.

Some aspects of these studies may prove useful to other researchers. The matched pairs design permits the use of a small sample. It also provides for tight control of blocking variables, such as amount of interaction and language proficiency. The same design could be used with different independent and dependent variables. The observation instrument that was developed and used in these studies could be useful to researchers and evaluators interested in measuring language use and verbal interaction. Finally, for teachers, peer tutoring may be a good second-language teaching technique in itself. It may also be a useful indirect technique since it may encourage children of different language groups to interact with each other when free to do so. Such practice should lead to greater proficiency in the second language.

References

Allen, V., ed. *Children as Teachers: Theory and Research on Tutoring.* New York: Academic Press, 1976.

DeAvila, E., and Duncan, S. *Language Assessment Scales, Level I.* 2nd ed. Corte Madera, Calif.: Linguametrics Group, 1977.

Dunn, L.M. *Peabody Picture Vocabulary Test.* Circle Pines, Minn.: American Guidance Service, 1965.

Hollifield, J. "Race Relations R and D Help Achieve Desegregation Goals." In *Educational R and D Report* (May 1978).

Johnson, D. *Child-Child Communication Test.* Unpublished test. Palo Alto, Calif.: School of Education, Stanford University, 1978.

Johnson, D., and August, D. *Language Use Observation Instrument.* Unpublished observation system. Palo Alto, Calif.: School of Education, Stanford University, 1978.

Johnson, D.W., and Johnson, R.T. "Cooperative, Competitive and Individualistic Learning." In *Journal of Research and Development in Education* 12, no. 1 (fall 1978).

Overall, P.M. *An Assessment of the Communication Competence in English of Spanish-Speaking Students.* Ph.D. dissertation, Stanford University, 1978.

Seliger, H.W. "Does Practice Make Perfect? A Study of Interaction Patterns and L2 Competence." In *Language Learning* 27, no. 2 (December 1977).

Stallings, J. *Learning to Look: A Handbook on Classroom Observation and Teaching Models.* Belmont, Calif.: Wadsworth Publishing Company, 1977.

Wong Fillmore, L. *The Second Time Around: Cognitive and Social Strategies in Second Language Acquisition.* Ph.D. dissertation, Stanford University, 1976.

Hortographía Himortal—
A Third Look:
Expanded Subcategorization of
Bilingual Spanish-English
Spelling Errors

John J. Staczek
Florida International University
Miami, Florida

A preliminary study[1] of the Spanish language spelling habits of Spanish-English bilingual students (kindergarten through university) revealed that spelling strategies of these bilinguals could be categorized as either Spanish based, English based, or simply random.* Subcategories, with appropriate linguistic descriptions and justification, were listed. Subsequent research[2] on the basis of a locally designed instrument consisting of word, phrase, and sentence dictations, as well as written story retelling and free composition, has led to some further subcategorization of the orthographic errors and strategies. The new data, categorized and described below, confirm the strategies described in 1977 and provide additional information on all categories, including the random errors, the basis for which seem to be perceptual problems such as the orientation of graphemic < p q b d > , aural misperceptions, and incomplete mastery of the orthographic conventions of either Spanish or English.

---

* See notes on pages 222-223.

Design and Rationale

The instrument designed for data elicitation consisted of a series of four twenty-word dictation lists for a total of eighty words; two twenty-five word, combination single word and phrase-level dictations; a six-sentence dictation list; and two short narrative listening comprehension paragraphs for subsequent written retelling. Free composition was also used to elicit data from the monolingual control group. The tests were administered over a three-day period in an effort to eliminate practice effect and boredom and to detract as little as possible from the daily classroom activities of the Spanish for Native Speakers (Spanish-S) classes. The items selected for the instrument are of high frequency, including several Spanish-English cognates. Many of the items have been taken from the preliminary informal collection reported on by Aid and Staczek.

Test group subjects included 384 students enrolled in six junior and senior high schools, both public and private, in the Miami area. Personal data from the students indicate a two- to fourteen-year range of formal Spanish or English language study. The participants are predominantly Cuban or Cuban American, with about 20 percent coming from other countries of the Hispanic Caribbean, Central America, and South America. Of the Cuban American group, several have come to the Miami area by way of Spain, and these students received a larger degree of formal instruction in Spanish than did the group as a whole. Control group subjects, monolingual Spanish speakers, were 120 eighth, ninth, tenth and eleventh grade Colombian students from Bogota. The control group subjects were asked to include a free composition for the database. One of the compositions, for its content, is cited at the end of this paper.

The spelling strategies revealed in the preliminary study were apparently developed as an independent accommodation to two different spelling systems available to the bilingual. The new data suggest a similar accommodation to the spelling systems of Spanish and English. It is my intent here to describe the findings from a purely descriptive point of view and not to judge them. The derived spelling strategies are an attempt on the part of the bilingual to cope with learning to write an acquired language, Spanish, while at the same time learning to read and write a learned language, English. An observation is in order with respect to the language requirement in the Dade County Public Schools. As is the case throughout much of the United States, the study of languages other than English is part of an enrichment program. Spanish would clearly fall within it. However, a program of Spanish for native speakers cannot be clearly delimited in a foreign language curriculum. Spanish-S, as it is called in Dade County, though it falls administratively in the Office of Bilingual Programs, is a language program of the language arts variety. It is not, and I emphasize not, a required course of study for Spanish-English bilinguals. Figures for 1978–1979 indicate that 13,000 students were enrolled in Spanish-S classes in Dade County. The only language that is required in the Dade County School System, as mandated by the Dade County School Board in July 1978, is English for Speakers of Other Languages (ESOL). The implication is that Spanish-English bilinguals receive formal instruction in English in ESOL classes and in other content-area classes, but do not receive the same kind of reinforcement in the language of the home, except perhaps for the daily fifty-minute class for those enrolled in Spanish-S. This fact, though one of several, is helpful in explaining partially the spelling strategies of the bilingual student.

Prior to the present study, the underlying sources of deviance from standard Spanish orthography were described as (1) intralanguage problems of a Spanish-based variety that arise because of inconsistencies or irregularities in the orthographic patterns of Spanish—for instance, graphemic < p b> , the sound/symbol correspondence of the voiceless alveolar fricative [s], and the like; (2) interlanguage problems of the English-based variety that arise because of interference based on a similarity of phonemes, morphemes, and graphemes; and (3) random errors for which attempts at categorization were deemed inappropriate.

Intralanguage Phenomena

In the Spanish orthographic system, it was expected that the monolingual students would have difficulty with spelling those words (1) where more than a single grapheme may be used to represent a single phonetic segment; (2) where two graphemes are in complementary distribution, yet have the same phonemic value; (3) where dialectal variation leads the writer to spell phonetically, on the basis of aural perception; and (4) where certain historical processes are independently and unwittingly resurrected.

Rather than approach the new data in terms of the classification of the preliminary data, I have found it more profitable to describe the new data in terms of a standard and all its intralanguage variants in order to emphasize the degree of deviance and the multiplicity of forms. Although the frequencies of occurrence are pointed out, no attempt is made at statistical interpretation. Those data are simply tabulated as follows:

Standard	Variants	Frequency
1. HAY	ay	10
	aí	2
	ai	3
	ahi	3
	háy	3
	hoi	1
	hai	1
2. MUY	mui	10
	muí	2
	moi	1

3. MIS	miz	1
	mis	6
	mi	1
4. IBAN	hiban	39
	hivan	8
	ivan	33
	iba	1
5. CEBOLLA	sebolla	37
	cevolla	3
	sevolla	9
	sevoya	3
	sevoilla	1
	seboya	18
6. VISITAN	bisita	1
	bisitan	4
7. RECIBAN	recivan	19
	resiban	44
	resiba	1
	resivan	13
8. SIGUE	sige	40
	sigen	1
	cigue	3
9. ESTRICTO	extricto	6
	estrixto	1
10. RELACION	relazion	1
	relasion	9
11. HICIMOS	isimos	13
	hizimo	3
	icimos	3
	hisimos	13
	hizimos	4
12. AGENTE	ahente	2
	hajente	5
	ajente	7
	adjente	2
13. JARRO	jaro	14
	haro	5
	harro	5
	garro	2
	jarró	2

14. ACERCA	hacelca	3
	hacerca	11
	aserca	8
	aselca	2

The above data are consistent with the data collected from the monolingual Spanish control group. In gross terms, there seems to be nothing new under the sun that is not Spanish based. There does appear, however, to be a growing, though perhaps still minor, tendency toward the voicing of voiceless consonants in Spanish, as shown in the following examples:

Standard	*Variants*	*Frequency*
1. MELANCOLIA	melegonia	2
	melagolia	5
	melagoria	1
	malagolia	5
2. ACERCA	acerga	2
3. CASTIGAR	gastigar	2
4. PULGA	bulga	2

Other types of errors include the difficulty with consonant clusters; metathesis; intrusion of extra consonants or vowels; loss of consonant, vowel, or syllable; confusion in syllabification; and the like. These types of errors are seen below:

Standard	*Variants*	*Frequency*
1. RELACION	relason	2
2. CALIFICACIONES	calicafion	2
	caficaciones	1
3. ME SIENTO	me semto	2
	me siemto	1
4. RECIBAN	recinban	2
5. BIBLIOTECA	bivoteca	1
	didiloteca	1
6. ENTONCES	entocis	1
	entoses	1
7. ESTRELLA	esella	1
	esterlla	1

Many of the above examples, though infrequent, exhibit some degree of consistency across words and from writer to writer. Though one or another may seem arbitrary and independently motivated, the evidence suggests that there is an accommodation strategy at work.

Interlanguage Phenomena

The second class of errors alluded to in the preliminary study stems from the regularities and patterns of English orthography. Those errors were classified relative to four phenomena: (1) naming the alphabet, (2) spelling of the English vowels, (3) spelling of the English consonants, and (4) the transfer of English morphemes. The naming of the alphabet is a strategy employed by bilingual students whereby the learning of the second language affects the spelling in the first because greater emphasis is being placed on the learning of the second language and the techniques to teach it—namely, spelling aloud, alphabet repetition, and the use of phonics.

In an effort to summarize earlier categorizations, I chose to list the repeated errors for the purpose of dramatizing their frequency and multiplicity of style. The strategies suggested in 1977 continue to be employed, and the results are tabulated as follows:

Standard	Variants	Frequency
1. HAY	I	4
	Hi	2
2. MUY	my	1
	muey	1
	mue	1
3. MIS	miss	1
	mes	1
4. IBAN	eban	7
	evan	5
	evas	1
5. VISITAN	visentan	1
	besetan	1
	besitan	3
	decintan	1
6. CEBOLLA	ceboje	1
	cevoja	1
7. RECIBAN	reseban	2
	raseban	3
8. SIGUE	sege	1
	segian	1
	cege	1

9. QUESCO	geso	1
	ceso	1
	cheso	2
	guesso	2
10. CUÑADO	cunjado	1
11. BEISBOL	baseball	7
	basebol	2
	baesboll	1
	baesbal	1
	basboll	1
	beisbal	1
12. MOTOCICLETA	motocyclas	1
	motorcicleta	6
	motociqleta	1
	motocikleta	1
	motociquleta	1
	motocycleta	8
	motociqueta	1
13. DIJO	deho	2
	dejo	2
14. INTELIGENTE	intelligente	3
	intelijante	1
15. QUIERO	cero	3
	ciero	2

As with the intralanguage phenomena, there is in the above examples a certain predictability. Movement beyond the four categories described for English-based errors seems to be limited.

Random Errors

In the 1977 study there were too few data to suggest any kind of categorization of the random errors, errors that appeared to have their origin in arbitrary spelling assignments, as well as in totally misperceived cues and in incomplete mastery of either system. It was suggested at that time that the random forms defied systematic description and that mastery of either system had not yet begun. Ignorance of spelling conventions produced some anomalous errors but not enough to warrant classification. However, in the collection of the new data there began to appear some consistencies in the random category that suggest a categorization; namely, in terms of such visual-perceptual phenomena as the orientation of <g p q b d>, aural misperceptions, phonetic guesswork, and the simple lack of understanding of the conventions of a system.

The graphemes < g p q b d> , it is to be understood, are problematic for many students who are learning to write the Roman alphabet because of the mirror-image likeness of the symbols. It is not my intent to label these errors as unique to the Spanish-English bilingual but only to point out that among these bilinguals the perception and the consequent confusion of the letters do indeed present some spelling problems. Though the errors usually disappear by midadolescence among monolinguals, the errors here are common in the age group. It would appear that the strategy in dealing with this problem is more or less arbitrary, being neither Spanish nor English based but simply Roman alphabet based. Some of the confusion, in fact, results from the phonetic cue confusion over the < b v > distinction.

The occurrence of graphemic confusion of < g p q b d> is tabulated as follows:

Standard	Variants	Frequency
1. CABALLO	cadallo	3
2. VOCECITA	dosesita	2
3. BIBLIOTECA	didioteca	2
	didotica	1
4. QUESO	gueso	3
	gweso	2
5. PEQUEÑO	pegueño	2
6. QUIERO	guiero	2
	giero	3

This confusion also produces *todadía* from *todavía*.

Aural misperception of cues, including total misperception of phonetic features or surrounding environments, accounts for a number of random errors. In several cases, there is a recurring redundant palatal, from either oral to nasal or nasal to oral. Aural misperceptions occurred with the following frequencies:

Standard	Variants	Frequency
1. CUÑADO	puñado	2
	guyado	1
2. MELANCOLIA	melegonia	2
	melogonia	2
	melagoria	1
3. CEBOLLA	tevoya	3
	tevofoya	1
4. TANTO	santo	1
	canto	1

5. LECCIONES	tecchines	1
6. VOCECITA	bolsetita	1
7. GRINGO	gueringo	1
8. DESAYUNAR	decaunal	1
	desallnar	2
	diesala	1
9. BIBLIOTECA	bleboteca	2
	bibogeta	1
	bibletica	1
	biotegla	1
10. TODAVIA	dovinga	1

Phonetic guesswork, however it is accomplished, accounts for a number of inaccuracies in spelling. The student either totally misperceives and attempts to guess or, because of poor short-term memory, recalls a sound from a previous word or one at another boundary and consequently produces what might be termed a barbarism. The student may also recognize a feature of one sound yet write its corresponding grapheme in terms of another with a similar feature. Phonetic guesswork accounts for the following errors:

Standard	*Variants*	*Frequency*
1. GRINGO	trinco	2
2. AÑO	allo	3
	anllo	4
3. PRESENCIA	preciaca	1
4. AGENTE	ajuerte	1
5. PEQUEÑO	pecenllo	1
6. EXPLICADO	exbecado	1
7. DESAYUNAR	desallnar	2
8. MEJOR	mehoy	1
9. OJALA	uchalá	1
10. CALIFICACIONES	caniricanes	1
	califactiere	1

A lack of understanding of either phonetic or graphemic system leads to errors for which there are no apparent categorizations. There are documented cases where a student's misunderstanding or inability to spell correctly results from a lack of familiarity with an orthographic system, compounded by the fact that the student's aural ability is not at all matched by his writing or spelling ability. This lack of understanding of the graphemic system can be seen in the following examples:

1. FUIMOS A LOS CAYOS A PESCAR.
   Fmos as cajo a pezca.
   Fimos a lo callos a pecar.
   Fuymos a los callos a petar.

2. LA CASA BLANCA ESTA EN LA LOMA.
   La casa *blanra* está en la loma.
   La casa blanca está en la *roja*.

3. LOS NIÑOS JUEGAN CON LOS GATOS Y LOS PERROS.
   Los niños *jugegan* con los gatos y los perros.
   Los niños *guelgan* con los gatos y los perros.
   Los niños *gedan* con los gatos y los perros.

I would like to share one of the most enjoyable compositions, not because it contains any errors but because its theme gives one pause while conducting research of the type herein described. It comes from one of the students in the Bogota, Colombia, control group:

Los norteamericanos son faltos de imaginación porque debé primero mirar su idioma corregirlo y despues cuando lo tenga bien adaptado mirar los de los demásy criticarlos.

Pero no obstante sabén hacer las cosas y por esto se aprovechan de los paises subdesarrollados como el nuestro y hasta lográn apoderace de paises como Cuba pero luego se tienén que retirar cuando se les muestra que uno también pueden. . .

Conclusion

What I have undertaken is to study the problems in the spelling habits of Spanish-English bilinguals, to analyze them and to see what strategies are used in spelling. Doubtless, more needs to be done with the data and with more data to be collected from other bilingual areas in the United States. At the same time, similar research needs to be done in English as a second language. The goal of such research necessarily will have to be a program of teaching and remediation of the spelling rules of Spanish and English.

Notes

1. Frances Aid and John J. Staczek, "Hortographía Himortal: Spelling Problems Among Bilingual Students." Presented at the Symposium on Spanish and Portuguese Bilingualism, University of Massachusetts, November 18-19, 1977, and forthcoming in the *Bilingual Review*.

2. I would like to express my appreciation to the School of Education, Florida International University, for the Faculty Development Award in the Spring Quarter of 1978 for the design and preparation of the instrument and for the collection and collation of data, and to the Dade County Public Schools and Christopher Columbus High School for allowing me to use their students as subjects in the research project. Moreover, I would like to express my thanks to the 384 bilingual subjects in Miami and to the 120 monolingual subjects of Bogota, Colombia.